Studies in Digital Politics and Governance

This book series examines how and why digital technologies matter for democracy – whether in terms of coordinating social movements, elections, e-government, or digital inclusion. Relevant topics include, but are not limited to, digital democracy, electronic voting, online participation and civic engagement, and electronic campaigning. The series also covers studies on the impact of information technologies on policy issues such as smart cities and the applications of information technologies in a diverse range of areas, such as public health, education, and cybersecurity.

Studies in Digital Politics and Governance (DPG) welcomes monographs and edited volumes from a variety of disciplines and approaches, such as political science, public administration and computational sciences, which are accessible to academics, decision-makers and practitioners working at governmental and non-governmental institutions.

Gorden Moyo
Editor

An Anatomy of AI Surveillance in Africa

The Contradictions of Digital Technologies

Springer

Editor
Gorden Moyo
Fort Hare Institute for Social and Economic Research
University of Fort Hare
East London, South Africa

ISSN 2524-3926 ISSN 2524-3934 (electronic)
Studies in Digital Politics and Governance
ISBN 978-3-032-04268-2 ISBN 978-3-032-04269-9 (eBook)
https://doi.org/10.1007/978-3-032-04269-9

This Springer imprint is published by the registered company Springer Nature Switzerland AG
The registered company address is: Gewerbestrasse 11, 6330 Cham, Switzerland

This volume offers a comprehensive analysis of the growing engagement between China and African countries in the field of AI surveillance technology. It is a compelling read for anyone seeking a broad yet nuanced understanding of this complex and evolving relationship.—**Dr. Obert Hodzi, Senior Lecturer (Associate Professor), University of Liverpool, UK**

An Anatomy of AI Surveillance in Africa interrogates the malevolent role of Chinese surveillance technologies in Africa. The volume puts to rest reactionary claims that the Chinese Communist Party seeks to liberate the people of the Global South from the yoke of oppression, class war, and neocolonial conquest. ***—Michael Kwet, Postdoctoral Fellow of the Centre for Social Change, University of Johannesburg, South Africa, and Visiting Fellow of the Information Society at Yale Law School, USA***

Technology is a double-edged sword. This is the unequivocal case with digital technologies, in particular, artificial intelligence (AI) systems. AI can be used to drive inclusive development and shared prosperity. However, the same technology can be used to build autonomous weapons systems or develop AI surveillance systems. This book details and analyses such malignant and intrusive surveillance technologies in Africa. It is a thorough publication. Nevertheless, this does not have to be the African AI experience. Africans must leverage AI to address their challenges and enhance their quality of life.***—Prof. Arthur G.O. Mutambara, Full Professor and Director, Institute for the Future of Knowledge (IFK), University of Johannesburg, South Africa***

An Anatomy of AI Surveillance in Africa is far more than a study of technology; it is a profound interrogation of power. Gorden Moyo and his collaborators dismantle the polished façade of AI innovation to expose its insidious deployment in monitoring, classifying, and disciplining African lives. With a rare blend of scholarly rigor and ethical urgency, the book traces how facial recognition systems, automated plate readers, and similar tools travel from global centres of production to the streets of African cities, raising the unsettling question of whose safety they ultimately guarantee. In charting this trajectory, the volume reveals the entanglement of global geopolitics—from China's expanding digital footprint to Western exports—with the intimate realities of citizens stripped of choice and consent. The strength of the work lies in its empirical depth and analytical clarity and in its insistence on seeing the human beings obscured by data and devices. This is a timely, uncompromising, and necessary book that compels us to envision technologies that serve freedom rather than subjugation.***—Dr. Dhaval Kataria, Assistant Professor, Faculty of Business Administration, GLS University, Ahmedabad, Gujarat, India***

This timely and incisive book offers a critical examination of the growing deployment of intrusive surveillance technologies across Africa. It is an exciting contribution by African scholars in this new and evolving field, which is dominated by Western scholars. By unpacking the use of CCTV cameras, automated vehicle plate readers, facial recognition systems, and other AI-driven tools, the authors challenge the dominant narrative that frames these technologies as purely protective measures against cyberthreats and cyber-terrorists. Instead, the book compellingly argues that such tools are increasingly repurposed to monitor ordinary citizens often without their knowledge or consent, violating their democratic rights and privileges. Of particular significance is the book's analysis of China's expanding role as a key manufacturer, exporter, financier, and installer of AI surveillance infrastructure on the continent. It presents a sobering account of how these technologies are being used to construct digital surveillance states, raising urgent questions about privacy, sovereignty, and human rights in many countries lacking policies and the will to protect and uphold human rights. It is a powerful contribution to the growing discourse on digital authoritarianism and the future of civil liberties in the age of AI.—***Prof. Vusumuzi Maphosa, National University of Science and Technology, Zimbabwe***

Acknowledgements

This book is part of my research output as a fellow in the Institute of Social and Economic Research at the University of Fort Hare in South Africa. I am deeply indebted to the director of the institute, Prof. Philani Moyo, and his colleagues for affording me the opportunity to pursue this initiative under their ambit. I would also like to thank all the contributors to this project. Without them, this book would have never materialised.

My friends from across the globe who have offered me friendship, hospitality, and enlightenment comprise a group far too large to mention, but I trust that they know who they are and appreciate how much I feel beholden to them. However, it will be remiss of me if I do not mention a few of them, including Prof. Reinford Khumalo, Prof. Kirk Helliker, Prof. Sabelo Ndlovu-Gatsheni, Prof. Arthur Mutambara, Prof. Jonathan Moyo, Prof. Patrick Bond, Prof. Cornelias Ncube, Dr. Mkhululi Nyathi, Dr. Freidarike Satner, Dr. Khuphukile Mlambo, Dr. Samukele Hadebe, Dr. Qhubani Moyo, Dr. Peter Zwidekalanga Khumalo, Dr. Mbulisi Ndlovu, Dr. Douglas Nyathi, Dr. Gracsious Maviza, Dr. Divane Nzima, Dr. Mandla Maphosa, Dr. Mandlenkosi Mpofu, Dr. Mbuso Moyo, Dr. Zenzo Moyo, Dr. Shary Eppel, Dr. Macdonald Lewanika, Luke Mhlaba, Karen Dube, Sindiso Ngwenya, Nicolas Nyathi, Albert Nyathi, Dumiso Matshazi, Jason Braganza, Nigel Johnson, Joshua Mhambi, Albert Mhlanga, and Anele Ndebele.

I am also grateful to my civil society colleagues, including Prof. Eldred Masunungure, Dr. Charles Mutasa, Dr. Robert Munyukwi, Dr. Delta Sivalo, Zibusiso Dube, Tony Reelar, Arnold Tsunga, Otto Saki, Liberty Bhebhe, Zenzele Ndebele, Permanent Ngoma, Mbuso Fuzwayo, Useni Sibanda, Samukeliso Khumalo, Nonsikelelo Fayayo (nee Ndlovu) Melusi Moyo, Effie Ncube, Beloved Chiweshe, and many more.

My colleagues at the Public Policy and Research Institute of Zimbabwe (PPRIZ), including Dr. Rodrik Fayayo, Dr. Wayne Malinga, Nomagugu Mutandi Moyo, Ryan Chuma, and Daisyline Bhebhe, as well as Philani Mpofu, helped me remain sane in the face of a health scare. More importantly, my discussions with them helped me shape many of the perspectives contained in this book. I also benefitted a lot from my conversations and discussions with Research Fellows from PPRIZ, including

Prof. Favourate Sebele-Mpofu, Didmus Dewa, Vicent Moyo, Bhekimpilo Nhlabano Moyo, Tobias Guzura, Mbongeni Nhliziyo, Stevenson Dlamini, and Themba Chiveya.

The members of the Board of Governors at PPRIZ, Ambros Sibindi, Bakani Ncube, Ntombizodwa Khumalo, and Dr. Hilda Jaka, deserve special mention here. Also, my friends in the diplomatic community, such as Zandile Sifelani, Ndaba Ndlovu, Nikolai Hutchisnson, Jonathan McClean, Jenifer Schmidt, Francis Rwodzi, and Christopher Makuvaza, deserve a mention here.

This book also benefitted from the China-Africa Dialogue Series coordinated by PPRIZ, in particular, the participants, researchers, and presenters in the dialogue series, including Prof. Obert Hodzi, Dr. Jethro Mpofu, Dr. Basil Hamusokwe, Dr. Ronald Chipaike, Dr. Lucy Anning, and Dr. Emmanuel Matambo, whose contributions helped shape some of the arguments contained in this book. My words of gratitude also go to Thakazile Tshuma, who meticulously sorted out the references, and Dr. Agreement Ndlovu, who proofread the final manuscript. I also wish to express my thanks to the editorial team at Springer Nature, especially to Niko Chtouris, as well as the reviewers whose comments were most helpful in strengthening the book. Again, my special regards go to Prof. Arthur Mutambara, Prof. Obert Hodzi, and Prof. Michael Kwet for their endorsements of this book.

As I was finalising the manuscript of this book, I was diagnosed with a heart problem, which threatened the entire project. I am, therefore, grateful to my medical doctors, *viz.* Dr. Mbongeni Ndlovu (specialist physician), Dr. Leon Gwaunza (neurologist), and Dr. Kwenza Ncube (specialist physician), and the medical staff at Flex Clinic, Corporate Clinic, and Mater Dei Hospital in Bulawayo. In addition, a legion of friends and family members gave me overwhelming support and encouragement to stay the course and subsequently complete this work. Among them were Sidumo Bhebhe, Mqondobanzi Magonya, Benson Ntini, Frank Nyoni, Pastor Dr. Sikhumbuzo Ndlovu, Pastor Obadiah Mthungameli Ngwenya, Busani Ncube, George Mkhwanazi, Patience Mafu MaNkonjeni, Fortune Mlalazi, and many others.

Like all academic work, the writing of this book meant compromising on family responsibilities, and I wish to express my thanks to the members of my family, including my nephews, nieces, siblings, as well as children. In particular, Dumoluhle and Nomakhwezi acted as my research assistants as they kept the literature I needed flowing to me, while the youngest, Makhezulu Dumisile, was regularly called upon to fix my misbehaving laptop. The best is reserved for the last, Dr. Fedina Moyo, my wife. I do not have enough words to appreciate her unwavering support for me at all times. If this book has any value, all credit goes to the friends and family mentioned above. But approximations, errors, and excesses, if any, belong to me.

About This Book

This book analyses intrusive artificial intelligence (AI) surveillance technologies, including closed-circuit television (CCTV) cameras, automated vehicle plate readers, and facial recognition technologies, among others, that have become pervasive in Africa. Contrary to the official narrative that celebrates these technologies as ranged against cyber-criminals, cyber-terrorists, and cyber-espionage, this book argues that the tools are increasingly used to telemonitor ordinary citizens without their consent. It also argues that although countries such as France, Germany, Israel, Italy, the UK, and the USA are major exporters of AI surveillance tools to Africa, in recent years, China has emerged as the key manufacturer, promoter, exporter, financier, distributor, and installer of these technologies in many countries on the continent. Accordingly, the central proposition of this book is that the Chinese-made AI surveillance technologies have been used as scaffolds in the project of constructing Orwellian surveillance states in Africa. The book will be of interest to scholars, policymakers, diplomats, human rights defenders, civil society actors, as well as students of African politics, international relations, China-Africa relations, and security studies as well as surveillance studies.

Contents

Editor and Contributors

Gorden Moyo (PhD) is currently a Research Fellow at the Fort Hare Institute for Social and Economic Research at the University of Fort Hare in South Africa; Fellow at the University of the Free State in South Africa; Senior Lecturer in the Faculty of Humanities and Social Sciences at Lupane State University in Zimbabwe; Director of the Public Policy and Research Institute of Zimbabwe (PPRIZ); Member of the Editorial Board of the Sabella Abidde Publishing House, University of Alabama (USA); Member of the Board of Trustees of the Mass Public Opinion Institute (MPOI); Associate Member of the International Society for Development and Sustainability (ISDS), Japan; President of the Development Studies Association of Zimbabwe (DeSAZ); Member of the Southern African Development Parliamentary Forum Technical Group on Public Financial Management; ex-Minister of State in the Prime Minister's Office, ex-Minister of State Enterprises and Parastatals, and former Member of Parliament of the Republic of Zimbabwe (2009–2013); and former British Council Facilitator of the Pan-African Leadership Programme in 19 countries across Africa, including Botswana, Cameroon, Eritrea, Ethiopia, eSwatini, Ghana, Kenya, Lesotho, Liberia, Malawi, Mauritius, Namibia, Nigeria, South Africa, Tanzania, Uganda, Zambia, and Zimbabwe. He is a Chevening Scholar whose primary research interests are in global finance, international economic relations, developmental states, public leadership, military commercialism, Africa-China relations, and African agency, among others. He has published several articles in peer-reviewed journals and several book chapters. His most recent books include *African Agency, Finance, and Developmental States* (Palgrave Macmillan, 2021); *Making Politics in Zimbabwe's Second Republic: The Formative Project by Emmerson Mnangagwa* (Springer, 2023), co-edited with Prof. Kirk Helliker; *Africa in the Global Economy: Capital Outflows, Enablers and Decolonial Responses* (Springer, 2024); and *Global Storms and Africa in Global Politics: Contemporary Challenges and Decolonial Responses*, co-edited with Sabelo J. Ndlovu-Gatsheni (Springer, 2025).

Contributors

John H. S. Åberg Global Political Studies, Malmo University, Malmo, Sweden

Lucy Anning Center for Africa-China Studies, University of Johannesburg, Johannesburg, South Africa

Bazel Coster Chinyonga Peace and Governance, Bindura University of Science Education, Bindura, Zimbabwe

Ronald Chipaike Peace and Governance, Bindura University of Science Education, Bindura, Zimbabwe

Auxence Augustin KOA Political Science, University of Bertoua, Bertoua, Cameroon

Emmanuel Matambo Centre for Africa-China Studies, University of Johannesburg, Johannesburg, South Africa

Gorden Moyo Fort Hare Institute for Social and Economic Research, University of Fort Hare, East London, South Africa

Philani Moyo Fort Hare Institute for Social and Economic Research, University of Fort Hare, East London, South Africa

Allen Munoriyarwa Journalism, Walter Sisulu University, East London, South Africa

Bekimpilo Moyo Nhlabano Development Studies, Lupane State University, Lupane, Zimbabwe

Mbongeni Nhliziyo Department of Development Studies, Lupane State University, Bulawayo, Zimbabwe

Fort Hare Institute for Social and Economic Research, University of Fort Hare, East London, South Africa

Nevison Shumba Development Studies, Lupane State University, Lupane, Zimbabwe

Tafadzwa T. William Peace and Governance, Bindura University of Science Education, Bindura, Zimbabwe

Abbreviations

ADC	Africa Data Centres
AGOA	African Growth and Opportunity Act
AI	Artificial Intelligence
ANC	African National Congress
BRI	Belt and Road Initiative
CCP	Chinese Communist Party
CSOs	Civil Society Organisations
CCTV	Closed-Circuit Television
DA	Democratic Alliance
DFC	Development Finance Corporation
DRC	Democratic Republic of the Congo
DSR	Digital Silk Road
DTA	Digital Transformation with Africa
EPRDF	Ethiopian People's Revolutionary Democratic Front
EPC+F	Engineering, Procurement, Construction + Finance
FOCAC	Forum for China-Africa Cooperation
GAFAM	Google, Apple, Facebook, Amazon, and Microsoft
ICT	Information and Communication Technologies
IPE	International Political Economy
IR	International Relations
MP	Member of Parliament
MPDP	Media Policy and Development Project
NA	National Assembly
NGO	Non-Governmental Organisation
OAU	Organisation of African Unity
PAC	Pan-African Congress
PF	Patriotic Front
PGII	Partnership for Global Infrastructure Initiative
PRC	People's Republic of China
PPRIZ	Public Policy and Research Institute of Zimbabwe
SACP	South African Communist Party

SAPS	South African Police Service
SAT3-WASC	South Atlantic 3/West Africa Submarine Cable (a submarine communications cable)
SSC	South-South Cooperation
UN	United Nations
UNHCR	United Nations High Commissioner for Refugees
USA	United States of America
USAID	United States Agency for International Development
USTDA	United States Trade and Development Agency
ZANU PF	Zimbabwe African National Union Patriotic Front
ZDF	Zimbabwe Defence Forces
ZimRights	Zimbabwe Human Rights Association
ZTE	Zhongxing Telecommunication Equipment (a Chinese telecommunications company)
ZRP	Zimbabwe Republic Police

Chapter 1
The Contradictions of Surveillance Tech in Africa: An Introduction

Gorden Moyo

Abstract This chapter analyses intrusive Artificial Intelligence (AI) surveillance technologies, including closed-circuit television (CCTV) cameras, automated vehicle plate readers, and facial recognition technologies, among others, that have become pervasive in Africa. Contrary to the official narrative that celebrates these technologies as ranged against cyber-criminals, cyber-terrorists and cyber-espionage, this book argues that the tools are increasingly used to telemonitor ordinary citizens without their consent. It also argues that although countries such as France, Germany, Israel, Italy, the United Kingdom and the United States are major exporters of AI surveillance tools to Africa, in the recent years, China has emerged as the key manufacturer, promoter, exporter, financier, distributor and installer of these technologies in many countries on the continent. Accordingly, the central proposition of this chapter is that the Chinese-made AI surveillance technologies have been used as scaffolds in the project of constructing Orwellian surveillance states in Africa.

Introduction

An age of Artificial Intelligence (AI) surveillance technologies is emerging in Africa. Many countries on the continent are currently building stocks of telemonitoring tools, such as closed-circuit television (CCTV) cameras, drones, biometric identification systems, border management technology, automated vehicle plate readers, facial recognition technologies and video analytics, as well as a series of predictive policing tools. Some of these technologies have been deployed for objectionable purposes, including profiling and monitoring daily activities such as work, leisure, shopping, learning, communication, business and commercial transactions without the knowledge and approval of the affected population.

G. Moyo (✉)
Fort Hare Institute for Social and Economic Research, University of Fort Hare, East London, South Africa

G. Moyo (ed.), *An Anatomy of AI Surveillance in Africa*, Studies in Digital Politics and Governance, https://doi.org/10.1007/978-3-032-04269-9_1

The often offered reasons for the expanding AI surveillance technologies are that they have the potential to enhance crime prevention, traffic management, emergency response, counter-terrorism, counter-intelligence, border control, cybersecurity, business security, infrastructure protection and many more. Nevertheless, as will be demonstrated throughout this volume, this claim is a narrative of convenience intended to disguise the lived reality of the darker side of the AI surveillance tools in Africa. There is no doubt that protecting the interests of the state and its citizens against cyber-criminals, cyber-terrorists and cyber-espionage is a fundamental responsibility of governments and can be achieved through the ethical deployment of electronic technologies. However, the authors in this volume provide mounds of evidence from across the continent demonstrating that state agents have instrumentalised the digital surveillance tools and used them to violate human rights, political freedoms and civil liberties in the pretext of combating cybercriminals, cyber terrorists and cyberespionage, among other digital criminalities.

Needless to say, what is evident on the continent today is what Königs (2022) termed the 'Orwellian Surveillance states' and what Michel Foucault dubbed 'Panoptic States'. This simply means that in Africa, surveillance technologies have been repurposed, instrumentalised and deployed not necessarily for the public interest but as political tools used to stifle political dissent, entrench authoritarian rule and control information for the express interest of the ruling elite. Consequently, the rise of surveillance systems and practices across the continent has been characterised by the victimisation of opinion makers, government critics, public intellectuals, civil society activists, journalists, human rights defenders and opposition leaders, as well as minority populations.

The central proposition of this volume is that digital technologies are akin to the paradox of a bee. With its mouth, a bee produces honey, and with its tail, it produces a sting. Apparently, Africa has so far experienced more of the 'surveillance sting' than 'surveillance honey'. Countries such as Angola, Cameroon, Chad, Cote d'Ivoire, Egypt, Equatorial Guinea, Ethiopia, Ghana, Kenya, Morocco, Niger, Nigeria, Sudan, Tanzania, Togo, Uganda and Zimbabwe have essentially weaponised digital surveillance technologies in pursuit of political gains. Rather than using AI surveillance tools to fight crime and threats, state security agents have deployed them as technologies of subjectivation, algorithmic suppression and algorithmic exploitation of the citizens. By so doing, a number of African countries have been gravitating towards what some surveillance scholars (Gravett, 2020; Kwet, 2021; Nhanale & Verde, 2023; Ibrahim, 2024) view as 'digital authoritarianism', 'digital colonialism' and 'coloniality of surveillance' on the continent. In particular, digital authoritarianism refers to the use of digital information technology by authoritarian regimes such as Egypt, Sudan and Zimbabwe to surveil, repress and manipulate domestic and foreign populations (also see Gravett, 2020). However, a rejoinder is important at this point. It is not only the authoritarian states, such as Egypt, Sudan, Zimbabwe, China, Democratic Republic of North Korea, Russia and Saudi Arabia, that have used remote surveillance tools as political weapons. There are also claims that democratic states, including Botswana, South Africa, the United States, the United Kingdom and

Italy, are users of surveillance technologies. Perhaps the only major difference is that these countries have laws and regulatory frameworks that limit the malign use of AI surveillance technologies.

Drawing from the foregoing discussion, it may not come as a surprise to many that some of the paragons of democratic values and principles of the Global North, including countries like Germany, France, Israel, Italy, Japan, the United Kingdom and the United States, are the major manufacturers, exporters and suppliers of the controversial surveillance technologies to autocratic African states, such as Angola, Cameroon, Egypt, Morocco and Sudan among others. However, the focus of this book is not the Euro-Western suppliers of the intrusive surveillance technologies but China. It is instructive to note that China has become the largest surveillance state on earth. It is recognised as the largest producer, exporter, promoter, financier, supplier, distributor and installer of mass surveillance equipment on the continent (Beraja et al., 2023; Travers, 2024). Companies such as Dahua Technology, CloudWalk, Hikvision, Huawei and ZTE are the largest global suppliers of cutting-edge surveillance technologies empowered by artificial intelligence. At the same time, Chinese policy banks and financial institutions, including the National Aero-Technology Import and Export Corporation, China Exim Bank and China Development Bank, as well as the China Export and Credit Insurance Corporation, have provided billions of dollars in the form of cheap loans to African countries to procure AI surveillance technologies from Chinese companies. This has resulted in increased collaboration between Chinese tech corporations and African governments across various aspects of AI surveillance technologies across the continent.

In this context, several African governments have honed their new surveillance techniques, including their capacity to intercept and monitor electronic communications through the procurement and installation of equipment and software that enables remote control hacking and eavesdropping, as well as the deployment of video surveillance systems. It is for this reason that this volume sets out to gain a better understanding of the capabilities of surveillance systems in Africa. Overall, the book assesses the actors, motives, contradictions and implications of intrusive AI surveillance technologies on peoples' privacy, security, civil liberties and political freedoms.

Contextualisation of Surveillance Technologies

There is no better way to begin the decoupling of the intrusive AI surveillance technologies than the contextualisation, conceptualisation and textualisation, as well as historisation, of the notion and practice of surveillance in Africa. As used in this volume, the term surveillance refers to the tracking of citizens' movements, activities, conversations, correspondences and communications including recording of metadata by state agents(Gravett, 2020; Königs, 2022; Munoriyarwa & Mare, 2023; Sheombar & Skelton, 2023; Monahan, 2025; Sheombar & Skelton, 2025). In the same vein, digital surveillance can be viewed as real-time tele-monitoring of citizens' geolocation, financial transactions, browsing history, social media posts and 'likes' (Sheombar & Skelton, 2023). Digital surveillance practices are aided by digital technologies such as CCTV cameras, biometric identification systems, border management technology, automated vehicle plate readers and facial recognition technologies, as well as AI, among others. All these are used to monitor public spaces, intercept internet and telecommunication traffic, track the movements of both people and data, among others (Königs, 2022). Notably, African governments have acquired and continue to acquire AI-powered facial recognition systems, cloud computing infrastructures and smart policing initiatives for both benign and malign purposes. As mentioned, former Euro-Western colonial and imperialist powers such as Germany, France, Italy, Japan, the United Kingdom and the United States, as well as those countries that stood on the side of the colonised, including China and Russia, are today the major producers, providers and promoters of intrusive AI surveillance technologies to Africa. Their surveillance apparatuses come in the form of directly equipping of foreign intelligence and security forces; training of foreign intelligence and security forces; financing of their operations and procurement; facilitation of exports of surveillance equipment by industry and promotion of legislation which enables surveillance to reshape, reorder and reworld Africa's public sphere without the knowledge and consent of the majority of the people on the continent.

While the AI-powered surveillance technology is a recent phenomenon, surveillance systems and practices are not new in Africa. The biographies and histories as well as the contours of surveillance in Africa are traceable back to the hostile eras of slavery, colonialism, apartheidism and imperialism (Ogasawara, 2019; Kwet, 2018; Roberts et al., 2021; Munoriyarwa & Mare, 2023; Moyo, 2024; Monahan, 2025; Sheombar & Skelton, 2025; Moyo, forthcoming). The current grammar of digital surveillance is linked to the phenomena of globalisation, globalism and the Fourth Industrial Revolution. In the past, surveillance practices and technologies were deployed to control and dominate the colonised populations, perpetuate colonial power and maintain social control over the colonised and the Fanonian's *Les Damnes de la Terre*-The Wretched of the Earth. In apartheid South Africa and colonial Namibia and Zimbabwe, surveillance practices included searching for information, opening private correspondences, eavesdropping, monitoring of movements, passbook, national identification cards, spatial containment, profiling of suspected enemies of the state, conducting stop and search, spying on and infiltration of activist groups by law enforcement agents and police terror techniques (Monahan, 2025). These programs were designed to keep a close eye on citizens and gather information about their activities so as to intimidate, arrest, detain, prosecute and sentence them, as well as treat them as non-beings. Crucially, colonial surveillance was also used to enable the extraction of taxes from the black Africans as well as to monitor the struggle for independence (Munoriyarwa & Mare, 2023).

Needless to say, surveillance regimes in Africa were devised by foreign colonisers, imperialists, intellectuals and profit-seeking capitalists. As such, surveillance was often racialised and gendered, with black people being subjected to more intense surveillance and control compared to other races. Viewed from this perspective, surveillance is not just a tool of modern states, but also a legacy of colonialism, apartheidism and imperialism. As conceptualised by decolonial thinkers, surveillance did not end with the end of administrative colonialism in the 1960s, 1970s, 1980s and mid-1990s, when most African countries got their juridical political independence (Moyo, 2021). Like many colonialities, including coloniality of power, knowledge, nature, markets, economy, finance and many more, coloniality of surveillance is strong and alive in Africa and other Global South regions. It has been transformed, renovated and reborn in the digital and AI 'maternity ward'. Foreign powers such as the United States, the United Kingdom, China, Germany, Israel, Italy and Russia have played midwifery roles in the reshaping of surveillance tools in Africa today. As such, the AI surveillance technologies are part of the neoliberal and imperial toolkits that are deployed by the powerful in pursuit of their financial and economic interests, as well as geostrategic agendas over human and social justice in Africa. Decolonial thinkers, such as Achille Mbembe, Adebayo Adedeji, Adebayo Olukoshi, Amilca Cabral, Amina Mama, Archie Mafeje, Bade Omnimode, Bernard Ngubane, Charles Abugre, Cheik Anta Diop, Chinua Achebe, Claude Ake, Dani Nabudare, Demba Dembele, Dennis Brutus, Eshetu Chole, Fantu Cheru, Frantz Fanon, George Nzongala-Ntalaja, Ibbo Mandaza, Issa G. Shiviji, Jacques Delpechin, Jimi Adesina, Leonce Ndikumana, KankwendaM'Baya, Kwesi Prah, Mahmood Mamdani, Ngugi waThiong'o, Pauline Hountondji, Paul TiyambeZeleza, Peter Anyang' Nyong'o, Sabelo Ndlovu-Gatsheni, Sam Moyo, Samir Amin, Steve Bantu Biko, Thandika Mkandawire, Toyin Falola, Tukumbi Lumumba-Kasongo, Valentine Mudimbe, Walter Rodney, Yao Graham, Yash Tandon and Yasmine Fall, among others, have written tomes about the struggles of Africa and Africans under the difficulty structures and systems laid down by colonial and imperial forces, including surveillance apparatuses (Moyo et al., 2020; Moyo, 2021, 2024). The decolonial scholars and researchers have condemned the various colonialities, including surveillance that has outlived administrative colonialism.

It should be reiterated here that after independence, many African countries inherited colonial-era surveillance practices and systems. There is no doubt that colonial surveillance systems have been passed down from colonisers to 'liberators', and some African leaders today use them to telemonitor and victimise their citizens just as the colonisers and apartheidists used to do at the height of their rule (Sheombar & Skelton, 2025). Quite clearly, Africa is currently characterised by coloniality of surveillance, meaning that the ongoing tele-monitoring of citizens represents the continuities of the colonial era practices, systems, laws and institutions. To be clear, decolonial thinkers such as Anibal Quijano, Arturo Escobar Enrique Dussell, Nelson Maldonado-Torres, RamonGrosfoguel, Sabelo Ndlovu-Gatsheni, Steve Martinot and Walter Mignolo have long argued that colonialism did not reach its expiry date at Africa's independence. It has outlived administrative colonialism and it exists in the form of control of the economy, finance, trade and investments, among others. As explained, the discussions in this volume are framed within the discursive context of coloniality of surveillance technology.

The main difference between colonial and contemporary surveillance systems is that today surveillance is largely digitised, whereas in the past, it was largely human-driven. Again, whereas in the past the surveillance powers of the state were directed largely at particular individuals who were deemed to be dangerous to the colonial state, today surveillance is directed at every citizen in the country, of course, opinion makers, government critics, public intellectuals, civil society activists, journalists, human rights defenders and opposition leaders, as well as minority populations are still given special attention (Munoriyarwa & Mare, 2023). Today, countries such as Angola, Cameroon, Chad, Cote d'Ivoire, Egypt, Equatorial Guinea, Ethiopia, Ghana, Kenya, Morocco, Niger, Nigeria, Tanzania, Uganda, Zambia and Zimbabwe have doubled mass surveillance of all aspects of economic, political and social lives (Sheombar & Skelton, 2023). One of the most worrying observations in this volume is that African governments are currently involved in a process of renovating, retooling and reproducing coloniality of technology through deploying intrusive AI surveillance technologies against their own citizens in partnership with foreign actors who are only concerned with profits and geostrategic objectives over human rights, civil liberties and political freedoms.

Lastly, it must be noted that the digital surveillance of Africans is not limited to African countries. In fact, the digital surveillance of Africans outside Africa in countries like the United States, the United Kingdom, France and China is a growing concern. Their phones and emails are monitored and intercepted; their biometric data, including fingerprints and facial recognition scans, among others, are sometimes required, and not those for non-Africans. This is a clear example of the coloniality of surveillance in Global Africa. This is an area for future research, as the contributors in this volume did not pay much attention to the racialised AI surveillance in Global Africa.

Legal and Regulatory Landscape

One of the concerns raised in this volume is that the rise of AI surveillance and digital technologies in Africa is not backed by the requisite regulatory frameworks that protect and safeguard the rights of citizens. The contributors in this book decry the fact that many African countries are still using some antiquated colonial and apartheid legal and regulatory instruments. This is a clear exemplar of the continuities of colonialism in Africa and the observation is true with many other countries of the Global South. The old colonial and apartheid laws present a fertile ground to 'irrigate' intrusive surveillance practices and systems in Africa that were erected to keep the black majority exploited, marginalised, oppressed, peripherised, subalternised, suppressed and otherised, as well as stuck on the other side of the abyssal lines. Countries like Namibia, South Africa and Zimbabwe still retain some of the draconian laws that were enacted by the settlers at the height of colonialism and apartheid. What is even more disturbing is that where African countries have made changes to the colonial and apartheid laws, those changes have been only tokenistic and cosmetic, meant to placate the restive population. For instance, countries such as Chad, Malawi, Mozambique, Tanzania, Tunisia, Uganda, Zambia and Zimbabwe have enacted legal provisions requiring mandatory compliance by third parties to government interception requests. These kinds of laws tend to undermine democratic principles, human rights, civil liberties and political freedoms in the same fashion that the colonial and apartheid frameworks dehumanised, denigrated and subjugated Africans. In particular, Zimbabwe has passed a battery of legislation, including the Interception of Communication Act of 2007 and the Cyber and Data Protection Act of 2021, as well as the Official Secrets Act, among others. Similarly, Mozambique enacted laws that limit the freedoms of the press, such as Law nr. 12/75 of State Secrecy and Law nr.19/92 of Crime against the State Security (Nhanale & Verde, 2023). Moreover, Mozambique, Namibia and Zimbabwe have approved regulations for compulsory registration of SIM cards, thereby removing anonymity from mobile phone communications. These practices are not dissimilar to the colonial and apartheid laws in terms of their motives and implications for the citizens.

As previously mentioned, most of the laws intended to govern the digital lives of the people in Africa have been promulgated under the guise of data protection, electronic transactions, cybersecurity and national security that are contrary to the principles of fundamental human rights, civil liberties and political freedoms defined in the constitutions (Nhanale & Verde, 2023). As noted, some of these laws do not only allow surveillance to be brazenly implemented but also compel providers of telecommunication services to facilitate communication interception, restrict encryption usage; stipulate the mandatory collection of biometric data; demand the localisation of personal data; and bestow law enforcement agents broad search and seizure powers reminiscent of apartheid South Africa where the blacks were subjected to inhumane treatment by state agencies. In this context, the citizens are 'stripped naked', they have no privacy and their rights only exist on paper.

Available evidence indicates that with a combination of colonial-inspired laws and lack of data protection laws in Africa, the people are perennially exposed to privacy infringements, violation of human rights, violation of civil liberties and political freedoms. This is further worsened by the lack of institutional checks and balances, thereby exposing citizens to political surveillance, suppression, subjugation and dehumanisation by state agents (Jili, 2020). It is therefore not unreasonable to conclude that the current surveillance laws and regulations are reproducing colonial habits, practices, behaviours, attitudes, norms, values, principles, cultures and ideologies. This is in direct contrast to the initial excitement about digital technologies as presumed vectors of transformation from authoritarianism to democracy. At the same time, there were claims that technology would help African governments prevent crime, enhance emergency response, counter terrorism, counter intelligence and espionage, and promote cybersecurity and business security. On the contrary, many African governments have deployed the surveillance apparatuses to control and dominate the people, suppress political freedoms and perpetuate the practices of authoritarian governance (Nhanale & Verde, 2023:4). These are symptoms of continuities of colonialities of power, technologies, markets and economy as articulated by heterodox (decolonial and dependency) scholars.

Given the potential of AI surveillance systems to reproduce and perpetuate colonial power structures in Africa, the authors in this volume are unanimous in canvassing for greater transparency, accountability and progressive regulation in the deployment of AI surveillance systems in Africa. Progressive forces in Africa, including the independent media, academics and civil society, among others, are called upon to push back on the darker side of AI surveillance technologies. This is in line with the African Union Commission on Human Rights and Peoples Rights, which has already called for a nuanced regulation and deployment of surveillance technologies to protect human rights, privacy, civil liberties and political freedoms across the world (Mongae, 2024; Nishnianidze, 2024).

The Emergence of the Surveillance State

It is almost trite to say that Africa is witnessing the emergence of a Surveillance State, also known as the Panopticon State. This is a state in which the government, in partnership with some tech companies, collects and analyses vast amounts of data on citizens in order to punish political dissent, even though the stated objective is to monitor cybercriminals and cybercrime. The reality is that the Panopticon State is a modern version of an apartheid surveillance state. Although AI surveillance is practiced in various forms of governance, including the democratic states of the Global North, its negative effects are more pronounced in authoritarian states, such as Iran, the Republic of North Korea, Russia, Saudi Arabia and China, among others. The contributors in this volume focus on the Chinese Panopticon State, which is increasingly adopted as a model in many African countries, including Cameroon, Cote d'Ivoire, Egypt, Equatorial Guinea, Ethiopia, Ghana, Kenya, Morocco, Niger, Nigeria, Tanzania, Uganda, Zambia and Zimbabwe. There is no doubt that under President Xi Jinping, the Chinese government has turned China into the largest surveillance state, a techno-dystopia and the biggest 'digital prison on earth' (Gravett, 2020; Sheombar & Skelton, 2023; Sakarombe et al., 2025). Clearly, China has the most developed surveillance system and the most comprehensive institutional framework to implement its surveillance laws and policies. Its political leadership is committed to controlling and dominating the Chinese population.

To be clear, China is not currently beholden to the Silicon Valley-based tech giants, such as Google, Apple, Facebook, Amazon and Microsoft (GAFAM). For instance, instead of Google, the main search engine in China is Baidu. Instead of Google's YouTube, China has Bilibili. Instead of Facebook and Twitter, China has Weibo. Instead of Instagram, there is Xiaohongshu. Instead of Amazon, there are companies like Taobao and Jingdong (aka JD.com). In lieu of WhatsApp or other messaging apps, China has WeChat-which along with AliPay, is also used for payments, as alternatives to Google Pay and Apple Pay. Above that, China has TikTok, one of the most popular social media platforms on Earth. This serves to demonstrate the fact that China is a digital power in its own right and is currently involved in a cut-throat geoeconomic competition with the United States on the digital technologies global value chains.

The surveillance system of China is organised as a programme dubbed 'The Great Firewall', also known as 'The Golden Shield Project'. The system is one of the largest of its kind on earth and is designed to maintain strict control over the use of the Internet within China and especially the restive regions of Xinjiang, Tibet and Hong Kong, which have seen a significant increase in digital surveillance in recent years (Nishnianidze, 2024). The Great Firewall system is a brutal version of the United States' PRISM and MUSCULAR, the United Kingdom's Temporia and Russia's SORM programmes (for a more detailed discussion of these surveillance systems, see Nishnianidze, 2024). These are just a few examples of surveillance programmes that currently exist at the global level. The Chinese Great Firewall project enables the authorities to monitor citizens' behaviour and maintain social control by identifying and eliminating any potential threats to the security of the government and the Chinese Communist Party (CCP). Under this programme, the Chinese government has installed thousands of sensory systems in the restive region of Xinjiang. The surveillance tools include CCTV cameras with facial recognition, automated license plate recognition and infrared capabilities. As previously mentioned, China is not the only country that has constructed an elaborate surveillance system. The Spanish government has also constructed a massive surveillance network in the region of Catalonia, in northern Spain. The Spanish government came up with what is called 'the Catalan Protocol for Prevention, Detection and Intervention in Processes of Violent Extremism in Spain' (Mejias & Couldry, 2024a, b). This is a preventive techno-social system established to monitor the restive Muslim population in the country. The Spanish government's surveillance practices in Catalonia have been criticised for their lack of transparency and potential infringement on human rights. Nevertheless, the example of Catalonia demonstrates that surveillance is not confined to autocratic states, such as Iran, the Republic of North Korea, Russia, Saudi Arabia and China, but even democracies have been constructing surveillance states across the globe.

Not unexpectedly, many African countries have been building surveillance states in the image of China and other surveillance models across the world. In particular, China has been exporting its model as part of Beijing's geopolitical, geoeconomic and geostrategic agendas in Africa and the rest of the Global South. The Digital Silk Road, a component of the Belt Road Initiative, is the primary conduit for transferring digital technologies from China to Africa and the rest of the Global South (Sheombar & Skelton, 2023). The Digital Silk Road encompasses multiple technology areas, including 5G, data centres, e-commerce, Smart Cities, smartphones, undersea fibreoptic cables, Internet of Things and Artificial Intelligence, among others.

Evidently, Africa has seen a significant surge in imports of Chinese surveillance technologies in recent years. As reported by the Carnegie Endowment for International Peace in 2020, Chinese companies have supplied surveillance equipment to at least 24 African countries (Pamment, 2020). On average, China supplies approximately US$1 billion worth of digital surveillance tools annually in the form of loans to countries such as Cameroon, Chad, Cote d'Ivoire, Egypt, Ethiopia, Kenya, Malawi, Morocco, Nigeria, Rwanda, South Africa, Zambia and Zimbabwe (Matsengarwodzi, 2023). Thus, apart from the Chinese debt pile-up as a result of infrastructure loans, the procurement of surveillance technologies is deepening the debt crisis on the continent. Whilst the question of Beijing's interests on Africa's natural resources, markets and de-Taiwanisation, has long occupied researchers and scholars of geoeconomics, geopolitics and international relations as well as global power structures, the recent explosion of China's AI surveillance technology in Africa is proving to be a new area of concern (also see Polyakova & Meserole, 2019; Moyo, 2022; Travers, 2024). As noted earlier, African governments have justified the acquisition of surveillance technologies by using security, crime prevention, traffic management, emergency response, counter-terrorism, counter-intelligence and espionage, border control, cybersecurity, business security and infrastructure protection, as cover for their surveillance frenzy.

Needless to say, the pile up of surveillance technologies has some negative ramifications on human rights violations, right to privacy, freedom of expression, freedom of assembly and many more. For example, evidence from Tanzania and Uganda indicates that citizens' privacy and digital human rights are in danger from digital surveillance technologies since these technologies have been instrumentalised as tools for Foucauldian control and oppression by state agencies (Sheombar & Skelton, 2023). A study carried out by Murray et al. (2023) confirms that remote surveillance systems and practices have had chilling effects on the general population. The study explains that digital surveillance has prompted self-censorship and unwillingness to engage with individuals or organisations suspected to be subject to surveillance. Crucially, it has affected the ability of civil society to organise and mobilise society. It is for these reasons that the contributors in this volume view Chinese surveillance technologies as part of coloniality of power with adverse effects on freedom of expression, freedom of assembly, self-determination and reminiscent of colonialism.

The Contradictions of Safe Cities Project

The rise of surveillance states in Africa is inextricably linked to the growth of Chinese Smart or Safe Cities on the continent. To be sure, these cities are the new vehicles through which surveillance technologies are being exported to Africa. The terms 'Smart Cities' and 'Safe Cities' will be used interchangeably in this volume. It is interesting to note that many things these days have been christened smart or safe, take for example, smart phones, smart cars, smart borders, smart parking, smart buildings and smart energy, among others. The irony of Smart and Safe cities is that some of them are neither 'smart' or 'safe'. Take, e.g. cities like Harare, Maputo and Johannesburg that have embraced the Smart City concept; they are neither Smart nor Safe in the literal sense of these two terms. In the context of this discussion, the Safe Cities are equipped with a range of interconnected track devices, video cameras and software that are used to monitor work, leisure, shopping, learning, communication, business and commercial transactions of the citizens. Most of the surveillance apparatuses that are installed in many African cities were supplied by Chinese companies, especially Dahua Technology, CloudWalk, Hikvision, Huawei and ZTE. The major recipients of surveillance technologies for Safe/Smart Cities have been countries such as Benin, Egypt, Ghana, Kenya, Morocco, Niger, Rwanda, South Africa, Tunisia, Uganda and Zambia. The Zimbabwean government is implementing its Smart Zimbabwe 2030 Master Plan, which seeks to transform the country through technology. Under this programme, the country has constructed National Data Centres in Harare and Mazowe. It is also building its US$60 billion Zim Cyber City project (Nhanale & Verde, 2023). In Nairobi, Kenya, Huawei installed 1800 high-definition cameras and 200 high-definition traffic surveillance infrastructures (Harrisberg & Bhalla, 2023; Sheombar & Skelton, 2023). There are many more Smart City initiatives underway across the African continent today. As Travers (2024) correctly observed, most of the deals entered by African governments with Chinese companies such as CloudWalk, Hikvision and Huawei have been completed without public consultation and or parliamentary approval.

On paper, the goals of Smart Cities are good. These include enhanced policing, improved public transport, enhanced public safety, better healthcare services, green infrastructure and improved urban planning, among others (Jili, 2020, 2022). The Rustenburg City argues that its Smart City project aims to develop the local economy, enhance citizen participation, improve public safety and transportation, expand the scope of government services and implement digitalised public utilities through leading technologies (Jili, 2019). It is the irony of history that the same surveillance technologies are used by governments for malign reasons. For example, the surveillance packages of Smart Cities have a sophisticated capacity to collect and transmit data to central command and control data centres in real time, where the data are analysed and used to punish opinion makers, journalists, government critics, opposition leaders and civil society activists.

It is, however, the argument of this volume that despite the much-celebrated idea of Smart Cities, available evidence indicates that these cities have not achieved their stated goals of promoting the development of the local economy, improving public safety and transportation and expanding the scope of government services in Africa so far. On the contrary, it has been reported that crime rates have increased in Johannesburg, Maputo, Mombasa and Nairobi despite the installation of massive surveillance systems in these African cities (Gagliardone, 2021; Nhanale & Verde, 2023; Passalacqua & Polito, 2024). Moreover, in a strange twist of logic, countries with surveillance systems have seen increased arrests, harassment and clampdown on political dissent rather than criminals, thieves, terrorists, smugglers, drug and human traffickers. In light of this observation, it is worth reiterating the point that instead of enhancing the quality of life, surveillance systems are deployed as tools that violate individuals' privacy rights, freedom of expression, freedom of the press, freedom of movement, political rights, rights to health, education, dignity and access to information (Kwet, 2018; Nhanale & Verde, 2023; Laibuta, 2024; Sakarombe et al., 2025).

Key Actors in the Surveillance Sector

Drawing from the foregoing discussion, it can be noted that the three key actors on the digital surveillance ecosystem in Africa are the African governments along with the state agencies; tech companies such as Dahua Technology, CloudWalk, Hikvision, Huawei and ZTE; and the global actors such as China and the United States. Taken together, these actors take advantage of Africa by unfair and unethical means for financial, political, diplomatic and economic benefits.

First, China's interest in exporting its surveillance technologies to Africa is driven by its geostrategic goal of expanding its global influence, and strengthening its position as a global leader of the digital sector. At the same time, China aims to advance its diplomatic ambitions, corporate interests and technological prowess. By providing surveillance technologies to African countries, China seeks to deepen its bilateral ties as well as secure African markets. It is not only China that is involved in the surveillance business in Africa. Other powers, including Germany, Israel, Italy, the United Kingdom and the United States, are equally playing geopolitical chase-games with technology on the continent. China is only reified here because of the intensity and specific projects such as the BRI, DSR and the Smart Cities initiatives that have taken root faster than any other known programmes since administrative colonialism and apartheid days. Additionally, Beijing's surveillance agenda is tied to its domestic and social control agenda. By exporting these technologies, China can legitimise its own surveillance state model in the eyes of the world.

Second, it will be demonstrated that some African governments, including those of Cameroon, Egypt, Ethiopia, Morocco, Rwanda and Zimbabwe, are driven by their desire to control and dominate their citizens as a power retention strategy. As noted, digital surveillance has been used to maintain authoritarian control, suppress dissent and monitor government critics and opposition activists. There are also concerns that in the process of building surveillance states, some African governments are pillaging state resources through opaque borrowing, opaque tendering processes and underhand dealings. To be clear, the intersection of corruption and digital surveillance imports is a growing concern in Africa, though not much research has been done in this area. Clearly, some African governments are involved in what some scholars have termed 'algorithmic dispossession'. This refers to the way AI surveillance tools are used by the ruling elite to facilitate the centralisation of power leading to the deprivation of the majority of the citizens (Travers, 2024).

Third and final, tech companies, including startups, are major players in the surveillance ecosystem in Africa. It should be recalled that foreign companies played a role in the colonial project. These include companies such as the British South African Company, the Germany East African Company, the Imperial British East African Company, the Royal Niger Company and the United Africa Company, that were used as tools for primitive accumulation, accumulation by dispossession and extractivism in Africa and the Global South (Coleman, 2019; Benyera, 2023). Today, Silicon Valley-based and Shenzhen-based tech companies: Amazon, Alibaba, Apple, Baidu, ByteDance, Facebook, Google, Microsoft, Netflix, Tencent, TikTok, Xiaomi, ZTE, are all over Africa for the same reasons that their colonial predecessors pursued during the colonial and apartheid era. The Chinese companies Dahua Technology, CloudWalk, Hikvision, Huawei and ZTE are aligned with Beijing's objectives of creating spheres of influence, growing markets, building partnerships and collaborations with African governments and domestic tech companies in shaping the region's technological and political landscape. Crucially, the companies are after profits through exports, debts and minerals, which are exchanged for technologies.

Overall, there is a general agreement among the authors in this volume that the losers from the deployment of the AI surveillance systems and practices in Africa are the people. It is reasoned out that the majority of the people are unable to exercise their fundamental rights out of fear of being surveilled by state agents who have access to their private lives-both online and offline. Clearly, the African populations are increasingly under surveillance conditions that have eroded the enjoyment of their fundamental rights, civil liberties and political freedoms, among other outcomes of the darker side of AI surveillance technologies.

Methodology

As mentioned, this book provides a prognosis of the actors, drivers, motives, contradictions and implications of the controversial digital surveillance in Africa. The analyses in this volume are pursued primarily from the standpoint of heterodox approaches, including dependency theories, world systems theory and decolonial perspectives. A prime concern of the authors is to confront the tensions, contradictions and motives of the rise of digital surveillance tools in Africa. The book draws from the review of the emerging literature on digital surveillance in Africa, including academic literature, books, reports, policy documents and media reports. Databases such as GoogleScholar, JSTOR and ResearchGate were utilised to access peer-reviewed journal articles, book chapters and conference papers. There are also empirical chapters in this volume where the contributors conducted in-depth interviews with experts, government officials, policy makers, journalists and media professionals, civil society, business and Chinese digital companies, as well as former security officials. Additionally, case studies of countries such as Cameroon, Cote d'Ivoire, Ethiopia, Ghana, Nigeria, South Africa, Uganda, Zambia and Zimbabwe were carried out. The volume is necessarily synthetic and its remit is very extensive and multifaceted.

Although the authors in this volume came from different epistemological and disciplinary backgrounds and offer different perspectives on digital surveillance, there is a currency that runs across the chapters in this volume: the perverted history of surveillance, the explosion of AI surveillance tools, the instrumentalisation of digital surveillance and the implications of surveillance on human rights, privacy, political freedoms and civil liberties. Together, the authors provide a map to make sense of the emerging surveillance state in Africa. However, the focus of the book on the darker side of the actors, such as algorithmic oppression, algorithmic exploitation and algorithmic dispossession, does not make it a miserablist narrative. Instead, the book should be received as a wake-up call to policy makers who are encouraged to rethink their digital policies and practices to protect human rights and freedoms in an evolving digital world.

Structure of the Book

The chapter after this introduction, by *Allen Munoriyarwa* provides theoretical, historical and contemporary contexts of electronic surveillance in Africa. He argues that the growth of Chinese surveillance technologies in Africa is part of a ‘nuclear option’ strategy by the Chinese Communist Party (CCP) to eliminate and obliterate other surveillance technology players from the Global North and other parts of the world seeking a place in the burgeoning African surveillance market. As such, the author views the explosion of Chinese electronic surveillance tools in Africa as part of a geoeconomic competition largely between the United States and China, the two global powers that are contending for global supremacy. Munoriyarwa rightly argues that the CCP seeks to use its surveillance start-up techs as ‘menus of manipulation’ in its growing desire to control Africa in the ‘new scramble for Africa’. This chapter contributes a new perspective on what is ethically at stake when African states monitor their citizens.

Ronald Chipaike, Bazel Chinyonga and Tafadzwa William concur with Munoriyarwa’s argument on digital surveillance apparatuses being deployed by Beijing as geoeconomic tools in its bid to rise to the helm of the global governance order. However, the trio focuses more on the implications of Chinese surveillance technologies on the state of democracy, the rule of law and human rights in Africa. The authors also note that surveillance technologies have been deployed by African governments to monitor government critics, public intellectuals, civil society activists, journalists and opposition politicians’ communications and collect citizens’ private and sensitive information. Contrary to the tendency of condemning China, this chapter argues that African governments have agency and are the ones who import and abuse technology. As such, the three authors view the activities of African governments as pro tanto objectionable practice. They conclude by calling for civil society and other non-state actors to play a key role in pushing back against the weaponisation of remote surveillance practices in Africa.

Auxence Augustin KOA discusses how remote surveillance technologies from China have transformed Cameroon into a panoptic state. The concept of the panoptic state is conceived in this chapter as a state where the government has complete domination and control over its citizens. The concept was first introduced by the French philosopher Michel Foucault. KOA argues that Cameroon is now a fully blown Foucauldian panoptic state where movements of opinion makers and government critics are tracked and monitored. He further argues that the construction of the panoptic state in Cameroon is part of a shifting configuration that situates and installs Chinese models of remote surveillance in the country.

Nevison Shumba and Bhekimpilo Nhlabano Moyo's chapter discusses the complexities surrounding the deployment of surveillance technologies in Zimbabwe and the benefits and risks they pose to human rights, governance and digital sovereignty. The duo argues that surveillance tools have a dual role, that is, they can reduce crime while at the same time, and they can be used to violate human rights, personal privacy and civil liberties. This chapter attempts to expose the paradoxes, ironies and contradictions in the deployment of electronic surveillance in Zimbabwe. Although the authors do not use the concept of coloniality, their case study of Zimbabwe provides a typical example of algorithmic coloniality. The authors conclude their chapter by canvassing for a regulatory framework that is in line with international human rights standards.

Emmanual Matambo's chapter deploys constructivism as a theoretical framework to examine the role of national identity and interest in South Africa's embrace of Chinese technologies. Constructivist theory is a social science approach that explains how social reality is constructed through social interactions, norms and values. This framework is carefully deployed to analyse how African governments socially construct the values and beliefs that shape the implementation of their digital surveillance projects. The chapter focuses on the presence of Chinese tech entities in South Africa, in particular, Huawei, Hikvision and smartphone manufacturers. It interprets South Africa's endorsement of Chinese technologies and postulates possible hazards that are partly based on Article 7 of China's National Intelligence Law. This law enjoins all Chinese entities to aid the Chinese government's intelligence gathering. The chapter has three main arguments: firstly, that South Africa embraces Chinese technologies; secondly, this embrace lies in South Africa and China's intersubjective identities. Thirdly, Article 7 of China's National Intelligence Law poses risks for the use of tech companies in South Africa for China's quest for political control.

Lucy Anning's chapter discusses how the rise of Chinese technologies aggravates existing governance challenges in Africa. Like Shumba and Moyo's chapter, Aning's chapter raises critical questions about privacy, freedom and state control in Africa. In particular, the author argues that with the increasing prevalence of electronic surveillance programmes and systems in Africa, the extent to which the right to privacy is safeguarded has become a pressing issue. Anning also delves into the regulatory shortcomings of African nations. She argues that African countries are characterised by weak legal frameworks and inadequate oversight mechanisms, which means that the continent is vulnerable to external tech dominance over and above the abuse of technology by state agencies.

Mbongeni Nhliziyo's chapter examines the intricate interaction between African agency, Chinese digital technologies and the emergence of surveillance states in Africa. This chapter introduces the valuable concept of authoritarian diffusion. This concept refers to the process by which authoritarian regimes spread and influence other countries, in this case by using their technologies. Nhliziyo's chapter explores how the perceived success of China's model of digital control, combining economic growth with stringent surveillance, entices African states, particularly those already leaning towards authoritarianism. It argues that African governments actively procure these technologies under the guise of addressing pressing domestic public security challenges, including crime, terrorism, banditry, piracy and infrastructure deficits. The author concludes his chapter by advocating for an African agency that could promote inclusive digital governance, safeguard individual liberties and counter the potential for digital authoritarianism.

Gorden Moyo's chapter focuses on the tensions between digital sovereignty and digital surveillance. He argues that some African countries have used digital sovereignty to justify digital surveillance. In doing so, some African governments have doubled their purchase of surveillance tools from China under the guise of de-Westernisation. Moyo argues that countries such as Burkina Faso, the Central African Republic, Niger and Zimbabwe have been canvassing for de-imperialisation, de-westernisation and delinking from the Euro-Western orbits of power and economy. As part of this delinking agenda, they have been looking towards the Global East for investment, trade, finance and technology. However, Moyo notes that instead of using digital sovereignty to protect the continent from the malign foreign influence, some African governments have used it to entrench their rule, punish their critics and enrich themselves through opaque imports of digital technologies. The chapter concludes by elevating the idea of decolonial agency that is presented as having the potential to protect the general population from the weaponisation of digital surveillance.

Lucy Anning's second chapter focuses on the Forum on China-Africa Cooperation (FOCAC). Unlike in her earlier chapter, which discussed how the rise of Chinese technologies aggravates existing governance challenges in Africa, in this one, Anning argues that FOCAC has positioned itself as a transformative catalyst for Africa's industrialisation and digital economy, fostering South-South cooperation through infrastructure, technological transfer and economic integration. The author presents a more optimistic role of China in Africa while raising concerns about the negative implications of its electronic surveillance. To support her argument, the chapter interrogates the proliferation of Chinese surveillance technologies within FOCAC's framework, exploring its implications for Africa's industrial and digital sovereignty. The chapter concludes by underscoring Africa's urgent need for strategic engagement that safeguards economic autonomy while leveraging China's developmental support.

John Herg's chapter makes use of different international relations (IR) theories, including realism, constructivism, world systems analysis and postcolonialism, to provide different analytical 'cuts' of how US-China rivalry plays out on the African continent in relation to digital technologies. These theoretical approaches offer different lenses through which to analyse digital surveillance in Africa, highlighting the complex interplay of power, identity, norms and technology in shaping digital surveillance systems and practices on the continent. The goal of the author is not to arrive at a preferred theory, but to show different aspects of a multifaceted reality by using various IR perspectives. Herg argues that viewing digital surveillance from different approaches, paradigms, prisms and perspectives is likely to enhance our understanding of the drivers, actors, motives, contradictions and implications of the emerging surveillance culture in Africa.

The last chapter by *Philani Moyo and Gorden Moyo* provides a postscript. It offers a synthesis of actors, motives, contradictions and implications of AI surveillance technologies in Africa. It also reinforces the argument made throughout the book that AI surveillance technologies in Africa have been deployed in ways that violate the fundamental rights of the citizens, despite the fact that these rights are guaranteed in national constitutions, regional and international conventions, as well as in domestic legislation. The chapter concludes with a clarion call for the decolonisation of digital technologies in Africa and the rest of the Global South.

References

Benyera, E. (2023). *The fourth industrial revolution and the recolonisation of Africa; The coloniality of data*. Routledge. www.routledge.com/

Beraja, M., et al. (2023). *Exporting the surveillance state via trade in AI*. https://www.wsj.com/articles/

Coleman, D. (2019). Digital colonialism: The 21st century scramble for Africa through the extraction and control of user data and the limitations of data protection Laws. *Michigan Journal of Race & Law, 24*(2), 417. https://doi.org/10.36643/mjrl.24.2.digital

Gagliardone, I. (2021). *Chinese digital tech in Africa: Moral panics and the messy reality of surveillance*. https://blogs.lse.ac.uk/cff/2021/05/20/chinese-digital-tech-in-africa-moral-panics-and-the-messy-reality-of-surveillance/

Gravett, W. (2020). Digital neo-colonialism: The chinese model of internet sovereignty in Africa. *African Human Rights Law Journal, 20*(1), 125–146. https://doi.org/10.17159/1996-2096/2020/v20n1a5

Harrisberg, K., & Bhalla, N. (2023). *The rise of surveillance tech in Africa: What you need to know*. Context. https://www.context.news/surveillance/the-rise-of-surveillance-tech-in-africa-what-you-need-to-know

Ibrahim, A. (2024). *How digital authoritarianism in Africa threatens citizens' human rights*. https://www.africanliberty.org/2024/11/14/how-digital-authoritarianism-in-africa-threatens-citizens-human-rights/

Jili, B. (2019). Chinese surveillance tools in Africa. *China, Law and Development, 8*. https://www.aspi.org.au/report/mapping-chinas-tech-giants

Jili, B. (2020). *The spread of surveillance Technology in Africa Stirs Security Concerns*.

Jili, B. (2022). The spread of Chinese surveillance tools in Africa. In I. C. Daniels, B. Erforth, & C. Teevan (Eds.), *Africa–Europe Cooperation and Digital Transformation* (1st ed., pp. 32–49). Routledge. https://doi.org/10.4324/9781003274322-3

Königs, P. (2022). Government surveillance, privacy, and legitimacy. *Philosophy and Technology, 35*(1). https://doi.org/10.1007/s13347-022-00503-9

Kwet, M. (2018). *Digital colonialism: US Empire and the new imperialism in the global south* (SSRN Scholarly Paper No. 3232297). Social Science Research Network. https://doi.org/10.2139/ssrn.3232297

Kwet, M. (Ed.). (2021). *The Cambridge handbook of race and surveillance*. Cambridge University Press. https://books.google.co.zw

Laibuta, M. (2024, December 3). *State surveillance in Kenya breaches citizens' right to privacy*. African Liberty. https://www.africanliberty.org/2024/12/03/state-surveillance-in-kenya-breaches-citizens-right-to-privacy/

Matsengarwodzi, D. (2023). *Colonial legacy of surveillance: Hidden world of surveillance technology in the African continent*. https://institute.aljazeera.net/en/ajr/article/2423

Mejias, U. A., & Couldry, N. (2024a). *Data grab: The new colonialism of Big Tech and how to fight back*. WH Allen. https://www.penguin.co.uk/book

Mejias, U. A., & Couldry, N. (2024b). *Data grab: The new colonialism of Big Tech and how to fight back*. Chicaco University Press. https://www.degruyterbrill.com/document/doi/10.7208/chicago/9780226832319/html

Monahan, T. (2025). Surveillance in trump's America. *Surveillance & Society, 23*(1), 1–16. https://doi.org/10.24908/ss.v23i1.19220

Mongae, M. (2024). *The opportunities and risks of leveraging technology in Africa*. ACCORD. https://www.accord.org.za/analysis/the-opportunities-and-risks-of-leveraging-technology-in-africa/

Moyo, G. (2021). African agency, finance and developmental states. *African Agency, Finance and Developmental States*, 1–235. https://doi.org/10.1007/978-3-030-72412-2/COVER

Moyo, G. (2022). China-Taiwan Geoeconomic competition for diplomatic recognition: Battling for the soul of Africa. In S. O. Abbide (Ed.), *Taiwan in Africa: Seven decades of certainty and uncertainties*. https://books.google.com

Moyo, G. (2024). Africa in the global economy: Capital flight, enablers, and Decolonial responses. *Advances in African Economic, Social and Political Development, Part, F2469*, 1–173. https://doi.org/10.1007/978-3-031-51000-7/COVER

Moyo, G., Nhliziyo, M., & Fayayo, R. (2020). The entanglement of Zimbabwe in the US-China Geoeconomic frictions: Defining winners and losers. *iBusiness, 12*(03), 81–102. https://doi.org/10.4236/ib.2020.123006

Munoriyarwa, A., & Mare, A. (2023). *Digital surveillance in southern Africa: Policies, politics and practices*, 1–220. https://doi.org/10.1007/978-3-031-16636-5/COVER

Murray, D., Fussey, P., Hove, K., Wakabi, W., Kimumwe, P., Saki, O., & Stevens, A. (2023). The chilling effects of surveillance and human rights: Insights from qualitative research in Uganda and Zimbabwe. *Journal of Human Rights Practice, 16*(1), 397–412. https://doi.org/10.1093/jhuman/huad020

Nhanale, E., & Verde, R. (2023). *The context and the international drivers of surveillance in the SADC* (Media Policy and Democracy Project (MPDP). University of Johannesburg's and the University of South Africa's. https://www.academia.edu/

Nishnianidze, A. (2024). Surveillance in the digital age. *European Scientific Journal, 20*, 1–25. https://doi.org/10.19044/esj.2024.v20n37p1

Ogasawara, M. (2019). Mainstreaming colonial experiences in surveillance studies. *Surveillance and Society, 17*(5), 726–729.

Pamment, J. (2020). *The EU'S role in fighting disinformation: Taking Back the initiative*.

Passalacqua, C. C., & Polito, C. (2024). *The Chinese supply of surveillance technology to Africa going beyond the authoritarian bias*. LUISS. https://sog.luiss.it/

Polyakova, A., & Meserole, C. (2019). *Exporting digital authoritarianism: The Russian and Chinese models* (Democracy and Disorder Series) (pp. 1–22).

Roberts, T., Mohamed Ali, A., Farahat, M., Oloyede, R., & Mutung'u, G. (2021). *Surveillance law in Africa: A review of six countries*. https://doi.org/10.19088/IDS.2021.059

Sakarombe, E., Chimwamurombe, F., Masuku, S. S., Mupanga, J., & Mutume Tanaka, E. C. (2025). The coloniality of Chinese surveillance technologies in Africa. *International Journal of Research and Innovation in Social Science*. https://doi.org/10.47772/IJRISS.2025.9020107

Sheombar, A., & Skelton, S. K. (2023). Follow the surveillance: A Breadcrumb Trail of surveillance technology exports to Africa. In *IFIP advances in information and communication technology, 696 AICT* (pp. 241–261). https://doi.org/10.1007/978-3-031-50154-8_19

Sheombar, A., & Skelton, S. K. (2025). Who supplies digital surveillance technologies to African governments? *Digital Surveillance in Africa*, 183–210. https://doi.org/10.5040/9781350422117.CH-8

Travers, L. (2024). *Algorithmic coloniality? The case of chinese artificial intelligence technology and Zimbabwean surveillance 15*(2).

Gorden Moyo (PhD) is currently a Research Fellow at the Fort Hare Institute for Social and Economic Research at the University of Fort Hare in South Africa; Fellow at the University of the Free State in South Africa; Senior Lecturer in the Faculty of Humanities and Social Sciences at Lupane State University in Zimbabwe; Director of the Public Policy and Research Institute of Zimbabwe (PPRIZ); Member of the Editorial Board of the Sabella Abidde Publishing House, University of Alabama (USA); Member of the Board of Trustees of the Mass Public Opinion Institute (MPOI); Associate Member of the International Society for Development and Sustainability (ISDS), Japan; President of the Development Studies Association of Zimbabwe (DeSAZ); Member of the Southern African Development Parliamentary Forum Technical Group on Public Financial Management; ex-Minister of State in the Prime Minister's Office, ex-Minister of State Enterprises and Parastatals, and former Member of Parliament of the Republic of Zimbabwe (2009–2013); and former British Council Facilitator of the Pan-African Leadership Programme in 19 countries across Africa, including Botswana, Cameroon, Eritrea, Ethiopia, eSwatini, Ghana, Kenya, Lesotho, Liberia, Malawi, Mauritius, Namibia, Nigeria, South Africa, Tanzania, Uganda, Zambia, and Zimbabwe. He is a Chevening Scholar whose primary research interests are in global finance, international economic relations, developmental states, public leadership, military commercialism, Africa-China relations, and African agency, among others. He has published several articles in peer-reviewed journals and several book chapters. His most recent books include *African Agency, Finance, and Developmental States* (Palgrave Macmillan, 2021); *Making Politics in Zimbabwe's Second Republic: The Formative Project by Emmerson Mnangagwa* (Springer, 2023), co-edited with Prof. Kirk Helliker; *Africa in the Global Economy: Capital Outflows, Enablers and Decolonial Responses* (Springer, 2024); and *Global Storms and Africa in Global Politics: Contemporary Challenges and Decolonial Responses*, co-edited with Sabelo J. Ndlovu-Gatsheni (Springer, 2025).

Roberts, T., Mohamed Ali, A., Farahat, M., Oloyede, R., & Mutung'u, G. (2021). Surveillance law in Africa: A review of six countries. Institute of Development Studies. https://doi.org/10.19088/IDS.2021.059
[illegible], L., Chiumbu, [illegible], Munoriyarwa, A., [illegible], Mare, A. (2025). [illegible] surveillance technologies [illegible] [illegible] Media. https://doi.org/[illegible]
[illegible] (2021). [illegible] surveillance [illegible] technologies [illegible] Africa. [illegible] (pp. 247–263). https://doi.org/10.1007/[illegible]
[illegible], A., & [illegible], S. (2022). [illegible] surveillance technologies [illegible] government [illegible] Surveillance [illegible] (pp. [illegible]). https://doi.org/[illegible]
[illegible] (2023). [illegible] surveillance [illegible] artificial intelligence in [illegible] [illegible] (2023).

Charles Mutasa (PhD) is currently a Research Fellow at the [illegible] Institute for Social and Economic Research at the University of Fort Hare in South Africa. [illegible] Fellow at the University of the Free State in South Africa, Senior Lecturer in the Faculty of Humanities and Social Sciences, Lupane State University in Zimbabwe, Director of the [illegible] Institute of Zimbabwe (PPRIZ), Member of the Editorial Board of the [illegible] Studies Publishing House, University of Alabama, USA, Member of the Board of Trustees of the Mass Public Opinion Institute (MPOI), Associate Member of the International Society for Development and Sustainability (ISDS), Japan, [illegible] Development Studies Association of Zimbabwe (DSAZ), Member of the Southern African Development Community [illegible] Technical [illegible] Ministry of State in the Prime Minister's Office [illegible] of the Republic of Zimbabwe [illegible] Leadership [illegible] countries across Africa including Botswana, Cameroon, Nigeria, Ethiopia, [illegible] Ghana, Kenya, Lesotho, Liberia, Malawi, Mozambique, Namibia, Nigeria, South Africa, Tanzania, Uganda, Zambia and Zimbabwe. He is a [illegible] researcher [illegible] governance, socio-economic development issues [illegible] United Nations, and [illegible]. He has published several articles in peer reviewed journals and several book chapters. His most recent books include [illegible] (2021), [illegible] The [illegible] (2023), [illegible] Palgrave Macmillan [illegible] (2021), [illegible] and [illegible] Development [illegible] [illegible].

Chapter 2
The 'Sinofication' of Surveillance in Africa: Exploring Emerging Dynamics

Allen Munoriyarwa

Abstract This chapter provides a refreshing and productive exploration of the 'Sinofication' of Africa-Chinese relations through the global trade of surveillance technologies. The chapter answers the question: In what ways are Chinese surveillance technology companies influencing African surveillance practices and cultures? Through interviews with a myriad of actors ranging from policymakers, former parliamentarians, digital technology experts, lawyers and human rights activists, the chapter makes two interrelated arguments. It argues, firstly, that the growth of Chinese surveillance technologies in Africa is part of a 'nuclear option' strategy by the Chinese Communist Party (CCP) to eliminate and obliterate other surveillance technology players from the Global North and other parts of the world seeking a place in the burgeoning African surveillance market. Secondly, the CCP seeks to use its surveillance start-up techs as 'menus of manipulation' in its growing design to control Africa in the 'new scramble for Africa'. It concludes by noting the inherent dynamics of this growing relationship and how it is likely to morph in the future.

Introduction

Between 22 and 23 June 2023, the Media Policy and Democracy Project (MPDP) held a conference in Johannesburg. Some conference attendees raised several important concerns about China. Some attendees noted during the deliberations that there is a growing surveillance culture amongst African countries, especially in Southern Africa, where the MPDP had conducted several studies on the issue. It was further noted that China and its tech corporations were central to this growing surveillance culture. Chinese technology corporations were at the forefront of supplying African regimes with surveillance technologies like CCTV, facial recognition

A. Munoriyarwa (✉)
Journalism, Walter Sisulu University, East London, South Africa
e-mail: amunoriyarwa@wsu.ac.za

G. Moyo (ed.), *An Anatomy of AI Surveillance in Africa*, Studies in Digital Politics and Governance, https://doi.org/10.1007/978-3-032-04269-9_2

technologies, and various other software associated with surveillance (MPDP, 2021). Earlier on, in region-wide research, the MPDP (2021) noted that Chinese start-ups have effectively become the region's main suppliers of surveillance technologies. Jili (2022) has argued that the growing influence of Chinese tech companies is being felt across Africa.

Chinese surveillance technologies have come to Africa through various initiatives. For example, some technologies have come through the Chinese-sponsored 'smart-city' initiatives (Chiumbu, 2021; Munoriyarwa & Chiumbu, 2022). In countries like Zimbabwe and Mozambique, the militaries of these countries have become major importers of Chinese surveillance technologies (Nhanale and Verde 2023; Munoriyarwa, 2022). All these developments point to two critical developments around digital surveillance. First, this points to the fact that established Chinese and start-up tech companies are increasingly becoming influential as suppliers of surveillance technologies. Secondly, as Jili (2022), Munoriyarwa (2022) and Chiumbu (2021) have noted, the Chinese Communist Party (CCP) and Chinese banks, like the Export-Import Bank of China (CHEXIM), amongst others, are funding these companies. This means these Chinese technology companies are backed by some of the most powerful financial institutions that see an opportunity in this trade and the ruling party in China, which sees surveillance technology as part of a broader geopolitical strategy to influence Africa.

This chapter examines how Chinese surveillance technology start-ups influence African surveillance practices and cultures. Extant literature has explored the growth of China's surveillance technologies on the African continent. Furthermore, existing literature has noted how these surveillance technologies are being weaponised in public spaces and communication surveillance. There is a dearth of research on how these surveillance technologies influence the dynamics of surveillance in Africa and how Chinese surveillance technologies are 'Sinofying' surveillance practices on the continent. Africa is largely a net importer of surveillance technologies. Any player who controls the surveillance technology market in Africa is, one can argue, therefore, likely to control the global trade in surveillance because Africa is turning out, gradually, to be a huge importer of these technologies. However, China's growing dominance is not happening in a vacuum. It is happening against the background of weak civil society opposition to it, collusion between the CCP and African regimes that are increasingly becoming authoritarian and the rise of a 'middlemen culture' in surveillance trade that drives these start-up techs from China. In this regard, African countries are importing not only Chinese surveillance technologies but also their surveillance cultures. As noted, the growth of Chinese tech companies falls within this broad design by the CCP.

This chapter draws on interviews with selected members of specific communities of practice. These were journalists, members of the Zimbabwe National Assembly, lawyers, human rights activists and other media activists who were accessible to the researcher. The chapter also draws on document analysis from different countries in Africa, where interviewees were not accessible. The documents include policy documents, state policy pronouncements, credible news reports, civil society reports, and publicly available reports by researchers that are publicly available. Therefore, the chapter builds on both primary and secondary data. As noted earlier, the fieldwork for this chapter was conducted between April 2023 and December 2023. The data are also part of a larger research project on digital surveillance by intelligence agencies. A total of 14 interviews were conducted during this period. Interviewing respondents in Zimbabwe is not easy. The semi-authoritarian nature of the state blocks respondents from speaking. The consequences of speaking and revealing information are huge for even the most interested informant. It is even worse on a subject as 'sensitive' as security intelligence. There is always a palpable fear that speaking would lead to reprisals. This fear is understandable in Zimbabwe, where intelligence agencies have a history of brutalising citizens (Muvingi, 2008). Zimbabwe's intelligence and security agencies have a well-documented history of violently abusing citizens (Tom & Chekera, 2022). Therefore, speaking about them is often treated as both a taboo and an invitation for trouble.

However, the disillusionment of the post-coup period has opened up windows of opportunity for researchers, as some of the retired members have started to open up and speak about some illegalities within these agencies. More media reports have also started to surface, chronicling excesses within these agencies, and they have become a credible source of data for researchers. The data was analysed using thematic analysis methods commonly used for interviews. Documents were analysed using documentary analysis, which is a common hermeneutic approach in the analysis of documentary data. Security forces in semi-authoritarian regimes do not often operate as democratic institutions. They are often weaponised and personalised for individual gains. This is the case in Zimbabwe, where security agencies often operate in the service of the ruling Zimbabwe African National Union-Patriotic Front (ZANU-PF) party to suppress and repress even legitimate opposition.

Chinese Technologies in Africa

Several lines of thought have generally emerged in scholarship relating to Chinese technologies in Africa. There is a 'sceptical view' that sees China as exporting technologies of repression and other forms of harm to Africa (Munoriyarwa, 2022; Tawiah et al., 2021). The overall argument of this view is that China is not only importing surveillance technologies but its dealings with African regimes are carefully calculated so that China exports critical technologies that would be used to suppress, through surveillance, any legitimate opposition to regimes in Africa (Taylor, 2010). Furthermore, this view argues that while China's influence in Africa is expanding (Matambo, 2019), the country is uncomfortable with regimes that mimic Western democracy (Kaburu, 2020). Thus, China has developed a neo-colonial relationship with Africa, in which it seeks to shape African politics in its own image (Deych, 2018; Lumumba-Kasongo, 2011). Therefore, as the argument goes, China is selling both technologies and a culture of surveillance that would be strategic to the survival of the CCP (Munoriyarwa & Chiumbu, 2022). Scholars of this view further argue that what China generally wants is for its African allies to follow, its 'hardcore' surveillance culture (Deych, 2018), like the Chinese social credit system (Mac Síthigh & Siems, 2019), or its hard suppression of the Uighur population within its own borders (Murphy et al., 2022). What this means is that Chinese surveillance technologies are spreading across Africa, and this is happening alongside other measures associated with the Chinese model of political control and repression and the entrenchment of extremely repressive surveillance practices. Thus, China is exporting both technologies and a culture that, in the long run, will serve the CCP. To achieve this, China is employing several methods. These include the ruling CCP supporting Chinese start-up technology firms' investments in Africa (Polyakova & Meserole, 2019). Thus, the CCP actively supports technology companies like Huawei, Hikvision, Tencent, and Xiaomi, which are producing advanced AI-driven technologies. In addition to this, other researchers (see, e.g., Segal, 2018) have noted that it is now difficult to separate China's technology companies from China's own foreign policy (Huang & Tsai, 2022). These technology companies are inherently part of the CCP's foreign policy because they help the party realise its ideals (Lumumba-Kasongo, 2011), especially the imperative to strangle any forms of democracy like privacy, free speech, freedom of movement and thought. China, furthermore, openly supports its banks to advance grants and loans to African countries to enable the global trade in these technologies, in addition to building other infrastructures (Matambo, 2019). For instance, China National Aero-Technology Import and Export Corporation (CATIC), China Exim Bank and China Development Bank have been critical in advancing loans to African governments and institutions in this regard (Acker & Brautigam, 2021).

Other scholars (Huang & Tsai, 2022; Munoriyarwa & Chiumbu, 2022) note that the recent advances in smart city projects across Africa have everything to do with China advancing its repressive surveillance technologies. Thus, smart cities are the new vehicle through which surveillance technologies and cultures are being exported to Africa. China's planning is strategic in this regard. The Chinese regime is not at all comfortable with democratic regimes in its orbit of allies. This explains why it would be ideal to export its surveillance cultures. For African ruling regimes, that are increasingly becoming authoritarian in contexts like Zimbabwe, Chinese surveillance technologies come with special 'advantages'. These include the absence of end-user requirements and the availability of loans and grants to smoothen the process of trading in these technologies (Huang & Tsai, 2022). According to Onjala (2018), this partly explains why Africa's debt to China is increasing.

Furthermore, China's surveillance technologies offer opportunities for an emerging class of 'middlemen' involved in this trade. These middlemen encourage this trade and spur it on, as it offers huge financial rewards. They are (the middlemen) linked to mostly corrupt African political regimes (Beraja et al., 2023). They see an opportunity for huge financial rewards and have been at the centre of sustaining this trade. These middlemen have morphed into sizeable companies in order to 'legitimise' their work. Munoriyarwa and Mare (2023) note further that the trade in repressive Chinese surveillance has been enabled through a public discourse of 'fearpolis'. The key takeaway in this literature is that China is exerting an oversized influence on African countries through the export of its technologies. More so, these technologies are not just 'innocent' technologies imported for policing, law, public order and national security. They have become technologies of repression used against legitimate political opposition in most African countries where they have been exported. There is, furthermore, a growing symbiotic relationship between Chinese start-up technology companies and African governments. According to Hawkins (2018), this symbiotic relationship is based on the latter's ever-growing appetite for surveillance technologies and the former's desire for both markets and data on which to train its new technologies (Hawkins, 2018).

International Political Economy of Surveillance

For this chapter, I draw on the theoretical insights of International Political Economy (IPE) (see the works of Mendonça & Demuner, 2016; Smith, 1989; Viotti & Kauppi, 2012 and many others). Broadly, IPE draws on political economy, which deals with the relationship between the state and the market (Smith, 1989). It also draws on the discipline of international relations that deals with the questions of relations -cooperation (or lack thereof) between and amongst players as represented primarily in the nation-state and by other actors like global Non-Governmental Organisations (NGOs) or Civil Society Organisations (CSOs). IPE highlights 'the umbilical relationship between power and money, state and market, authority and the economy' (Munoriyarwa & Chiumbu, 2022:213). As a conceptual tool, IPE seeks to understand the global political issues that spread worldwide (Ballam & Dillman, 2019). IPE seeks to establish who the actors are on global issues, their power in discourses and practices around these issues, and how much interest they have. At a global level, actors are usually powerful (Rudd, 2019). Actors' powers are often transnational (Ballam & Dillman, 2019). In other words, IPE interrogates problems that span an entire world (Ballam & Dillman, 2019), establishing interconnections of actors at a global level.

Furthermore, IPE seeks to understand the global political dimensions that account for the use of power by domestic groups, states, transnational organisations, Non-Governmental Organisations (NGOs), and transnational corporations. All these actors decide how goods and other resources, such as security products, are distributed (Ballam & Dillman, 2019). Thus, IPE sees a complex relationship that ties the state, the market, and society as interrelated actors.

Three perspectives dominate IPE. The first perspective is the realist approach to IPE (see Gilpin, 2003). This approach foregrounds the nation-state as the central actor in international relations, always acting rationally (Gilpin, 2003). The economic liberalism approach acknowledges an array of actors in an intricately interdependent relationship at a global level. The economic liberalism approach, unlike the realist one, acknowledges the existence of other actors beyond the state. Lastly, there is the structuralist approach, which is rooted in Marxism (Munoriyarwa & Chiumbu, 2022). Structuralist approaches acknowledge that the global world is an arena of fierce competition (Hoogvelt, 1997). Furthermore, structural approaches to

IPE argue that ownership of the means of production, or any form of domination of the productive areas, means that the producers will, ultimately, dominate global relations. This domination of the means of production has led to the division of the global world into the centre (wealthy states) and the periphery (poor states).

Drawing on this framework, I explore how China's dominance of the global surveillance industry has given it power at a global level as an actor in its field. Furthermore, I explore how Chinese start-up technology companies and African regimes constitute a symbiotic relationship of mutual benefit in the trade in surveillance technologies.

The Spread of China's Surveillance Technologies in Africa

Since Xi Jinping, the current Chinese leader (as of 2024), assumed power in 2012, China has aggressively expanded its influence on many continents. However, this influence has been most notable in Africa and East Asia. Many African countries are gradually importing Chinese surveillance technologies (Jili, 2021; Feldstein, 2021; Munoriyarwa & Chiumbu, 2022). By 2024, most African countries had become net importers of Chinese technologies (Mare & Munoriyarwa, 2026). There is hardly any African country that does not import Chinese technologies. Two different but related forces are pushing Chinese surveillance technologies into Africa. The first force is the ruling CCP. The CCP has, in the past two decades or so, made a conscious decision to establish close relations with African regimes. And this has marked the beginning of Chinese influence on the continent. One former Member of the Zimbabwean National Assembly (MNA) said,

> China-Africa relations are extensively driven from the top echelons of the CCP. The party is very aggressive in this. This explains the huge number of delegations our government has frequently sent to China…even when nothing tangible comes out of these visits; they are good for the optics (sic)… (Respondent 1, former MNA member).

The CCP cannot, however, push this on its own. Over time, it has used Chinese start-ups and well-established technology companies to exert its influence. Gravett (2020) notes that most Chinese technology companies are private enterprises governed by market forces and profit motives. However, they report and are held accountable by the CCP because, in the broader scheme, they are part of the CCP's foreign influence strategy. Some examples of these companies include Hikvision, one of the world's leading manufacturers and suppliers of surveillance cameras (see Munoriyarwa & Mare, 2023), ZTE, and a private enterprise, Huawei, which retains close ties with the ruling party (Gravett, 2020). A former ZANU-PF National Assembly (NA) member during the Mugabe era said,

> We could not travel to China to meet the Chinese government delegation without attending shows hosted by these companies to showcase their technologies… The CCP carefully arranged this, and whatever negotiations and agreements we entered into with these companies, the CCP was very interested in that as well…(Respondent 2, former NA member).

The existence of a wilfully aggressive (in foreign policy terms) CCP party and emerging technology companies has created a fertile ground around which Chinese start-up techs and the CCP have expanded their influence on the African continent. China's CCP and technology companies share this broad vision of politics and profit.

We cannot discount the growing appetite for these technologies among many African regimes. Several African regimes are beginning to unravel under the threats of organised public opposition, disillusionment, internal defections and other legitimate challenges to their authority. For example, Zimbabwe's ruling party, ZANU PF, tottering under the weight of its own inefficiencies, corruption, and poor service-delivery record, has become a key actor in purchasing surveillance needed to suppress and repress legitimate opposition. It has been instrumental in importing surveillance technologies for its civilian surveillance institutions, like the Zimbabwe Republic Police (ZRP) and the military, the Zimbabwe Defence Forces (ZDF) (see MPDP, 2021; Munoriyarwa, 2022; Dhlela, 2021). Zimbabwe is not the only one; it is just a prominent example of how surveillance technologies from China are circulating within official institutions targeted at legitimate opposition. One former opposition NA member said,

> We are very aware that the regime built an arsenal of these technologies from China. The so-called deals from China are making these technologies available outside the transparent channels of the state… the ZANU PF regime abuses its power and uses these technologies against us' (Respondent 5, former opposition MNA member).

However, in the Zimbabwe context, even members of the ruling party are not spared from surveillance by their own party. So, the circulation of surveillance technologies in Zimbabwe is generally about hierarchies of power. This can also be true about much of Africa. In the Zimbabwe case, Vice President Kembo Mohadi once complained, the first time he resigned from the government on 21 March 2022, that 'I am a victim of information distortion, voice cloning and sponsored spooking and political sabotage…'.

Several intertwined actors can be identified in the supply matrix of surveillance technologies. Chinese technology companies like Dahua, Tencent and Huawei are already opening African subsidiaries. For example, Dahua has opened branches in Morocco, South Africa, Tanzania and Zimbabwe. These are strategic decisions these technology companies make, driven and supported by the CCP. By opening subsidiaries within Africa, they are creating direct links that make them dominate the surveillance technology market, which, at the moment, is a very lucrative market. They can also outwit other buyers who are not directly linked to the market and the strategic decision-makers. One technology activist said,

> Major surveillance technology players from China are establishing offices and contracts in Africa. This is their market…and they want to dominate it. They want to be close to government officials who decide who buys what. They want to be close to top government officials (Respondent 8, technology experts from Zimbabwe).

China has begun to treat its surveillance technology companies as central to its foreign expansion strategy. Zimbabwe remains a critical example of China's expansion of surveillance technologies, as I have demonstrated in the previous sections of this chapter. Recently (in 2023–24), many China-driven projects that promote a Chinese version of surveillance have been launched. For example, the Zimbabwe government agreed with Chinese companies to set up a cyber-city in Mount Hampden, Harare. This followed the completion of a China-funded parliament in Zimbabwe. Several cyber-companies are sprouting around Zimbabwe, using Chinese technologies to install surveillance cameras and other surveillance technologies around cities and roads in Zimbabwe.

For example, on 30 August 2024, on his visit to China, the President of Zimbabwe, Emmerson Mnangagwa, signed a Memorandum of Understanding (MOU) with Huawei to supply 'digital technologies'. Chinese tech companies are already shaping Zimbabwe's surveillance practices in several ways. The MPDP (2021) report noted many of these ways, and there is no reason to belabour this point here. However, much more recently, Chinese techs have launched a rather aggressive move to further consolidate their surveillance technologies' dominance in the country. Already, in 2024, two smart city projects, supported by Chinese technologies, are being rolled out in Mt. Hampden, Harare and Bubi, Matabeleland North. Huawei has also launched a multi-billion-dollar surveillance camera project in Bulawayo. These examples show how Chinese techs have overrun Zimbabwe's surveillance technology market.

Chinese Start-Up Technology Companies as a 'Nuclear Option' for the Ruling CCP

There is little doubt that the CCP's major objective is to export its social, economic and political ideology across the many countries of the world (Sun, 2016). Africa has, in this grand CCP scheme, become a major target. Arguably, Africa is offering a fertile opportunity to spread CCP ideology. African liberation parties are faltering. They are quickly losing support. This has left them with China to look up to for survival lessons. In its own home, China has provided invaluable lessons, ranging from the authoritarian control of religions like Christianity (Yang, 2017) to the suppression of civilians to the outright suppression of ethnic groups like the Uyghur (Stern, 2021). All these have served as examples to which the ruling liberation parties have looked up for vicarious lessons. China has started to leverage such already existing relations to push forward its digital authoritarianism model, propagated through its tech companies. In fact, as some respondents noted, most ruling parties have had several years of tech relations with China, which have given them the tools to suppress legitimate opposition. One informant noted,

> When you hear that China is an all-weather friend, we mean that it has been doing everything here. It has supplied the technologies that have helped the ruling party to surveil us…we know that since the days of Morgan Tsvangirai, China and Iran have supplied the state with technologies used against us even when we are a legitimate opposition. We knew we had always been targets (Respondent 3, former opposition Member of Parliament MNA).

However, the new (surveillance) technology-based relationship between China and African countries, which has firmed over the years, is only the latest in several other relationships. For instance, the CCP launched a political party training programme across Africa. The programme, according to Sun (2016), has three basic components: (1) lectures at a Chinese education or training institution, (2) field trips to a local government for first-hand experience and meetings with local officials, farmers, and businesses, and (3) cultural programmes to familiarise participants with Chinese traditional culture. This training brought many liberation movements like the African National Congress ANC and ZANU-PF close to the CCP. And it is the genesis of this relationship that has enabled Chinese technology companies to infiltrate the African surveillance market. One respondent noted,

> The question of technology companies like Huawei, Dahua and others like ZTE coming here to supply different surveillance technologies is not supposed to surprise anyone. ZANU PF cultivated these relationships a long time ago. Remember, the CCP has been an ally of ZANU PF since time immemorial. These are relations that date back a long time. China was very strategic about this (Respondent 4, former ZANU PF MNA).

But where liberal democratic values have taken root, China's ideological push has not gone beyond influencing specific political parties. These cadre trainings represent China's weaponisation of its tech companies to complement these efforts. This explains Huawei's aggressive investments across African countries. For example, how has the technology company invested in North Africa (Kadi, 2022) and Southern Africa (Munoriyarwa & Mare, 2023). The investments are part of the CCP's weaponisation of its technology companies, a move that previously would be unthinkable (like nuclear war itself). One respondent noted,

> There is no moment you can discuss China's investments in Africa without talking about its technology companies. They are always the torchbearers of any discussion about China in Africa. To me, the reason is that they sell more than technologies…they sell a culture of surveillance that China very much wishes to export to Africa… in addition to other forms of political and economic domination… (Respondent 7, Human Rights Lawyer).

Several drivers explain why China has been able to weaponise its technology companies as 'menus' of manipulation in furthering its dominance of the surveillance technology market. I have already identified the insatiable appetite for suppression amongst some African ruling parties like ZANU-PF. But beyond this, external factors have driven much of China's success.

China's Technology Companies as 'Menus of Manipulation'

Chinese technology companies are manipulatable instruments within Beijing's global power strategy. This is why Beijing has perfected its brand of authoritarian capitalism that allows it to control these technology companies through a unique version of ownership that, amongst other practices, allows government shareholding and deployment of political cadres into the governing structures of these technology companies (Gravett, 2020). For example, Gravett (2020) notes that Beijing owns shares in ZTE and Huawei, amongst other surveillance technology manufacturing companies. Datenna (n.d.) notes that Beijing's manipulation of its tech companies includes the acquisition of 'golden shares' in the strategic techs within China. According to Datenna (n.d.), golden shares are a special ownership tool through which a Chinese government-controlled entity can exercise outsized influence in a company's decision-making through a small, symbolic ownership share that, on paper, looks insignificant. The CCP, through the Chinese government, influences practices within these techs by manipulating its ownership of these golden shares. Through its control of these golden shares, we have a crucial insight into how Beijing's state interests spill into these techs' quotidian practices.

However, Beijing still intends to see these companies as both profit-making companies and, simultaneously, 'political' ones that can sync neatly with its strategic global goals, one of which is to dominate the flow and trade of surveillance technologies. Originally, as Respondent 7 further noted, China had envisaged that its tech companies would be 'props' for its economic interests. One respondent notes thus,

> China's objectives have changed over time. First of all, its own authoritarianism has hardened at home. You cannot think of China without thinking of the hard suppression policies on its own citizens... and over time, China realised that it has allies in Africa...with no respect for human rights and bent on destroying any opposition to their power... then China realised that actually these surveillance tools have a market...... (Respondent 7, Human Rights Lawyer).

Beyond the imperative of profit-making, Hawkins's research has noted that Chinese surveillance technology companies are also searching for data on which to train new surveillance technologies, such as surveillance software algorithms. Hawkins (2018, no page), notes thus,

> In 2015, the Chinese government launched its Made in China 2025 plan to dominate cutting-edge technological industries. This was followed up last year with plans for the country to be a world leader in artificial intelligence by 2030 and build a US$150 billion industry. The developing world is a big part of these ambitions. But China doesn't just want to dominate these markets. It wants to use developing countries as a laboratory to improve its own surveillance technologies.

Because these technology companies already have their own commercial imperatives, they have their own agency. Since there are many, they have basically become an integrated network of actors dominating the global surveillance market. A technology expert said,

> There is always a process through which Beijing has manipulated its technology companies into its global political orbit. It starts with the political actors establishing (diplomatic) links and economic networks abroad. After that, they propose to trade in surveillance technologies through government officials, military and other security attaches. In recent times, the process has included journalists. In Zimbabwe, state media journalists are now part of China's target. They legitimise and sanitise the involvement of China's technology companies in the public eye. If you complain about issues of costs and sustainable funding of technology acquisition, Chinese banks like CHEXIM and the China Exim Bank are brought into the equation (Respondent 8, technology expert).

What China brings to the surveillance trade is a 'one-stop-shop' approach. All the processes, from establishing contact to financing and acquisition, are done by actors who are closely aligned with Beijing. This gives Beijing more power and control of the surveillance trade at a global level since its technology companies, while having agency, do not operate outside the ruling party's realm of influence. Beijing's power, therefore, lies in its ability to intervene in purchasing and distributing these surveillance technologies. However, one respondent sees what they call 'Beijing's powerful but invisible hand' in the global surveillance technology trade ecosystem. A human rights Lawyer said,

> I think the CCP might not be at the forefront of pushing the trade in surveillance technologies. But one thing for sure is that its hand is big in this trade and maintains an underground level of invisibility. It has power that allows it ultimate say in where the surveillance technologies end up. This capability underlines its ability to manipulate technology companies within its borders (Respondent 10, Human Rights Lawyer, Harare).

Therefore, the relationship between the CCP and surveillance technology-producing companies inside China involves strategic manipulation and deliberate weaponisation. It is true that while profit-oriented, China's technology companies are also politically-oriented in serving the elite. Hence, these technology companies and the ruling elite are two sides of the same coin. What drives this 'Sinofication' of surveillance practices is both these technology companies and the ruling CCP itself, whose cooperation produces a 'syndicate of actors' in the surveillance trade. Yet beyond these drivers, several other factors within Beijing and in African countries like Zimbabwe have added impetus to Beijing's quest for dominance of the global trade in surveillance, or at least dominance of the African surveillance market.

Many such companies have sprouted across Africa. As Munoriyarwa and Mare (2023) noted, these middleman companies fuel the global trade in surveillance technologies in several ways. These include engagement in aggressive marketing of these technologies for profit; some of them are linked to the ruling elite and can fuel this trade through their links with political elites who, in turn, benefit from the trade. There are two dangers with the 'middleman approach' to trade in surveillance technologies. First, these middlemen may fuel an uncontrollable and dangerous black market of surveillance technologies. There is already a precedent. In April 2021, the South African Police Service (SAPS) was fighting with an assorted mixture of thugs from Zimbabwe, South Africa, and Botswana. Twelve were killed, and others were arrested. The incident is now referred to as the 'Rosettenville shooting'. Amongst the items recovered from the robbers were cellphone grabbers and sophisticated listen-in technology. This is what happens when middlemen enter the global trade in surveillance. No one plays by the rules and sophisticated surveillance technologies end up in the hands of criminals. The second danger is that of capture. These local middlemen, eager to lay their hands on this lucrative trade, may be captured by Chinese suppliers. This will make the surveillance trade more profit-making than human rights-oriented.

Drivers and Consequences of the ‘Sinofication’ of Surveillance

The chapter sought to answer the question: How do Chinese surveillance technology start-ups influence African surveillance practices and cultures? The chapter first scoped the extent of Chinese surveillance technology companies’ influence in Africa.

We have given an example of an authoritarian system like the ZANU PF-led government of Zimbabwe. To expect such a dictatorial system, with no respect for human rights and no value for human life, to run a transparent surveillance culture is equivalent to expecting a chicken to hatch an elephant. As noted in the findings, China uses its tech companies through the Smart City/Cyber City projects already sprouting in Zimbabwe and other African countries (Da Vinha, 2024). One or more Chinese technology companies are involved in every smart city project being developed. For instance, during the Patriotic Front (PF) reign in Zambia under Edgar Lungu, Huawei was at the forefront of championing Zambia’s smart city concept, and it was already completing a huge Zambia data centre project.

However, China’s growing dominance is not happening in a vacuum. It is happening against the background of weak civil society opposition to it and collusion between the CCP and African regimes that are increasingly becoming authoritarian. Regimes like the Zimbabwean one are increasingly relying on repressive measures and outright rigging of election processes in their country. This often triggers the need for more repressive measures when dealing with a restive and disillusioned population. Surveillance of populations has become a weapon of choice for these African leaders. Zimbabwe is well-known for surveilling even its legitimate opponents (MPDP, 2021) and China is also known for supplying the hardware (MPDP, 2021). Added to this is the rise of a ‘middleman culture’ in the surveillance trade that drives these techs from China. In essence, African countries are importing not only Chinese surveillance technologies but also their surveillance cultures. As noted, the growth of Chinese start-up techs falls within this broad design by the CCP. Several African-based companies have sprouted to act as middlemen. For example, Tendy Three Investments (TTI) has become a big middleman in the surveillance technology trade in Zimbabwe.

Added to the dangers above is the fact that Civil Society Organisations (CSOs) in countries like Zimbabwe are not yet speaking out about these dangers. Very few organisations focus on surveillance as a human rights issue about individual privacy. In fact, the South Africa-based, Intelwatch, successor to MPDP, and the Public Policy and Research Institute of Zimbabwe (PPRIZ) have started raising public awareness of these issues in Africa. The expectation would be that as China keeps expanding its surveillance trade on the African continent, more organisations would be at the forefront of raising public awareness and or fighting existing and possible future abuses. This has not been the case. For example, China’s surveillance technologies do not have end-user expectations. They do not have human rights observation protocols. This makes them usable in Africa, where most countries’ leaders have no appetite for human rights.

There are grounds for transparency on which Chinese technologies should be resisted. Firstly, no one knows how these technologies work, the data they were trained on, and their technical affordances. These technologies have to be 'second-guessed' by end users. Second, how China treats its own citizens and 'lesser citizens' like Uighurs gives us a clue of what can generally be expected from Chinese technology organisations. China has normalised within its borders a deep-rooted culture of surveillance, like the infamous Chinese credit system. It is largely expected that this culture will be exported with these technologies. For example, the Chinese social credit system will likely be transferred to African countries since these technologies enable it. As one respondent noted,

> You cannot import these technologies without ending up with the cultures and practices around which they are made and used in their own countries. Why are countries like Zimbabwe avoiding Western technology corporations that sell such technologies? It is because they are looking up to China. China provides them with a surveillance model that they envy so much... (Informant 11, Opposition MNA).

The lack of transparency of purchases of these technologies makes their usage look even murkier. In addition to the ones noted in this discussion, the obvious consequence is that Chinese technology companies will use Africa as a dumping ground for their surveillance technologies that may not work effectively in their context over time. Chinese tech companies will intensify a dumbing-down culture in Africa, which will further intensify unmonitored possession of these technologies and further human rights violations.

Conclusion

The chapter has made two interconnected arguments. First, I argued that the Chinese surveillance technology companies are part of Beijing's ruling elites' 'nuclear option'—a last resort option to extend their power by, among other methods, weaponising these technology companies. This explains why Beijing maintains a tight grip on some technology companies, such as ZTE and Huawei. Therefore, I argued secondly that Beijing views China-based surveillance technology companies as falling within its menu of manipulation—crucial institutions among a gamut of others that can be used to project global power. China, hence, seeks to extend to, as Hawkins (2018) notes, dominate the global trade in surveillance technologies. But, beyond seeking domination of the global surveillance trade market, I have argued that China seeks to export its surveillance cultures to surveillance technology recipient countries in Africa. China's ultimate goal is to destroy or weaken liberal democracy and replace it with its hard authoritarian governance model, characterised by repressive and violent population control. Surveillance is one way, as we have already noted within China itself, through which this hard surveillance-driven repressive culture can be maintained. Early scholars of colonisation in Africa noted that the flag followed the bible (Crouch and Stökl, 2013; West, 2016). These discourses emphasise the importance of the bible to Western colonial domination of Africa. This is equally true when we look at China's growing dominance of Africa. They are couched in discourses of Internet Technology (IT) development, technology cooperation, cybersecurity, and smart city focuses. Yet, at the centre of all these discourses is Beijing's ambitious goal to dominate the production of technologies, their global trade, and, in the process, export to African countries its cultures and practices of surveillance. Furthermore, the chapter notes that Chinese tech companies are the weapons of the CCP, which it uses to expand Chinese influence in Africa. The chapter, however, ends on a sceptical and cautionary note. The continued growth of Chinese tech companies' influence in Africa is a harbinger of a carefully coordinated and orchestrated anti-human rights crusade on the African continent. Future research can focus on several other unexplored areas. For example, future research may explore the (in)effectiveness of current responses to the Sinofication of surveillance in Africa and the ramifications of this growing trend across Africa. Future research may also benefit from further interviews with a variety of respondents. This chapter, however, provided a fundamental examination from which future research could benefit.

Acknowledgements The interviews on which this chapter was built were enabled by funding from the British Academy project called, 'Watching the Watchers: Strengthening Public Oversight of Intelligence-driven Surveillance'. Professor Jane Duncan headed the project as the Principal Investigator (PI). It is accessible here: https://www.gla.ac.uk/research/az/watchingthewatchers/.

References

Acker, K., & Brautigam, D. (2021). *Twenty years of data on China's Africa lending* (Research report no. 04/2021). Johns Hopkins University. https://www.econstor.eu/handle/10419/248245

Ballam, D. N., & Dillman, B. (2019). *Introduction to international political economy* (Vol. 10, 7th ed.). Routledge. https://ejournal.um.edu.my/index.php/mjir/article/view/36614

Beraja, M., et al. (2023). *Exporting the surveillance state via trade in AI.* https://www.wsj.com/articles/

Chiumbu. (2021). Chinese Digital Infrastructure, Smart Cities and Surveillance in Zambia. Accessible at: http://www.mediaanddemocracy.com/uploads/1/6/5/7/16577624/zambia_report.pdf

Crouch, C. L., & Stökl, J. (2013). *In the name of God: The Bible in the colonial discourse of empire*. Brill.

Da Vinha, L. (2024). Smart for whom? Africa's smart cities and digital authoritarianism. *International Journal of Intelligence and CounterIntelligence, 37*(3), 941–959. https://doi.org/10.1080/08850607.2023.2284629

Datenna. (n.d.). *China's crackdown on Big Tech: The role of golden shares*. Datenna. https://www.datenna.com/resources/chinas-crackdown-on-big-tech-the-role-of-golden-shares/

Deych, T. L. (2018). China in Africa: Neo-colonial power or 'win-win' strategy? *Outlines of Global Transformations: Politics, Economics, Law, 11*(5), 119–141. https://doi.org/10.23932/2542-0240-2018-11-5-119-141

Dhlela, D. (2021). Zimbabwe in danger of sleepwalking into a surveillance stat https://www.newsday.co.zw/theindependent/tennis/article/15765/zim-in-danger-of-sleepwalking-into-a-surveillancestate

Feldstein, S. (2021). Surveillance in the illiberal state. In Sajó, András, Renáta Uitz, and Stephen Holmes, eds. Routledge handbook of illiberalism. *London: Routledge* (pp. 351–364).

Gilpin, R. (2003). Sources of American-Japanese economic conflict. *International relations theory and the Asia-Pacific, 1*(3), 299–322.

Gravett, W. (2020). Digital neo-colonialism: The Chinese model of internet sovereignty in Africa. *African Human Rights Law Journal, 20*(1), 125–146. https://doi.org/10.17159/1996-2096/2020/v20n1a5

Hawkins A (2018). *Beijing's big brother tech needs African faces —Foreign policy*. FP. Available at: https://foreignpolicy.com/2018/07/24/beijings-big-brother-tech-needs-african-faces/

Hoogvelt, A. (1997). Globalisation and the postcolonial world. *Macmillan Education UK*. https://doi.org/10.1007/978-1-349-25671-6

Huang, J., & Tsai, K. S. (2022). Securing authoritarian capitalism in the digital age: The political economy of surveillance in China. *China Journal, 88*(1), 2–28. https://doi.org/10.1086/720144

Jili, B. (2021, December 22). *Chinese surveillance tech in Africa, with*. Merics. https://merics.org/en/podcast/chinese-surveillance-tech-africa-jili-bulelani

Jili, B. (2022). The spread of Chinese surveillance tools in Africa. In I. C. Daniels, B. Erforth, & C. Teevan (Eds.), *Africa–Europe Cooperation and Digital Transformation* (1st ed., pp. 32–49). Routledge. https://doi.org/10.4324/9781003274322-3

Kaburu, M. (2020). Decision making and Kenya's foreign policy behaviour: The Moi and Kibaki presidencies in perspective. *Journal of language, Technology & Entrepreneurship in Africa, 11*(1), Article 1.

Kadi, T. H. E. (2022). *How Huawei's localization in North Africa delivered mixed returns*. Carnegie International Peace.

Lumumba-Kasongo, T. (2011). China-Africa relations: A neo-imperialism or a neo-colonialism? A reflection*. *African and Asian Studies, 10*(2–3), 234–266. https://doi.org/10.1163/156921011X587040

Mac Síthigh, D., & Siems, M. (2019). The Chinese social credit system: A model for other countries? *Modern Law Review, 82*(6), 1034–1071. https://doi.org/10.1111/1468-2230.12462

Mare, A., and Munoriyarwa, A. (2026). Disinformation Campaigns in Africa Actors, Consequences, and Responses. London: Bloomsbury.

Matambo, E. (2019). Constructing China's identity in Zambian politics: A tale of expediency and resignation. *Journal of African Foreign Affairs, 6*(3), 43–64. https://doi.org/10.31920/2056-5658/2019/6n3a3

Mendonça, F., & Demuner, D. (2016). The Neo-Gramscian school to international political economy, passive revolution and globalization. *Brazilian Political Science Review, 10*(3), 1–8.

MPDP. (2021). Drifting into darkness. The growth of surveillance in Zimbabwe. Report available at: https://www.mediaanddemocracy.com/uploads/1/6/5/7/16577624/zimbabwe_report_2nd_pages.pdf.

Munoriyarwa, A. (2022). The militarization of digital surveillance in post-coup Zimbabwe: 'Just don't tell them what we do'. *Security Dialogue, 53*(5), 456–474. https://doi.org/10.1177/09670106221118796

Munoriyarwa, A., & Chiumbu, S. (2022). Powers, Interests and Actors: The Influence of China in Africa's Digital Surveillance Practices. In *Farooq, A.K. Digital Dissidence and Social Media Censorship in Africa*" (pp. 209–229). London: Routledge. https://doi.org/10.4324/9781003276326-15

Munoriyarwa, A., & Mare, A. (2023). Digital Surveillance in Southern Africa. Switzerland: Springer International Publishing AG.

Murphy, L. T., Vallette, J., Elimä, N., Salcito, K., Thum, R., & Carter, L. (2022). *BUILT ON REPRESSION: PVC building materials' reliance on labor and environmental abuses in the Uyghur region*. https://doi.org/10.13140/RG.2.2.25154.04807

Muvingi, I. J. (2008). The politics of entitlement and state failure in Zimbabwe. *Peace Research: The Canadian Journal of Peace and Conflict Studies, 40*(1), 77–101.

Nhanale, E., & Verde, R. (2023). The Context and the International Drivers of Surveillance in the Southern African Development Community. Accessible at: https://share.google/h9wrmAHvyfDteZYKA

Onjala, J. (2018). China's development loans and the threat of debt crisis in Kenya. *Development Policy Review, 36*, O710–O728. https://doi.org/10.1111/dpr.12328

Polyakova, A., & Meserole, C. (2019). *Exporting digital authoritarianism: The Russian and Chinese models* (Democracy and disorder series) (pp. 1–22).

Rudd, K. (2019). US-China Relations in 2019. *Horizons: Journal of International Relations and Sustainable Development, 3*(13), pp.12–27.

Segal, A. (2018). When China rules the web: technology in service of the state. *Foreign Aff., 97*(10), pp. 34–44.

Smith, D. E. (1989). Feminist reflections on political economy. *Studies in Political Economy, 30*(1), 37–59.

Stern, J. (2021). Genocide in China: Uighur re-education camps and international response. *Immigration and Human Rights Law Review, 3*(1).

Sun, Y. (2016). Political party training: China's ideological push in Africa? *Africa in Focus*. https://scholar.google.com/

Tawiah, V. K., Zakari, A., & Khan, I. (2021). The environmental footprint of China-Africa engagement: An analysis of the effect of China—Africa partnership on carbon emissions. Science of the Total Environment, 756. https://doi.org/10.1016/j.scitotenv.2020.143603.

Taylor, I. (2010). *China's new role in Africa*. Lynne Rienner Publishers.

Tom, P., & Chekera, S. (2022). Labelling, torture, and law enforcement in Zimbabwe. In *Contesting torture* (1st ed., p. 22). Routledge. https://www.taylorfrancis.com/chapters/edit/10.4324/9780429343445

Viotti, P. R., & Kauppi, M. V. (2012). *International relations theory* (5th ed.). Pearson.

West, G. O. (2016). *The stolen bible: From tool of imperialism to African icon*. Brill. https://books.google.co.zw/

Yang, F. (2017). From cooperation to resistance: Christian responses to intensified suppression in China today. *The Review of Faith & International Affairs, 15*(1), 79–90. https://doi.org/10.1080/15570274.2017.1284415

Allen Munoriyarwa is an Associate Professor of journalism at Walter Sisulu University (WSU) in South Africa, in the Journalism Programme of the Marketing, Public Relations, and Communication Department. His research interests are AI, digital surveillance, and digital media. He administered the Media Policy and Democracy Project grant at the University of Johannesburg between 2020 and 2022. He is currently a researcher and administrator of the British Academy Project (PI: Professor Jane Duncan). This is a current project that can be followed here: https://www.gla.ac.uk/research/az/watchingthewatchers/. He co-authored one of the first books on digital surveillance in Southern Africa (*Digital Surveillance in Southern Africa: Policies, Politics and Practices*, Palgrave Macmillan, 2023). Allen is also a board member of one of the biggest civil society organisations on digital rights, surveillance, and protection of journalism in Africa, Intelwatch. It can be followed here: https://intelwatch.org.za/About.

Chapter 3
African Digital Authoritarianism and China's Role: Implications on Democracy and Human Rights

Ronald Chipaike, Bazel Coster Chinyonga, and Tafadzwa T. William

Abstract Chipaike, Chinyonga and William discuss the various technologies being deployed by African governments to control and police their publics. These include radio jamming, face recognition and telecommunications surveillance supplied by a variety of Chinese companies such as Huawei and Hikvision, among others. With such technology in the hands of leaders whose penchant for authoritarian governance is clear, the implications for civil liberties have largely been negative. As well, Chipaike, Chinyonga and William focus on how these technologies are acquired and how they have aided Chinese merchants, African governments and the Chinese government in its grand strategy of exporting the party-state system of governance to Africa. The increasing importation of these technologies is thus connected to the erosion of civil liberties and generally to increasing authoritarianism.

Introduction

The rapid advancement of digital surveillance technologies, which is largely pioneered by Chinese tech companies, has reshaped the socio-political landscape of many African nations. In recent years, African governments have increasingly turned to Chinese firms such as Huawei, ZTE, and Dahua Technology, among others, for sophisticated surveillance systems under the guise of national security and public safety enhancement (Woodhams, 2020). While these technologies offer promises of crime prevention, counterterrorism, and efficient governance, their deployment raises profound concerns regarding civil liberties, privacy rights, and democratic values in the region (Peterson & Hoffman, 2022). Research indicates a significant surge in the sale and adoption of Chinese surveillance technologies in Africa. According to a 2020 report by the Carnegie Endowment for International Peace, Chinese companies have supplied surveillance equipment to at least 24

R. Chipaike (✉) · B. C. Chinyonga · T. T. William
Peace and Governance, Bindura University of Science Education, Bindura, Zimbabwe
e-mail: bchinyonga@buse.ac.zw; twilliam@buse.ac.zw

G. Moyo (ed.), *An Anatomy of AI Surveillance in Africa*, Studies in Digital Politics and Governance, https://doi.org/10.1007/978-3-032-04269-9_3

African countries, fuelling a growing trend toward digital authoritarianism across the continent (Pamment, 2020). The allure of these technologies lies in their purported effectiveness in monitoring populations, tracking dissidents, and pre-empting security threats, which aligns with the security-centric agendas of many African governments.

The introduction of Chinese surveillance technologies in Africa has ignited debates on the ethical implications and human rights ramifications of such practices. Scholars argue that the mass surveillance capabilities facilitated by these technologies infringe upon fundamental rights to privacy, freedom of expression, and association (Gravett, 2020). The indiscriminate collection of biometric data, pervasive monitoring of online activities and the stifling of dissent through censorship mechanisms have raised red flags among civil society organisations, human rights advocates, and international observers (Damianos, 2021). Drawing from Zimbabwe, Ethiopia, Uganda and South Africa and empirical evidence, this chapter delves into the multifaceted dimensions of the Chinese digital surveillance ecosystem in Africa (Al-Bulushi, 2021). By examining specific instances of surveillance misuse, privacy breaches, and civil rights violations in countries like Ethiopia, Uganda, and Kenya, it seeks to underscore the urgent need for regulatory frameworks that safeguard individual liberties, promote transparency in technology procurement, and establish mechanisms for accountability and oversight.

In light of these developments, it is also imperative for African governments, regional bodies, and international stakeholders to engage in critical dialogues on the responsible use of surveillance technologies, the protection of civil liberties, and the promotion of democratic values in the digital age. This chapter contributes to the ongoing discourse on the intersection of technology, human rights, and governance in Africa, advocating for a rights-based approach to digital surveillance that upholds the principles of accountability, transparency and respect for fundamental freedoms.

It is, however, important to also take into cognisance the fact that the authoritarian-leaning governments of many African countries have traditionally used surveillance technologies to control their populations and spy on them. They have historically acquired such technologies from Israel, Europe, the USA and other regions (Corsi et al., 2020). It is therefore imperative to also seek to understand the agency of African leaders in their initiatives to acquire Chinese surveillance technologies. This will balance the narrative, which seems tipped toward accusing the Chinese government and Chinese tech companies more than African governments. Instead, more blame should be put on African leaders, who seem hungry for these kinds of technologies.

This chapter uses a qualitative narrative approach. It utilises secondary data sources such as scholarly and government publications, newspaper reports and reports of think tanks to analyse the trends around the purchase of surveillance technologies by African governments from Chinese companies. While the weaknesses of an approach purely based on secondary evidence are apparent, the insights deduced from such sources remain very important in analysing the state of affairs in the area of digital surveillance in Africa. Further, while it might have been more effective to zero in on a single case study, the phenomenon of Chinese surveillance technologies is still in its nascent stages in most African countries, to the extent that the single case would not be enough to produce richer data and comprehensive conclusions, hence, the resort to examples from different countries on the continent.

Chinese Surveillance Technologies in Africa

As China's influence in Africa expands, its surveillance technologies have become a focal point of discussion regarding both opportunities and risks for the continent. China's efforts to reclaim its rightful position in the international arena in the twenty-first century include building international credibility by providing security and economic advantages to other nations, which is crucial for its ambition to achieve global power status. Within this context, information and communications technology (ICT) plays a vital role in economic growth, and Africa faces a significant technology gap that more advanced economies, like China, can help bridge. China aims to support underdeveloped countries in improving their telecommunications networks, artificial intelligence (AI), cloud computing and surveillance capabilities, while also establishing cross-border and transcontinental fibre-optic networks and submarine cables. However, these technological partnerships are not without their risks; sensitive data transfers raise concerns about privacy and surveillance, potentially granting China an advantage over Western competitors in terms of access to critical information. This interplay between technological advancement and the potential for increased authoritarian control highlights the complexities surrounding the adoption of Chinese surveillance technologies in Africa, prompting ongoing debates about the implications for governance, civil liberties and national sovereignty.

China's involvement in Africa encompasses a range of technological advancements, including the provision of satellites, the development of fibre-optic connections and the construction of 3G, 4G and 5G networks. It offers access to its advanced technologies, such as facial recognition systems and the BeiDou navigation system. This evolving dimension of cooperation could impact the international system in various ways, for example, Africa's increased access to new military or dual-use technologies may enhance regime stability across the continent. Amin (2024) argues that such advancements empower African nations to bolster their defense capabilities, deterring both external threats and internal unrest. Increased military cooperation and technology transfers among African states could foster regional security alliances, contributing to more stable governance (Adeyemi, 2020). However, more subtle forms of China's involvement in Africa often go unrecognised as security-related. Investments in the telecommunications sector and the implementation of facial recognition technology within smart city initiatives are examples of this (Feldstein, 2020; Hawkins, 2018; Meservey, 2020). The expansion of Chinese fibre-optic networks and the growing use of BeiDou further illustrate this trend (Aluf, 2023; Blaubach, 2022). A comprehensive analysis of China's security engagement in Africa was recently conducted by Eisenman and Shinn (2023), highlighting the multifaceted nature of this involvement. Given China's increasing assertiveness, the failure to adequately recognise its security-related activities in Africa could lead to the oversight of potential future threats (Eisenman & Shinn, 2023).

China has been actively marketing its model of surveillance systems abroad, including both the hardware and software that facilitate these technologies. This model has the potential to establish surveillance societies that mirror China's own practices, especially in nations with poor human rights records where democratic institutions are either fragile or still emerging. As China continues to advance in information technology, the result has often been heightened repression rather than democratisation, especially in African countries that actively purchase the technologies (Mthembu-Salter, 2019). China has played a significant role in building cellular networks throughout the continent. Huawei alone has constructed 70% of the 4G network stations in Africa and is currently engaged in developing 5G networks in Ethiopia, Kenya, South Africa and Uganda (Kidera, 2022). The competitive advantages enjoyed by Chinese companies largely stem from their low pricing, which is bolstered by state subsidies (Fuller, 2016). This dominance in the telecommunications sector grants China access to substantial amounts of data, potentially undermining the national security of its African partners and their allies (Basin et al., 2018). To facilitate independent management of data flows and information, Huawei and ZTE have already established fibre-optic communication and e-government networks in more than 20 African nations, including Kenya, South Africa and Ethiopia. These countries have benefited from improved broadband infrastructure and digital governance capabilities, which have been crucial for enhancing public service delivery and supporting national security efforts. Moreover, Chinese companies are undertaking significant international projects to lay submarine cables, such as SeaMeWe-5, which links Southeast Asia, the Middle East, Western Europe and Africa; Africa Europe-1, connecting Southeast Asia to Europe via Egypt; SAT3-WASC, linking South Africa and Portugal along the western coast; and the extensive Africa Cable, which connects Africa with the United Kingdom. The dominance of China's interests is also evident in other sectors of technological cooperation, particularly regarding submarine cable connectivity, which is critical for the economies of coastal countries (Burdette, 2021).

In Africa, countries are increasingly adopting facial recognition technologies from companies such as CloudWalk, Hikvision and Huawei as part of their smart city initiatives. Smart city initiatives refer to the use of digital technologies, including surveillance systems and data analytics, to manage urban services, improve infrastructure and enhance the quality of life for citizens. These initiatives often aim to optimise public services, transportation, energy use and security through the integration of advanced technologies such as artificial intelligence, big data and the Internet of Things. This technology collects data from millions of individuals, enhancing Chinese Artificial Intelligence capabilities in recognising diverse ethnic groups' voices and faces (Hawkins, 2018). Notable implementations can be found in cities like Johannesburg, Nairobi, Accra and Kampala (Feldstein, 2020), with access to this extensive data giving China a significant competitive edge over

Western rivals, who have limited access to such sensitive information. However, the involvement of Chinese firms in Africa's technological landscape raises important concerns. Despite claims of independence, the 2017 National Intelligence Law requires all Chinese companies to 'support, assist and cooperate with state intelligence work', which raises alarm about potential data leaks and risks of 'back doors' in telecommunications infrastructure. While China's surveillance system is primarily confined within its borders, private companies are actively marketing their technologies to African clients (Feldstein, 2019). Backed by state funding, these firms have made significant inroads into African Information and Communication Technology markets; for instance, Huawei initially focused on improving internet connectivity in Kenya but shifted in 2014 to emphasise smart city solutions (Muzorewa, 2021). Proponents argue that public security technologies not only provide critical intelligence to authorities but also serve as deterrents against criminal activity, highlighting the complexities surrounding the implementation of Chinese surveillance technologies in Africa. Indeed, in China, such technologies have been deployed to drastically reduce crime rates.

The increasing acquisition of Chinese digital surveillance tools by African states represents a significant trend at the intersection of technology and governance on the continent. Reports indicate that approximately 22 African nations have contracted companies like Huawei and ZTE to implement advanced surveillance systems, typically framed under smart city initiatives. Huawei has constructed approximately 70% of Africa's 4G networks as of 2022, far outstripping European competitors and enabling significant improvements in connectivity across the continent (Dahir, 2022). This dominant market position has allowed Huawei to shape the digital infrastructure landscape in Africa. The Kenyan government has appointed Huawei as the principal adviser on its comprehensive master plan for information and communication technologies, which highlights the company's deep involvement in national infrastructure projects (Hansen, 2017). Similarly, ZTE Corporation has provided the Ethiopian government with critical infrastructure to monitor communications, particularly targeting opposition activists and journalists, raising significant human rights concerns (Mthembu-Salter, 2019). Moreover, Transsion Holdings, a Shenzhen-based company, has surpassed Samsung to become the leading smartphone provider in Africa, facilitating connectivity and also the widespread use of Chinese technology among consumers (Muzorewa, 2021). China Telecom's plans to lay a 150,000-kilometre fibre-optic network across 48 African nations further solidify China's influence in Africa's digital infrastructure and connectivity landscape (Aina, 2021). However, this growing reliance on Chinese technology raises critical concerns regarding human rights and civil liberties. Critics argue that these surveillance systems enable authoritarian regimes to monitor and suppress dissent, exemplified by Hikvision's deployment of 15,000 surveillance cameras in Johannesburg through a local provider, which illustrates the potential for invasive monitoring of citizens (Mthembu-Salter, 2019). While proponents of these technologies highlight their potential to enhance security and improve urban management, sceptics caution that the resulting surveillance societies may mirror China's own practices, particularly in nations with fragile democratic institutions. This duality raises vital questions about the implications of adopting such technologies, as African nations navigate the balance between leveraging foreign investment and maintaining civil liberties, ultimately shaping the future of governance and human rights on the continent.

A recent investigative report revealed that Huawei technicians in Uganda and Zambia assisted government officials in spying on political opponents, underscoring the ethical implications of such partnerships (Aina, 2021). In light of these developments, it is crucial for African nations to critically evaluate their technological dependencies and consider the long-term implications of adopting systems that may undermine civil liberties. Governments should prioritize the development of local technological capacity and invest in democratic frameworks that promote transparency and accountability. Additionally, international cooperation is essential to establish standards that protect digital rights and freedoms. By fostering an environment that values open dialogue and citizen participation, African countries can better safeguard their democratic aspirations against the encroachment of digital authoritarianism. While the allure of Chinese technology may offer immediate benefits, the potential erosion of digital freedoms and democratic values when such technologies get into the hands of undemocratic African governments presents significant risks that must be navigated carefully.

Implications of Chinese Digital Surveillance on Human Rights

China has been widely criticised for its extensive surveillance infrastructure, particularly in regions like Xinjiang, where its government has implemented a range of high-tech surveillance tools, including facial recognition, artificial intelligence and biometric data collection to monitor the population. This surveillance system is used not only to track individuals but also to intimidate and silence dissent, a tactic that aligns closely with the fears of self-censorship. China's surveillance regime curtails the freedom to communicate openly, especially for those who might voice opposition to the government.

In Africa, governments have increasingly turned to Chinese-made surveillance technologies to monitor their populations. These technologies, which include facial recognition, artificial intelligence and mobile tracking, enable governments to monitor citizens' activities closely, including their political engagements. This has clear parallels to the way China has used surveillance to stifle political dissent and control information within its own borders. Fear and intimidation characterise China's internal use of digital surveillance to track, control and suppress its citizens, particularly in politically sensitive contexts such as protests or elections (Chen & Kim, 2024a, b).

When such technologies are exported to African countries, they exacerbate the risks to free and fair elections. Digital surveillance can create a climate of fear that discourages citizens from expressing their political preferences, participating in campaigns, or even casting votes freely. In countries where elections are already contested, surveillance can be used strategically to monitor and suppress opposition parties, activists and voters who might challenge the ruling government. This parallels China's use of surveillance in its own domestic political campaigns, where dissenting voices are suppressed through both digital and physical surveillance systems. In China, the government has used digital surveillance technologies to monitor the behaviour of citizens in ways that undermine their privacy and limit their ability to express dissent. By tracking individuals' digital footprints, the government can not only know who is engaging with which political information but can also monitor their movement and behaviour at polling stations. The exportation of such surveillance tools to African countries similarly raises concerns about voter privacy. If governments monitor communications related to the electoral process, such as political discourse, campaign activities, or even individual voting behaviour, this compromises the confidentiality of the ballot.

The ability of governments to intercept communications and manipulate or suppress information about elections is directly relevant to the export of Chinese digital tools. In China, the government maintains strict control over internet content, censoring and suppressing information that does not align with state-approved narratives. In Africa, the introduction of Chinese surveillance technology can provide similar tools for governments to monitor online platforms, track communications and manipulate electoral discourse (Dube et al., 2023). This impacts the transparency and fairness of elections, making it more difficult for citizens to access independent, unbiased information about candidates and political issues. The connection between the use of Chinese surveillance technologies and the erosion of voting rights in Africa highlights the risks posed by the growing global reach of China's digital authoritarian model. These surveillance systems undermine electoral integrity, create an atmosphere of fear and self-censorship and compromise the confidentiality of the voting process, ultimately impeding citizens' ability to participate freely in democratic processes (Nguyen & Osei, 2022a, b). Just as China uses surveillance to maintain political control at home, African governments adopting Chinese surveillance tools may do so to similarly limit the free expression and political engagement of their citizens, thus undermining the democratic process.

China has positioned itself at the forefront of leveraging digital technologies to shape the narrative, control public opinion and suppress dissent within its borders. By blending state-sponsored digital surveillance, disinformation campaigns and stringent censorship, the Chinese government has developed a powerful digital infrastructure designed to maintain its authority. These tactics, ranging from internet disruptions and the criminalisation of online speech to mandatory registration of online content creators, are not merely confined to China but are emblematic of the growing trend of digital governance in authoritarian regimes globally.

In this digital age, China is notorious for orchestrating elaborate disinformation campaigns to manipulate public opinion and stifle criticism. These campaigns often take the form of fake social media accounts, coordinated posts of pro-government content and the deliberate spreading of misleading information aimed at discrediting opposition movements. A notable example is China's infamous '50-cent army', a group of paid internet commentators who are tasked with flooding the online space with government-friendly narratives, counteracting any discourse that challenges the Communist Party's hold on power (Chen & Kim, 2024a, b). This strategy ensures that the regime can dominate the digital landscape, preventing the rise of alternative viewpoints that could threaten its authority.

China also takes extreme measures to control access to information and restrict the free flow of online content. The 'Great Firewall of China' is a massive, state-run censorship and surveillance system that blocks popular foreign websites like Facebook, Twitter and Google, while simultaneously monitoring the activities of internet users. As Huang et al. (2023) note, internet disruptions are strategically deployed during politically sensitive events, such as protests or elections, to prevent citizens from organising or accessing information that could fuel opposition movements.

One of the most striking features of China's digital governance is the stringent regulation of online platforms and content creators. In China, the government mandates that all individuals using online platforms register their real identities. This ensures the authorities can easily track and monitor those engaging in political discourse or sharing sensitive content online. The requirement for mandatory registration of social media accounts provides the government with unparalleled control over who can participate in public discussions, making it easier to target individuals who challenge the state (Chen & Kim, 2024a, b). The criminalisation of certain forms of online speech, particularly content deemed 'false' or harmful to the state, further entrenches government control. Vague definitions of what constitutes 'false information' have led to the prosecution of citizens, journalists and activists who simply voice alternative political opinions. The Cybersecurity Law and related amendments to the criminal code empower the government to arrest individuals based on their online posts, particularly those critical of the regime (Chen & Kim, 2024a, b).

At the heart of China's digital authoritarianism lies an expansive surveillance network that tracks and monitors virtually every aspect of citizens' online and offline behaviour. The government has implemented far-reaching monitoring systems to intercept communications on social media platforms and messaging apps in real time. This surveillance extends beyond internet activities, incorporating the use of facial recognition technology in public spaces and the tracking of private digital communications. These measures, which infringe upon privacy and freedom of expression, prompt citizens to adopt self-censorship strategies to avoid attracting government scrutiny. As individuals, journalists and activists become increasingly aware of the pervasive nature of surveillance, many turn to privacy-enhancing tools such as encryption and secure communication channels to protect their sensitive information. In China, these strategies are not only used to safeguard online activities but also to evade monitoring of physical movements and behaviours by the state.

The freedom of assembly and association is vital to the functioning of democratic societies, allowing citizens to come together to express dissent, organise protests, or form advocacy groups. However, in many African countries, the expansion of state surveillance, often through Chinese-made digital technologies, has severely undermined this fundamental right. Chinese surveillance systems, such as facial recognition, real-time location tracking and internet monitoring, have been increasingly adopted by African governments as tools to suppress political dissent and control public mobilisation. These technologies enable authorities to track the movements of individuals, monitor their digital communications and identify key organisers of protests or political movements. As a result, activists, opposition leaders and even ordinary citizens who seek to engage in political discourse are increasingly fearful of surveillance, leading to a chilling effect that limits their ability to freely organise and protest against government actions (Amin, 2024). The erosion of trust caused by the pervasive presence of surveillance also leads to self-censorship, where individuals refrain from engaging in conversations, both online and offline, out of fear of retaliation. For example, in countries like Uganda and Ethiopia, Chinese surveillance systems are being used to track opposition activities and monitor social media platforms, which restrict the ability of citizens to associate and mobilise in a meaningful way. The adoption of these tools serves as a powerful deterrent to collective action, weakening the foundations of democratic engagement and social movements.

Moreover, the adoption of Chinese surveillance technologies in Africa also amplifies the state's ability to disrupt large-scale protests and monitor political gatherings. This surveillance is not limited to digital tools but often extends to physical monitoring through cameras, drones and other tracking systems that target public spaces where protests or meetings are likely to occur. The use of these tools is particularly alarming in countries where political opposition is already marginalised, and public gatherings are routinely monitored or disrupted. The result is a climate of fear where citizens begin to limit their participation in both formal and informal political events (Krukowska, 2024). China's model of suppressing political dissent by controlling the digital space is becoming a global export, influencing African governments to adopt similar tactics to suppress civil liberties and curtail the freedom of assembly and association. This growing surveillance infrastructure not only compromises privacy but also actively works to eliminate spaces for democratic expression.

Civic participation is a cornerstone of democratic societies, where citizens engage in decision-making, hold governments accountable and express their political preferences freely. However, in African countries adopting Chinese surveillance technologies, the digital tools used to monitor and control public discourse are systematically undermining this participation. Secure and open platforms for public debate are essential for a thriving democracy. When governments, often with the help of Chinese technology, implement extensive surveillance and censorship measures, they create an environment where citizens fear expressing their opinions, particularly on issues critical of the state. In China, the 'Great Firewall' and extensive censorship of social media platforms serve as a model for African nations where governments can manipulate the flow of information and monitor online communication. As African governments embrace these technologies, they implement similar tactics to suppress political opposition, limit access to critical news and restrict free expression online (Amin, 2024). This erosion of secure and reliable platforms reduces public trust in the democratic process, as citizens become increasingly concerned about the risks of engaging in political discourse on digital platforms. In countries like Zimbabwe, the use of Chinese surveillance technology has led to the monitoring of social media platforms and arrests of individuals for online expressions deemed critical of the government. This creates an atmosphere of fear where citizens are hesitant to voice their opinions or engage in civic activities.

Furthermore, the implementation of surveillance and digital control measures exacerbates the feeling of vulnerability among African citizens, limiting their participation in civic processes and elections. Citizens are less likely to engage in meaningful political discussions, participate in protests, or hold their leaders accountable when they fear that their communications and actions are being monitored. The decline in participation is not only due to the fear of state retaliation but also because many individuals feel that their efforts are futile in the face of such pervasive control. As surveillance technologies continue to be deployed, particularly those provided by Chinese companies, governments in Africa gain unprecedented power to manipulate and control the flow of information. This diminishes the quality of civic engagement, as it erodes public trust in institutions and the ability to make informed political decisions. As Deeks (2018) suggests, when citizens cannot access reliable information or express dissent without facing consequences, the civic space contracts, leading to the weakening of democratic foundations. The use of Chinese surveillance tools to monitor and censor online activity has broader implications for political participation, where even private and secure online spaces are infiltrated, further diminishing the conditions necessary for free and fair engagement in public life.

Zimbabwe

Zimbabwe has a longstanding tradition of state-led surveillance primarily aimed at political control rather than genuine crime investigation. Under Robert Mugabe's 37-year rule, the government utilised laws and security structures to execute targeted surveillance on politically significant individuals, alongside widespread monitoring of the general populace. Key legislation, such as the Interception of Communications Act and mandatory SIM-card registration, facilitated this extensive electronic surveillance (Mafunda, 2020). This culture of surveillance has persisted under the Emmerson Mnangagwa administration, which has signalled intentions to enhance these capabilities even further. A critical element of this evolution is the collaboration with Chinese firms, notably Cloudwalk Technology, which has reportedly entered into agreements with the Zimbabwean government to provide advanced facial recognition technology for law enforcement. By granting Cloudwalk access to the biometric data of Zimbabweans, the government not only aids in correcting prevalent racial biases in facial recognition algorithms but also empowers the company to expand its market presence internationally. Such partnerships are predicted to enable Chinese corporations to dominate around 44% of the global facial recognition technology market by 2023, raising concerns about privacy and human rights in Zimbabwe. As these developments unfold, the implications for civil liberties and political dissent remain significant, reflecting a broader trend of increasing state surveillance in the region.

One prominent Chinese company in this landscape is Huawei, which has established a dominant position in Zimbabwe's telecommunications sector. Huawei has secured significant contracts with the Zimbabwean government and state-owned enterprises, notably NetOne, the country's second-largest mobile network operator. The company's primary contribution has been supplying telecommunications equipment, which has been deployed nationwide by NetOne. In 2014, NetOne undertook a network upgrade facilitated by Huawei, supported by a US$218 million loan from China Exim Bank. This upgrade included the installation of 2G base stations and the expansion of 3G and 4G high-speed internet services (Moyo, 2019). By the end of 2017, NetOne secured an additional US$71 million financing agreement from China Exim Bank to further enhance its network infrastructure through Huawei's leadership (Chikodzi, 2022). Moreover, a state-mandated infrastructure-sharing agreement implies that the other two mobile network operators in Zimbabwe could also potentially utilise the telecommunications equipment provided by Huawei. Ultimately, Huawei's role in Zimbabwe highlights the complex relationship between technology, foreign investment, and national security in the evolving landscape of international relations.

Zimbabwe's relationship with Huawei was solidified in February 2020 when the country's Finance Minister granted the company a comprehensive tax exemption retroactive to December 2009. Huawei's collaboration with the Zimbabwean government on the Smart Sustainable Cities initiative, officially launched in March 2018, raises significant concerns. Reports from March 2020 indicated that Huawei had allegedly received US $20 million to initiate the installation of a network of public surveillance cameras as part of a broader Smart City Project, which has a projected budget of US$100 million over 5 years. Sources indicate that Hikvision is set to provide facial recognition software for this initiative (Chikanda, 2021). These developments unfold in a context where Zimbabwe lacks adequate privacy and data protection legislation governing the collection and processing of information obtained through this extensive surveillance system. The proposed smart cities initiative could result in continuous data generation and collection without appropriate safeguards. Furthermore, incidents in Zambia and Uganda have highlighted concerns regarding Huawei employees allegedly assisting governments in monitoring political opponents, leading to arrests in Zambia (Munyuki, 2020). Overall, these factors raise critical questions about the implications of such technological partnerships for civil liberties and governance in Zimbabwe.

Facial recognition technology from the Chinese company Hikvision is currently operational at airports and international border posts in Zimbabwe. The state-owned fixed-line telephony operator TelOne inaugurated two data centres with cloud capabilities in Harare and Mazowe in 2017, as part of a broader US$98 million network upgrade project implemented with Huawei. Despite significant concerns raised by the US and UK governments regarding the security of Huawei's telecommunications equipment, leading to a ban on its use in those countries, Zimbabwean authorities appear unfazed. In fact, the strained relations between Harare and Western nations, which have imposed sanctions since 2002, seem to have reinforced Zimbabwe's ties with China today. This growing partnership not only underscores a strategic pivot toward closer cooperation with Chinese technology firms but also reflects Zimbabwe's broader shift in alignment within the changing global landscape, highlighting the complexities of international relations.

Ethiopia

Ethiopia's government is increasingly utilising advanced cyber and phone surveillance technologies sourced from China to conduct widespread monitoring aimed at suppressing political dissent. A recent report by Human Rights Watch highlights that Ethiopia's state telecom company has spent the last 5 years integrating cutting-edge equipment from the Chinese telecom giant ZTE with additional spyware from European vendors. This collaboration has resulted in sophisticated surveillance tools encompassing social media, phone and Internet communications (Human Rights Watch, 2021). With this robust system operational, the ruling Ethiopian People's Revolutionary Democratic Front (EPRDF) coalition leverages its enhanced capabilities to target and intimidate political opponents. Historically, Ethiopia's authoritarian regime has closely monitored its citizens, but the introduction of these technologies has significantly augmented its surveillance capabilities, enabling the government to spy on local citizens, business people, journalists and even the extensive diaspora community abroad. Munyuki (2020) also asserts that this trend is part of a broader pattern across Africa, where governments increasingly adopt Chinese surveillance technologies to strengthen control over their populations under the guise of national security.

In recent years, various East African nations, including Ethiopia, Uganda, Kenya and Tanzania, have faced criticism for implementing stricter policies on free expression and cracking down on civil society and non-governmental organisations (Amnesty International, 2022). The rise of affordable and powerful spyware has allowed these governments to monitor dissent more effectively, posing a serious threat to democratic movements. Emphasises that states increasingly surveil activists and opposition figures, leading to harassment and arrests, which ultimately stifles political engagement. The implications of these surveillance practices extend beyond immediate political repression; they create a chilling effect on free speech, with citizens self-censoring due to fears of government reprisals. Furthermore, the lack of robust legal frameworks to protect privacy and data rights exacerbates the risks posed by these technologies (Munyuki, 2020). Despite the growing sophistication of surveillance technologies, internet connectivity in Ethiopia remains limited, with less than 1.5% of the population having access and only around 27,000 broadband subscribers nationwide. This presents a paradox: while the state deploys advanced technologies for monitoring, the majority of the population lacks access to the digital tools that could empower them politically. This dichotomy underscores the potential for increased control as digital infrastructure develops, amplifying the risks for those who seek to express dissent or engage in political activism. As these technologies proliferate across the continent, they not only enable authoritarian regimes to maintain control but also fundamentally undermine the prospects for democratic governance in Africa.

Uganda

Uganda has adopted some of the techniques espoused by the People's Republic of China (PRC) government. While it is unclear if the PRC has had a direct influence on Ugandan legislation, it has inspired a number of the legislative frameworks and practices that aid digital authoritarianism in the East African country. The PRC has consistently increased its influence on Uganda's socio-economic development through seemingly no-strings-attached credit packages, which President Museveni frequently acknowledges and praises. This non-interference stance in other nations' internal affairs gives their regimes more latitude to stifle opposition and democratic processes without incurring censure or penalties from China.

The Ugandan government or prominent public officials, on the other hand, have faced penalties from the United States, the United Kingdom and the World Bank for governance and human rights issues in 2023 and 2024. As a result, critics argue that the PRC's no-strings-attached policy encourages authoritarian inclinations in the countries with whom it works (Kurlantzick, 2016). The People's Republic of China (PRC) government has been a significant source of assistance in improving Uganda's digital communication and infrastructure. There are also allegations that the Chinese telecom corporation Huawei assisted security forces in spying on President Museveni's political opponents. The investigation detailed how Huawei specialists assisted Ugandan security agencies in infiltrating opposition leader Robert Sentamu Kyagulanyi's (Bobi Wine) encrypted communications, allowing them to follow his activities and sabotage his mobilisation rallies for the 2021 elections.

Huawei is also a major exporter of video surveillance equipment to Uganda, including facial recognition capabilities, which Ugandan authorities have used in ways that frequently violate privacy in the name of law enforcement, public security and urban management. The PRC has contributed more than US$ 110 million to Uganda's National Backbone Data Transmission Project, as well as the National Fibre-Optic Project. There are allegations that the national backbone and fiber-optic projects are part of a digital infrastructure that has increased the Uganda government's monitoring capabilities, violating the right to privacy and freedom of speech. There is significant evidence that African autocracies are using PRC technology and internet control models to undermine democratic achievements through surveillance and censorship.

Conclusion

This chapter concludes that the acquisition of surveillance technologies from China by African countries does appear to have negative implications on civil liberties. The pervasive monitoring of opposition politicians' communications, the collection of private data, as well as the deployment of facial recognition technologies are strategies whose deployment has resulted in instilling fear as well as self-censorship in those who seriously speak out against government abuses. However, what also needs to be made clear is that blame for the misuse of such technologies should not be entirely put on the Chinese government and Chinese tech companies, but largely on African governments that actively seek to acquire such technologies for their political and security agendas. It should be known that the authoritarian regimes in Africa were using such technologies imported from Europe, Israel and the United States, among other suppliers, before the emergence of China as a source. Thus, as the debate on this subject continues, there is a need to zero in on how decisions and initiatives to buy such technologies are made and to what extent these are influenced by external actors, such as the tech suppliers or the Chinese government. This will assist in giving a clear picture of what is really going on. Further, there is also a need for research on what specific percentage of surveillance equipment African governments are purchasing from China as opposed to that they purchase from the West. An enquiry has to be made in terms of how such surveillance technologies are acquired or procured and deployed in African democracies such as South Africa, Ghana and Botswana, among others in comparison to authoritarian states that dominate the continent. Finally, there is a need for civil society organisations, scholars and think tanks in Africa to highlight these issues and continue to push back against the incessant desire by their governments to acquire such technologies, especially those that are used to infringe on people's rights.

References

Adeyemi, O. (2020). The role of technology in regional security cooperation in Africa. *Journal of African Security Studies, 9*(2), 145–157. https://doi.org/10.1080/24104767.2020.1771501

Aina, T. (2021). The implications of Chinese telecommunications on African governance. *Journal of African Policy Studies, 15*(2), 115–110. https://doi.org/10.1016/j.japs.2021.03.005

Al-Bulushi, S. (2021). Citizen-suspect: Navigating surveillance and policing in Urban Kenya. *American Anthropologist, 123*(4), 819–832.

Aluf, S. (2023). China's infrastructure investments in Africa: Opportunities and challenges. *African Economic History, 51*(1), 37–56. https://doi.org/10.1007/s11528-022-00354-6

Amin, H. (2024). *The impact of Chinese AI on developing countries in sub-Saharan Africa* (Doctoral dissertation, San Francisco State University).

Amnesty International. (2022). *New York City, USA: Facial Recognition Cameras Reinforcing Racist Policing—New Research*. Retrieved December 2, 2024 from https://www.amnesty.org/en/latest/news/2022/02/usa-facial-recognition-technology-reinforcing-racist-stop-and-frisk-policing-in-new-york-new-research/

Basin, M., Kober, A., & Schmitt, A. (2018). The implications of Chinese telecommunications dominance in Africa. *International Journal of African Studies, 45*(3), 234–250. https://doi.org/10.1080/09668136.2018.1502874

Blaubach, J. (2022). The growth of Chinese telecommunication networks in Africa: A case study of fiber-optic expansion. *Telecommunications Policy, 46*(6), 102–115. https://doi.org/10.1016/j.telpol.2022.102135

Burdette, M. (2021). *The role of submarine cable connectivity in Africa's economic landscape*. TeleGeography Report. Retrieved November 30, 2024 from https://www.telegeography.com

Chen, L., & Kim, J. (2024a). Digital taxation and internet freedom: The impact on online expression. *International Journal of Information Technology and Management, 23*(1), 15–29. https://doi.org/10.1504/IJITM.2024.10004456

Chen, L., & Kim, S. (2024b). Digital control measures and democratic erosion: A global perspective. *Journal of Digital Governance, 10*(2), 145–160.

Chikanda, A. (2021). Surveillance in Zimbabwe: The implications of Huawei's smart cities initiative. *African Journal of Information and Communication, 27*, 1–20. https://doi.org/10.23962/10539/30615

Chikodzi, D. (2022). Huawei's investments in Zimbabwe: Telecommunications and beyond. *Zimbabwean Journal of Economics and Finance, 4*(1), 45–62. https://doi.org/10.1142/S0218438922000045

Corsi, A., Pagani, R. N., & Kovaleski, J. L. (2020). Technology transfer for sustainable development: Social impacts depicted and some other answers to a few questions. *Journal of Cleaner Production, 245*, 118522.

Dahir, A. L. (2022). *Huawei is powering Africa's internet, and the U.S. is worried*. Quartz Africa. Retrieved from https://qz.com/africa/2138957/huawei-dominates-africas-4g-network-construction

Damianos, N. E. (2021). *Digital authoritarianism and regime type: Measuring the impact of Chinese surveillance technologies on types of US alliances*.

Deeks, A. (2018). Digital control measures and their impact on civic engagement. *Journal of Civil Society, 14*(1), 20–35. https://doi.org/10.1080/17448689.2017.1392508

Dube, M., Moyo, A., & Chikwata, E. (2023). Digital surveillance and voting rights in Africa: Challenges and implications. *African Journal of Political Science, 17*(2), 98–115. https://doi.org/10.1016/j.afpol.2023.06.003

Eisenman, J., & Shinn, D. H. (2023). China's security engagement in Africa: A comprehensive analysis. *Journal of Asian Security and International Affairs, 10*(1), 33–58. https://doi.org/10.1177/23477970221097245

Feldstein, S. (2019). China's surveillance state and its implications for Africa. *The China Quarterly, 238*, 345–367. https://doi.org/10.1017/S030574101900032X

Feldstein, S. (2020). The role of technology in China's influence in Africa. *Journal of Current Chinese Affairs, 49*(1), 53–74. https://doi.org/10.1177/1868102620905598

Fuller, L. (2016). China's telecommunications strategy in Africa: An analysis of Huawei and ZTE. *Asian Journal of Comparative Politics, 2*(2), 174–191. https://doi.org/10.1177/2057891120966937

Gravett, W. (2020). Digital neo-colonialism: The Chinese model of internet sovereignty in Africa. *African Human Rights Law Journal, 20*(1), 125–146.

Hansen, S. J. (2017). Huawei's role in shaping African digital infrastructure. *African Security Review, 26*(3), 223–239. https://doi.org/10.1080/10246029.2017.1382678

Hawkins, R. (2018). Smart cities and surveillance: The role of Chinese technology in urban governance. *Urban Studies, 55*(14), 3151–3168. https://doi.org/10.1177/0042098017750501

Huang, Y., et al. (2023). Surveillance and self-censorship: Impact on democratic participation. *Journal of Communication Ethics, 16*(3), 289–304.

Human Rights Watch. (2021). *Ethiopia: The impact of surveillance technologies on human rights*.

Kidera, D. (2022). Huawei's influence in Africa's telecommunications landscape. *Telecoms Review, 22*(3), 12–17. https://doi.org/10.1109/TR.2022.9374762

Krukowska, M. (2024). China's security relations with Africa in the 21st century. *Security and Defence Quarterly, 46*(2), 4–23.
Kurlantzick, J. (2016). China's surveillance system and its export abroad. *The Washington Quarterly, 39*(1), 29–47. https://doi.org/10.1080/0163660X.2016.1158710
Mafunda, T. (2020). The role of surveillance in Zimbabwe's political landscape. *Zimbabwe Law Review, 12*, 67–84. https://doi.org/10.1093/zlr/12.3.67
Meservey, J. (2020). Technology and authoritarianism: Chinese influence in Africa. *Journal of International Affairs, 73*(2), 41–56. https://www.jstor.org/stable/26966154
Moyo, A. (2019). Telecommunications and governance in Zimbabwe: A historical perspective. *Journal of African Studies, 45*(3), 243–260. https://doi.org/10.1080/00141844.2019.1614383
Mthembu-Salter, G. (2019). Chinese technology and human rights in Africa. *Journal of Human Rights Practice, 11*(2), 214–230. https://doi.org/10.1093/jhuman/huz002
Munyuki, J. (2020). The implications of Huawei's involvement in African governance. *African Journal of Information Systems, 12*(3), 15–29. https://doi.org/10.2139/ssrn.3691082
Muzorewa, T. (2021). The impact of Chinese technology on Africa's digital landscape. *Telecommunications Policy, 45*(8), 102–118. https://doi.org/10.1016/j.telpol.2021.102118
Nguyen, T., & Osei, K. (2022a). Surveillance technologies and electoral processes: Safeguarding voting rights in the digital age. *African Journal of Democracy, 7*(1), 56–70.
Nguyen, T., & Osei, K. (2022b). The implications of digital surveillance on electoral integrity in Africa. *Elections and Democracy in Africa, 5*(2), 67–84. https://doi.org/10.1017/eda.2022.004
Pamment, J. (2020). *The EU's role in fighting disinformation: Taking back the initiative*.
Peterson, D., & Hoffman, S. (2022). *Geopolitical implications of AI and digital surveillance adoption*. Brookings Institution.
Woodhams, S. (2020). China, Africa, and the private surveillance industry. *Georgetown Journal of International Affairs, 21*, 158.

Ronald Chipaike (PhD) currently teaches international relations at Bindura University of Science Education. He specialises in researching Africa-China/Zimbabwe-China engagements as well as African agency in international engagements. Dr. Chipaike has presented papers in these research areas at various international conferences locally and across the world. He has also published widely in the same areas. Email: chipaiker84@gmail.com.

Bazel Coster Chinyonga holds a Bachelor of Science Honours Degree in Peace and Governance from Bindura University of Science Education. He is a teaching assistant at the Department of Peace and Governance at Bindura University of Science Education. He specialises in researching international institutions, transitional justice, and role of China in supporting African states. Email: bchinyonga@buse.ac.zw.

Tafadzwa T. William holds a Bachelor of Science Honours Degree in Peace and Governance from Bindura University of Science Education. Currently, he serves as a teaching assistant at Bindura University of Science Education. He is interested in researching issues about global governance, gender, and political economy. He is driven to explore these complex themes and their implications on contemporary societies. Email: twilliam@buse.ac.zw.

Chapter 4
Chinese Digital Technologies and the Construction of Surveillance States in Africa

Mbongeni Nhliziyo

Abstract Framed within the authoritarian diffusion theory, this chapter explores how the perceived success of China's model of digital control entices African states. While acknowledging concerns about the negative relationship of Chinese digital technologies with internet freedom, digital authoritarianism and neo-colonialism, this chapter reveals that African governments actively procure these technologies to address pressing domestic public security challenges such as crime, terrorism, banditry, piracy and infrastructure deficits. This agency, however, is often exercised within a context of weak legislative and institutional frameworks for data protection, creating opportunities for abuse and manipulation. Consequently, there is an urgent need for strengthening African agency to promote inclusive digital governance that safeguards individual liberties and counters the potential for digital authoritarianism.

Introduction

The People's Republic of China has made clear its intentions to command the digital world to become a 'cyber superpower' by 2050, and the centrality of this vision to its overall strategy for maintaining a stable Chinese state (Roberts et al., 2023). These intentions are not mere policy pronouncements but are supported by a number of major policy initiatives, governmental bodies and senior government officials pronouncements, including the Chinese President, Xi Jinping. In 2017, the Cyberspace Administration of China—a research institute of China's main cyber legislative body—argued that, 'if our party cannot traverse the hurdle represented by the Internet, it cannot traverse the hurdle of remaining in power for the long term' (Chang, 2018: 11; Kania, 2017: Online). Subsequently, in 2018, President Xi Jinping emphasised the fundamental interdependence of cybersecurity and national

M. Nhliziyo (✉)
Fort Hare Institute for Social and Economic Research, University of Fort Hare, East London, South Africa

G. Moyo (ed.), *An Anatomy of AI Surveillance in Africa*, Studies in Digital Politics and Governance, https://doi.org/10.1007/978-3-032-04269-9_4

security (Tan et al., 2025; Murniasari, 2024). The pronouncements of President Xi Jinping and the Cyberspace Administration of China, among others, underscore the People's Republic of China's developmental vision and digital technologies model, which prioritises political control alongside economic advancement (Austin, 2018). This approach holds considerable appeal for numerous developing nations in Africa, where the imperative of retaining political power often takes precedence.

The Digital Silk Road, a sub-component of the 2015 Belt and Road Initiative (BRI), a Chinese infrastructural programme with global reach, constitutes a key element of the People's Republic of China's (PRC) overarching digital strategy (Dollar, 2019). The Digital Silk Road (DSR) facilitates the expansion of Chinese technology companies into politically volatile markets, areas often avoided by other firms due to limited immediate profitability (Voo, 2022). This governmental backing fosters a technological reliance on Chinese technology within developing economies, potentially establishing long-term trade relationships and service dependencies for the maintenance and advancement of these digital infrastructures, thereby also cultivating political influence. The PRC's increasing digital technological footprint increases surveillance capabilities for both host countries and the PRC's security intelligence agencies, especially given Beijing's push to establish global standards for next-generation internet protocols (Erie & Streinz, 2021). Taken from this perspective, Gravett (2022) argues that Beijing's growing technological presence in Africa raises concerns about the potential for both digital authoritarianism and digital neocolonialism.

Consequently, the influence of the PRC in Africa concerning digital technologies and surveillance has been increasing. PRC utilises its technological prowess, coupled with economic and political leverage, to exert control over African nations (Abidde, 2022; Moyo, 2022a, 2022b; DiResta et al., 2020; Shahbaz, 2018; Gathii, 2012). Concerns regarding the potential misuse of surveillance technologies by African governments have been raised. In response, a Huawei representative in Kenya, Adam Lane, asserted that the company's role is limited to the development, installation, deployment and maintenance of technology, while the operational responsibility and policy adherence rest solely with the client, in this case, the Kenyan National Police Service (Francois, 2020). This highlights the contested nature of responsibility between vendor and client. It is also pertinent to note that many African nations acquiring PRC digital technologies have questionable democratic credentials, which aligns well with the PRC's approach to digital governance that diverges significantly from the globally accepted ideals based on the Western democratic principles of prioritising governmental interests over those of non-state actors (Jili, 2022).

A headline in The Economist (2022: Online) proclaims, 'China is helping Zimbabwe to build a surveillance state: Oppressive regimes stick together', arguing that the PRC is assisting the government of Zimbabwe in establishing an intrusive surveillance system. To this end, during a period of intense criticism regarding the repressive actions of Zimbabwean security officials, specifically in relation to the abduction of opposition member of parliament, Joan Mamombe and local councillor, Cecilia, in May 2020, President Emmerson Mnangagwa asserted that the government possessed the capability to 'trace where they walked, slept, and who they talked to' (The Economist, 2022: Online). This statement follows the modernisation of NetOne, Zimbabwe's state-owned telecommunications network, by Chinese telecommunications giants Huawei and ZTE and the development of a national data centre by a Chinese company, CloudWalk. President Mnangagwa's confirmation of the government's surveillance capacity, facilitated by PRC firms, raises concerns about data privacy and management within a nation that has a history of questionable democratic practices.

Evidence indicates a concerning trend of escalating digital surveillance, profiling and targeted online activities increasingly affecting African citizens, raising significant human rights concerns (Sheombar & Skelton, 2023). State actors across the continent are increasingly leveraging digital technologies to expand governmental surveillance prerogatives and substantially augment their monitoring infrastructure and technological capabilities, as evidenced by considerable financial investments in these domains (Roberts & Mare, 2025). Against this backdrop, Africa spends at least US$3 billion acquiring over 50 digital surveillance technologies from companies primarily based in Beijing but also including those in Washington, Brussels and Tel Aviv (Roberts et al., 2023). Consequently, the acquisition of these technologies not only amplifies vulnerabilities related to data protection and security, thereby undermining democracy, human rights and citizen agency but also incurs debt obligations.

As with many deals involving the African governments and the PRC firms, the adoption and subsequent implementation of these mass surveillance measures by African governments, which are ostensibly opaquely procured, often happen without public consultation or participation, prioritising state interests over cities' fundamental constitutional rights and freedoms. These (mis)steps pose a significant risk to individual liberties crucial for democratic governance (Gravett, 2022). Instructively, the growing prevalence of digital technological influence in Africa coincides with a perceived weakening of democratic norms globally, potentially endangering individual freedoms within the digital platforms. Consequently, ensuring the security of these digital platforms is paramount, as their susceptibility could facilitate the unfettered collection of personal data.

Recent reports (The Economist, 2022; Parkinson et al., 2019) allege that PRC telecommunication firms have assisted African governments, including Uganda, Zimbabwe and Zambia, in intercepting communications of opposition members and civil society actors. These allegations have heightened anxieties regarding the export of Chinese digital surveillance technologies to Africa (Munoriyarwa, 2022). Thus, Beijing is courting governments in Africa to create a network of countries that will follow its lead on internet policy. This chapter grapples with three interrelated questions: How are digital technologies enabling or undermining African agency in the context of surveillance states? What are the implications of the rise of surveillance states in Africa for democratic governance, human rights and social justice? How can African agencies be strengthened and exercised to promote democratic and inclusive digital governance in Africa?

This chapter utilised a qualitative design as a methodological approach. Sources of data collection included both primary and secondary sources. These include in-depth expert interviews and an extensive literature review of online articles. The qualitative design used key informant interviews and documentary analysis (books, online journal articles and publications focusing on governance and China-Africa relations, newspaper articles, etc.) as data collection instruments. Key informant interviews were conducted with university lecturers, experts from civil society and media practitioners on China-Africa relations, and these were purposefully sampled. Key experts included experts from the Public Policy and Research Institute of Zimbabwe (PPRIZ), which is running a China-in-Africa research programme. This chapter benefited significantly from the online and physical discussions conducted by PPRIZ. Data was also obtained from the China in Global South Project experts, their online podcasts and publications. This case study provides useful policy lessons that could be applied to African countries' engagement with China. The paper is structured as follows: the first section explores the Chinese digital technologies and the emerging surveillance states in Africa. The second section locates African agency within Chinese surveillance systems procurement, followed by the third section, which outlines the theoretical underpinnings of the study, the authoritarian diffusion theory. The fourth section presents the case of African agency amidst threatening digital authoritarianism, and the last section concludes the discussion.

Chinese Digital Technologies and the Rise of Surveillance States in Africa

The People's Republic of China's expanding digital technology presence in Africa is intertwined with its pursuit of Great Power status (Chang, 2023). These technologies support China's Global Security Initiative, a diplomatic effort promoting an alternative security model that contrasts with Western approaches (Nantlya, 2024). Table 4.1 highlights the Chinese model of digital control. This model is a form of the smart city and safe city models, which employs a network of interconnected technologies, including video cameras, tracking devices, software applications and cloud-based storage, to create a unified system (Chang, 2023). This integration of technologies and processes is designed to support public initiatives such as traffic management, policing activities and the optimisation of service delivery.

Projects like the smart city concept tend to obscure the line between initiatives focused on service provision and potentially intrusive surveillance practices (Jili, 2022). Consequently, the implementation of these technological tools raises concerns regarding civil liberties, especially within legal contexts characterised by the absence of strong regulatory mechanisms. China's Global Security Initiative, designed to foster international security cooperation, is perceived as a tool for increasing Chinese influence and challenging the US-led security framework (PPRIZ, 2024). However, PRC's internal security model, prioritising authoritarian

Table 4.1 The Chinese model of digital control

Key elements of the model	Practices
Development of the great firewall	Foreign social media, websites and messaging apps are blocked
Control of public space and surveillance	Individuals are regularly detained for online posts State critics are arrested
Violence, digital and safe city/ smart city	Activists are forcibly disappeared or tortured in detention Surveillance of public spaces using CCTV facial recognition
Technical attacks and internet interception	Dissidents suffer from persistent cyber-attacks and spear phishing
Social media monitoring and content removal	Posts that criticise officials are systematically removed Surveillance of social media interactions
Development of digital-ID systems and revoking access	Mobile and internet connectivity are denied as punishment for activism Surveillance using biometric scanning of face, iris and/or fingerprints
Online manipulation	Paid commentators downplay government criticism
Enactment of legislation and institutions for censorship	New laws tighten regulations on online media Implementing authoritarian cyber laws and exploiting and blocking data and content stored or transmitted in the digital domain
High-tech surveillance and mobile interception	Surveilling and tracking citizens Citizens' behaviour is monitored via artificial intelligence and facial recognition tools Content removal of posts that criticise Directing massive investments in new technologies to secure the Party's future

Source: compiled by author

control over individual freedoms, diverges from democratic policing principles (Jili, 2022). Instances such as COVID-19 enforcement, the Xinjiang human rights situation and the policing strategies employed in Hong Kong to suppress dissent highlight the limitations and potential negative consequences of this model, demonstrating its capacity to effectively silence opposition (PPRIZ, 2024).

The increasing Chinese digital technologies' footprint across the African continent is closely linked to the growth of surveillance states on the continent (see also Table 4.1). Surveillance states are defined by governments' pervasive monitoring of citizens, encompassing data collection, storage and the observation of individual actions (Bayar, 2023). While proponents often cite national security, social stability and counter-terrorism efforts as justifications for these measures (Romaniuk & Marton, 2023), the potential for abuse, including the suppression of dissent and the curtailment of fundamental freedoms, is significant. Chinese legislation, such as the 2017 National Intelligence Law, the 2021 Data Security Law, the 2015 National Security Law and the 2016 Cybersecurity Law, provides a legal foundation for extensive state access to personal data, thus restricting individual liberties. This legal framework contributes to the development of a global network of states that adhere to the PRC's security policies, potentially jeopardising democratic governance and human rights (Gravett, 2022). Therefore, strengthening African agency is considered essential for the promotion and protection of democracy in Africa. Table 4.1 illustrates the key elements and practices of the Chinese model of digital surveillance that many undemocratic African countries find appealing and seek to emulate.

PRC's ambition to become a cyber superpower, noted above, as articulated by President Xi Jinping (Chang, 2023), is being actively pursued through the expansion of Chinese telecommunications companies, particularly in the Global South. These companies are increasingly dominant in the construction of critical telecommunications infrastructure, providing the PRC with opportunities for data access through both legal and extra-legal channels (Jili, 2022). Evidence of this access includes the 2018 discovery of data exfiltration from the African Union headquarters, a building constructed and networked by the PRC, to Shanghai over a five-year period. Similar accusations of Chinese surveillance have been levelled by the Kenyan government, which is also a major recipient of Chinese loans amounting to US$9.8 billion and the developing countries' information communication and technology infrastructure and policy advice (Nhliziyo and Ncube, forthcoming). These instances suggest that Chinese telecommunications investments are strategically aligned with the Chinese government's broader global objectives. Additionally, through her actions, the PRC gains competitive advantages over African countries and Kenya, in this context, in trade negotiations and political and business dealings. This can be viewed as a strategy in which the PRC protects its political and economic interests on the continent. Unfortunately, in doing so, Beijing practised imperialism by other means (Roberts et al., 2023), reinforcing existing Sino-African politico-economic inequalities.

To this end, the United States and Australia have taken steps to limit the use of Chinese digital technologies, particularly those from companies like Huawei and ZTE, within their telecommunications networks (Shahbaz, 2018). These actions stem from security concerns related to these companies' potential ties to the Chinese state-party government. However, many developing nations, particularly those with significant infrastructure needs and security challenges, are actively partnering with Chinese digital firms (Dollar, 2019).

The Chinese companies, such as Yitu, Hikvision and CloudWalk, are at the forefront of developing advanced surveillance technologies, leveraging artificial intelligence and facial recognition to identify potential threats to public order. This technology is increasingly exported to governments with poor human rights records (Chang, 2023). A prime example is the agreement between Zimbabwe and CloudWalk to establish a national facial recognition system. This deal, negotiated without citizen input, involves the transfer of biometric data on millions of Zimbabweans to the PRC to train CloudWalk's AI algorithms, specifically focusing on darker skin tones (Nur Hussein, 2023). This not only raises concerns about data privacy and security but also potentially contributes to Zimbabwe's growing debt burden. This collaboration benefits both Chinese companies and the Chinese government. By providing data from diverse populations, such as those in Zimbabwe, these companies enhance the effectiveness and marketability of their surveillance technologies to authoritarian regimes globally (Travers, 2024).

African Agency and the Acquisition of Chinese Surveillance Technologies

The increasing use of Chinese surveillance technology in African countries raises concerns about potential human rights abuses. PRC's own extensive surveillance system, exemplified by the Golden Shield Project and Smart Cities Project, relies on advanced technologies like AI, big data and biometrics, coupled with a restrictive legal and political framework (Austin, 2018; Qiang, 2019). China's concept of 'cyber sovereignty', emphasising national control over data flows, further distinguishes its approach from other technology vendors, particularly given the legal and political context in which these tools are developed and promoted in Africa (Jili, 2022; Qiang, 2019). African leaders persist in acquiring surveillance technologies from the PRC. This choice stems from the accessibility and affordability of Chinese systems, coupled with the perceived potential of this technology to mitigate persistent infrastructural deficiencies and domestic public security concerns (Jili, 2023). This section explores the agency of African actors in the adoption of Chinese public surveillance systems.

Although numerous studies suggest that PRC's expanding technological influence is driven by Beijing's ambitions to achieve global technological leadership and establish a China-centric technological network, notably through its Digital Silk Road (PPRIZ, 2024; Dollar, 2019; Nhliziyo & Ncube, forthcoming), these analyses often overlook Africa's technological needs—African agency. African agency is defined as the capacity of African political elites, acting on behalf of their nations, to influence outcomes or regulations (Lala, 2020). Within the context of international engagements, African agency refers to the ability of African actors to engage in negotiations and bargaining with external actors in a way that advantages Africans themselves (Chipaike & Knowledge, 2018: 1; Nhliziyo, 2025). Therefore, it constitutes a self-aware and self-serving form of social action.

African leaders are acquiring Chinese technological systems with the stated intention of improving the lives of their citizens. A significant factor driving this procurement is the struggle faced by African nations in combating public insecurities that negatively impact their economies and the well-being of their populations (Nhliziyo, 2025). These insecurities include, but are not limited to, terrorism, banditry, organised crime and piracy (Ojo et al., 2023). This challenge is compounded by substantial infrastructural deficits and an increasing need for contemporary infrastructure to achieve the Sustainable Development Goals and the African Union's Agenda 2063, which envisions 'the Africa we want'. Consequently, government officials in countries such as Kenya, Uganda, Ethiopia, Zimbabwe, Zambia and South Africa are engaging with Chinese companies to assist in fulfilling diverse domestic objectives (Jili, 2023). As an example, the Ugandan government has procured surveillance technology from Huawei in an effort to mitigate the rising crime rate within its cities and to bridge existing gaps in digital infrastructure (Parkinson et al., 2019).

In Kenya, the nation's experience with terrorist attacks carried out by Islamist militants has been a key driver in the adoption of surveillance systems. These systems are intended to address a range of service delivery needs, encompassing real-time surveillance, evidence gathering and video analysis to support policing efforts (Parkinson et al., 2019). South Africa's persistently high crime rates serve as the principal motivation for the state's adoption of public security platforms, which are viewed as a tool for managing this ongoing threat. While this demand is undoubtedly a reaction to concerns regarding crime and governance, it also reflects governmental initiatives aimed at addressing infrastructural deficiencies and strengthening state digital capabilities (Jili, 2023). Therefore, the implementation of Chinese surveillance technologies in South Africa is intended to address both structural challenges and social issues, such as crime.

In light of the preceding points, Chinese digital surveillance platforms are understood to be components of a broader, state-directed effort to leverage technology in addressing structural challenges and thereby facilitating development. Nevertheless, the growing presence of Chinese surveillance technology in South Africa—the largest economy on the African continent—has prompted anxieties regarding the extent of Beijing's influence over Africa's digital infrastructure. PRC has minimised its involvement in enabling state surveillance of citizens, instead, attributing sole responsibility for any related misconduct to the state actors themselves (Jiang, 2010). This stance aligns with its established policy of non-interference, a cornerstone of its foreign policy approach (Moyo, 2022a).

African policymakers perceive digital surveillance systems as potential solutions to the long-standing challenges confronting their nations. This perspective challenges assumptions that the adoption of Chinese surveillance technology is solely a manifestation of Beijing's ambition to propagate digital authoritarianism. Instead, African governments procure these systems, including those from Chinese firms, as elements of a wider digital infrastructure project aimed at closing infrastructure gaps while integrating various tools whose deployment is expected to address domestic issues such as violent crime, banditry and terrorism (Jili, 2023). These objectives, however, are not accompanied by sufficiently strong legal frameworks to safeguard civil liberties. It is within this context that certain regimes are exploiting this legal deficiency for their own benefit. The implementation of public security platforms presents policymakers with the complex task of developing appropriate data policies and privacy measures to manage the increasing datafication and surveillance.

Surveillance State Development in Africa

Digital surveillance is the use of the internet or mobile technologies to monitor, intercept, or exploit sensitive data, information, or communication (Roberts & Mare, 2025). Practices of digital surveillance include internet interception, mobile interception, social media monitoring, public space surveillance and digital identity systems. Internet interception: surveillance of private internet communication; mobile interception: surveillance of private mobile phone communications (see also Table 4.1). In many African states, including Algeria, Egypt, Ghana, Malawi, Morocco, Nigeria, Uganda, Zambia and Zimbabwe, amongst other countries, pervasive surveillance in Egypt is manifesting, aiding the political interests of the regimes there. These surveillance practices are eroding citizen rights and agency. In many cases, state surveillance profiles citizens to micro-target them for identifying their political preferences and psychological vulnerabilities (Munoriyarwa & Mare, 2023).

To provide a more nuanced understanding of the development of surveillance states and the PRC's role therein, this chapter employs Thomas Ambrosio's theory of authoritarian diffusion. The authoritarian diffusion theory posits that the perceived successes of authoritarian regimes increase the likelihood of emulation by other nations (Ambrosio, 2010, 2012). PRC's emergence as a significant power within the Global South, alongside its promotion of its development model to developing nations, offers a contemporary illustration of this phenomenon (Moyo, 2020). Specifically, PRC's model as a party-state, characterised by concurrent economic growth and the suppression of individual freedoms, holds appeal for numerous African states (Hall & Ambrosio, 2017). This is particularly pertinent considering the historical context of these states, many of which experimented with single-party rule following independence, albeit with limited economic success.

The authoritarian diffusion theory rests primarily on two foundational arguments. The first centres on the concept of appropriateness. This suggests that as authoritarianism gains legitimacy, the likelihood of autocratic norms and practices spreading across the international system also increases (Ambrosio, 2010). Elkins and Simmons (2005: 7) contend that policy diffusion is evident when 'the policy decisions of one government alter the conditions under which other governments base their decisions'. In the context of authoritarian diffusion, the ascendance of authoritarian powers, exemplified by the PRC in this study, coupled with the comparative decline of democratic nations in establishing global standards, may contribute to a perceived greater appropriateness of authoritarian governance (Ambrosio, 2010; Elkins & Simmons, 2005).

The global decline of democracy has been documented (Shahbaz, 2018), and recent geopolitical shifts present further challenges to democratic ideals (Moyo et al., 2020). The logic of the 'appropriateness' framework suggests that the power of prevailing understandings of what constitutes acceptable behaviour influences decision-makers to align themselves with goals and practices perceived as socially legitimate (Lee & Strang, 2006: 886). Consequently, nations may adopt specific practices to signal their commitment to dominant international values and to avoid the negative consequences of nonconformity (Ambrosio, 2010). While Chinese values may not be universally accepted as 'international values', they, nonetheless, represent a challenge to established international norms, particularly those historically championed by the United States and its allies, which have significantly shaped the global system. Essentially, the PRC is developing a different world order, one that accommodates its own distinct values. Evidence of this shift can be seen in the higher attendance of African nations at the Chinese-led Forum on China-Africa Cooperation compared to the United Nations' General Assembly. However, the Kingdom of Eswatini is a notable exception, experiencing a form of stigma due to its disagreement with the PRC regarding the status of Taiwan (Moyo, 2022a).

A further core component of the diffusion theory is the concept of effectiveness. The more visible the political and economic achievements of authoritarian regimes become, the greater the probability that other states will emulate them (Ambrosio, 2010). Effectiveness, in this context, concerns how the successes of authoritarian states elevate the likelihood of their being perceived as models to be followed (Hall & Ambrosio, 2017). Elkins and Simmons (2005: 10) suggest that effectiveness, as a diffusion mechanism, involves prior adoptions providing information regarding 'the benefits and drawbacks of adopting' a particular behaviour. Distinct from appropriateness, which influences the broader context or environment within which choices are made, effectiveness is a learning process. Through this process, policymakers gain a clearer understanding of which strategies are successful and which are not, based on the experiences of other states (Ambrosio, 2012).

The theory of authoritarian diffusion posits that regimes seeking to consolidate their power will actively search for models that seem conducive to their objectives (Ambrosio, 2010). The perceived 'success' of a particular autocratic approach can be demonstrated by the capacity of authoritarian governments to achieve economic growth, as exemplified by the PRC's capitalist dictatorship, or to shield themselves from political pressures (Hall & Ambrosio, 2017). Gerrits (2008: 14) argues that these states not only explicitly reject the principles of international democracy promotion but have also revitalised a new model of development with considerable international allure, characterised by a forceful approach to political and economic modernisation. The PRC's rapid economic expansion, coupled with the preservation of social order and political control, has resulted in the emergence of a 'China model' as a potential alternative to the democratic-capitalist model of development (Mills et al., 2020). This model has been characterised by Diamond et al. (2009:80) as representing 'the model of a very successful and dynamic authoritarian regime'.

African leaders have demonstrated a significant interest in emulating the PRC's developmental trajectory. For instance, Madagascar's president, Marc Ravalomanana, expressed to Chinese officials, 'You are an example of transformation... We in Africa must learn from your success' (Kurlantzick & Link, 2009: 23). Likewise, prominent political figures such as Yoweri Museveni of Uganda, Paul Kagame of Rwanda and Emmerson Mnangagwa of Zimbabwe are leveraging their interactions with the PRC to bolster state surveillance capabilities directed at their respective populations, a move that implicitly challenges liberal democratic values. In 2017, Mnangagwa publicly stated that his government was contemplating the adoption of the Chinese development model as a viable alternative for Zimbabwe. Which it did, but only that it strengthens the ruling party's power (Hodzi, 2020: 899).

Ambrosio (2010) further posits that several mechanisms can be identified as either reinforcing or augmenting perceptions of appropriateness and effectiveness. These contributing factors include geographical proximity, established linkages, the influence of international organisations, the prestige associated with great powers and the impact of reference groups. The authoritarian diffusion theory provides a framework for understanding both the demand and supply aspects of African leaders' procurement of Chinese surveillance technologies. It offers insights into the development of surveillance states within Africa, potentially framing the PRC's involvement as a calculated strategy aligned with its broader global ambitions. This ambition, it is argued, seeks to establish a world order reflecting 'Chinese characteristics' and grounded in Chinese values. While the theory does not offer specific methodologies for measuring authoritarian diffusion, it is relevant to this study in exploring the potential impact of the PRC's growing engagement with African states on the long-term prospects for democracy in these nations. Furthermore, it contributes to an understanding of whether African elites are exercising genuine agency in adopting Chinese technologies or if their actions constitute what might be described as a form of negative agency.

African Agency in the Face of Digital Authoritarianism

This section emphasises the significance of African agency in the context of increasing digital authoritarianism. The Afrobarometer (2021) report indicates that a majority of Africans favour democratic governance over authoritarian models, expressing a preference for freer societies. Within the realm of digital governance, Africans lean towards 'a more open, free approach, which provides open platforms for private actors and civil society organisations' (Jili, 2023). Consequently, the rise of Chinese-procured, financed and built technologies poses a potential threat to this aspiration and to the values of African people and the African Union, as articulated in the African Charter on Human and Peoples Rights and the African Charter on Democracy and Elections, both of which have been ratified by member states (African Union, 1986, 2004). Therefore, for democracy to endure in the digital age, collaborative efforts among African governments, elites and civil society are essential to identify effective solutions to the challenges of social media manipulation and abusive data collection (Moore, 2022). This is especially crucial given the presence of invasive and intrusive technologies originating from the PRC.

The secretive nature of Chinese digital technology agreements, akin to other Chinese engagements (Moyo, 2020), positions these deals as instruments employed to curtail civil liberties. Consequently, multilateral and cross-sectoral collaboration becomes essential to fostering digital literacy, identifying malevolent actors and preventing them from utilising tools to fraudulently amplify their influence (Jili, 2023). Regarding data protection, users must be empowered to safeguard their privacy against unwarranted intrusions by both governmental entities and corporations. Global internet freedom can and should serve as a countermeasure to digital authoritarianism and the well-being of global democracies hinges on this (Shahbaz, 2018). Without such understanding, citizens are unable to hold Chinese firms and their governments accountable for any breaches of their commitments to democratic principles.

The PRC's ambition to achieve dominance in the field of artificial intelligence by 2030 necessitates increased scrutiny of the moral and ethical implications of this technology, especially from democratic nations (Shahbaz, 2018). The enforcement of ethical guidelines for both governmental bodies and private sector entities will require ongoing vigilance from civil society organisations, investigative journalists and official oversight bodies. These oversight bodies may play a crucial role in preventing the transfer of sophisticated technologies which have the potential for both beneficial and harmful applications from countries like the PRC (Moore, 2022). This preventative role could be exercised by demonstrating the viability of an alternative model for internet governance. Such a demonstration would involve addressing issues like social media manipulation and data misuse in a way that upholds human rights while simultaneously preserving a global, open and secure internet. Furthermore, it would require the development of new media legislation that prioritises the protection of populations from disinformation rather than focusing on the exertion of political control within the online environment.

Conclusion

In conclusion, this exploration of Chinese digital technologies and the construction of surveillance states in Africa reveal a complex interplay of agency, ambition and potential consequences. While the PRC's technological advancements and economic influence offer attractive solutions to pressing infrastructural and security challenges faced by African nations, the adoption of these technologies, particularly surveillance systems, raises profound concerns about the erosion of democratic governance, human rights and individual liberties. The attraction of the 'Chinese model', with its emphasis on economic growth coupled with stringent social control, presents a huge challenge to the democratic aspirations of many Africans. However, African agency, though often constrained, is not absent. Governments, driven by a desire to address local insecurities and developmental needs, actively seek out these technologies, highlighting a demand-driven aspect to the proliferation of Chinese surveillance tools. The authoritarian diffusion theory illuminates how the perceived success of the PRC's model can influence other nations, particularly within the context of a perceived decline in Western democratic dominance. Ultimately, the future of digital governance in Africa hinges on the ability of African citizens, civil society organisations and governments to assert their agency. This requires a concerted effort to promote digital literacy, establish robust legal frameworks for data protection and privacy and foster multilateral cooperation to counter the encroaching tide of digital authoritarianism. Only through such vigilance and proactive engagement can Africa ensure that technology serves the interests of its people and reinforces, rather than undermines, the foundations of democratic societies. The stakes are high, and the choices made by African governments will shape the trajectory of African governance in the digital age.

References

Abidde, S. O. (Ed.). (2022). *Taiwan in Africa: Seven decades of certainty and uncertainties*. Bloomsbury Publishing PLC. https://books.google.co.zw

African Union. (1986, October 19). *African charter on human and peoples' rights*. https://au.int/en/treaties/african-charter-human-and-peoples-rights

African Union. (2004). *African charter on democracy, elections and governance*. African Union. http://archive.ipu.org/idd-E/afr_charter.pdf

Afrobarometer. (2021). *Afrobarometer*. Mass Public Opinion Institute (MPOI). https://afrobarometer.org/

Ambrosio, T. (2010). Constructing a framework of authoritarian diffusion: Concepts, dynamics, and future research. *International Studies Perspectives, 11*(4), 375–392. https://doi.org/10.1111/J.1528-3585.2010.00411.X

Ambrosio, T. (2012). The rise of the 'China model' and 'Beijing consensus': Evidence of authoritarian diffusion? *Contemporary Politics, 18*(4), 381–399. https://doi.org/10.1080/13569775.2012.728029

Austin, G. (2018). *Cybersecurity in China*. https://doi.org/10.1007/978-3-319-68436-9

Bayar, T. (2023). Surveillance states. In *The Palgrave Encyclopedia of Global Security Studies* (pp. 1435–1438). Palgrave Macmillan. https://doi.org/10.1007/978-3-319-74319-6_295

Chang, S. (2018). *Cybersecurity under Xi Jinping: A new model for broad control in China*. Center for the Digital Future. https://www.digitalcenter.org/columns/cybersecurity-under-xi/

Chang, Y. Y. (2023). China beyond China, establishing a digital order with Chinese characteristics: China's growing discursive power and the Digital Silk Road. *Politics & Policy, 51*(2), 283–321. https://doi.org/10.1111/POLP.12524

Chipaike, R., & Knowledge, M. H. (2018). The question of African agency in international relations. *Cogent Social Sciences, 4*(1). https://doi.org/10.1080/23311886.2018.1487257

Diamond, L., Rolfe, E., & Stephenson, H. (2009). *The Brown Journal of World Affairs, 15*(2), 77–86.

DiResta, R., Miller, C., Molter, V., Pomfret, J., & Tiffert, G. (2020). *Telling China's story: The Chinese Communist Party's campaign to shape global narratives*.

Dollar, D. (2019). *Understanding China's belt and road infrastructure projects in Africa*. Brookings. https://www.brookings.edu/articles/understanding-chinas-belt-and-road-infrastructure-projects-in-africa/

Elkins, Z., & Simmons, B. (2005). On waves, clusters, and diffusion: A conceptual framework. *The Annals of the American Academy of Political and Social Science, 598*, 33–51. https://doi.org/10.1177/0002716204272516

Erie, M. S., & Streinz, T. (2021). The Beijing effect: China's digital silk road as transnational data governance. *New York University Journal of International Law and Politics, 54*. https://heinonline.org/HOL/Page?handle=hein.journals/nyuilp54&id=5&div=&collection=

Francois, N. (2020, January 8). *Huawei's surveillance tech in Kenya: A safe bet?* ACRP. https://africachinareporting.com/huaweis-surveillance-tech-in-kenya-a-safe-bet/

Gathii, J. T. (2012). Beyond China's human rights exceptionalism in Africa: Leveraging science, technology and engineering for long-term growth. *Columbia Journal of Transnational Law, 51*. https://heinonline.org/HOL/Page?handle=hein.journals/cjtl51&id=680&div=&collection=

Gerrits, A. (2008). Democracy research and democracy promotion under the shadow of semi-authoritarianism. In *World International studies committee conference, Ljubljana, Slovenia, July* (pp. 23–26). https://scholar.google.com

Gravett, W. H. (2022). Digital neocolonialism: The Chinese surveillance state in Africa. *African Journal of International and Comparative Law, 30*(1), 39–58. https://doi.org/10.3366/ajicl.2022.0393

Hall, S. G. F., & Ambrosio, T. (2017). Authoritarian learning: A conceptual overview. *East European Politics, 33*(2), 143–161. https://doi.org/10.1080/21599165.2017.1307826

Hodzi, O. (2020). African political elites and the making(s) of the China model in Africa. *Politics & Policy, 48*(5), 887–907. https://doi.org/10.1111/polp.12380

Jiang, M. (2010). Authoritarian Informationalism: China's approach to internet sovereignty. *SAIS Review of International Affairs, 30*(2), 71–89. https://doi.org/10.1353/SAIS.2010.0006

Jili, B. (2022). The spread of Chinese surveillance tools in Africa. In I. C. Daniels, B. Erforth, & C. Teevan (Eds.), *Africa–Europe cooperation and digital transformation* (1st ed., pp. 32–49). Routledge. https://doi.org/10.4324/9781003274322-3

Jili, B. (2023). *Africa's demand for and adoption of Chinese surveillance technology* [Issue Brief]. https://dfrlab.org

Kania, E. B. (2017, September 27). *The party's 'Hurdles': The internet, propaganda, and power.* https://www.cnas.org/publications/commentary/the-partys-hurdles-the-internet-propaganda-and-power

Kurlantzick, J., & Link, P. (2009). China: Resilient, sophisticated authoritarianism. In *Undermining democracy 21st century authoritarians* (pp. 13–28). Freedom House.

Lala, F. (2020). *Africa in the changing global order: Does African agency matter in global politics?* (pp. 127–143). Springer. https://doi.org/10.1007/978-3-030-21603-0_7

Lee, C. K., & Strang, D. (2006). The international diffusion of public-sector downsizing: Network emulation and theory-driven learning. *International Organization, 60*(4), 883–909. https://doi.org/10.1017/S0020818306060292

Mills, G., Obasanjo, O., van der Merwe, E., & Desalegn, H. (2020). *He Asian aspiration: Why and how Africa should emulate Asia—And what it should avoid.* Oxford University Press. https://scholar.google.com/

Moore, S. M. (2022). China's next act. How sustainability and technology are reshaping China's rise and the world's future. *EBSCOhost. Foro Internacional, 62*(4), 935.

Moyo, G. (2020). China's development finance to Africa and the spectre of debt distress. In *The Palgrave handbook of African political economy* (pp. 557–572). Palgrave Macmillan. https://doi.org/10.1007/978-3-030-38922-2_30

Moyo, G. (2022a). China-Taiwan Geoeconomic competition for diplomatic recognition: Battling for the soul of Africa. In S. O. Abbide (Ed.), *Taiwan in Africa: Seven Decades of Certainty and Uncertainties*. Bloomsbury Publishing PLC. https://books.google.co.zw

Moyo, G. (2022b). Piercing the veil of non-interference doctrine: China's expanding military footprint in Africa. The Palgrave Handbook of Africa and the Changing Global Order, 805–823. Palgrave Macmillan https://doi.org/10.1007/978-3-030-77481-3_39.

Moyo, G., Nhliziyo, M., & Fayayo, R. (2020). The entanglement of Zimbabwe in the US-China Geoeconomic frictions: Defining winners and losers. *iBusiness, 12*(03), 81–102. https://doi.org/10.4236/ib.2020.123006

Munoriyarwa, A. (2022). The militarization of digital surveillance in post-coup Zimbabwe: 'Just don't tell them what we do. *Security Dialogue, 53*(5), 456–474. https://doi.org/10.1177/09670106221118796

Munoriyarwa, A., & Mare, A. (2023). *Digital surveillance in southern Africa: Policies, politics and practices* (pp. 1–220). Palgrave Macmillan. https://doi.org/10.1007/978-3-031-16636-5/COVER

Murniasari, M. (2024). China's cybersecurity governance as part of foreign and security Policy. *Security Intelligence Terrorism Journal (SITJ), 1*(2), 164–177. https://doi.org/10.70710/SITJ.V1I2.23

Nantlya, P. (2024). *Reimagining African Agency in Africa-China Relations—Lessons from FOCAC 2024*. Africa Center. https://africacenter.org/spotlight/reimagining-african-agency-in-africa-china-relations-lessons-from-focac-2024/

Nhliziyo, M. (2025). African agency in the context of a new world dis(order). In G. Moyo & S. J. Ndlovu-Gatsheni (Eds.), *Global storms and Africa in world politics* (pp. 327–342). Springer Nature. https://doi.org/10.1007/978-3-031-83868-2_20

Nur Hussein, S. (2023). Win-win or win lose? An examination of china's supply of mass surveillance technologies in exchange for African's facial ids. *The Pretoria Student Law Review, 16*(1), 10.29053/PSLR.V16I1.4506.

Ojo, J. S., Oyewole, S., & Aina, F. (2023). Forces of terror: Armed banditry and insecurity in North-west Nigeria. *Democracy and Security, 19*(4), 319–346. https://doi.org/10.1080/17419166.2023.2164924

Parkinson, J., Bariyo, N., & Chin, J. (2019). Huawei technicians helped African governments spy on political opponents. *Wall Street Journal, 15*, 15. https://scholar.google.com/

Public Policy and Research Institute of Zimbabwe (PPRIZ). (2024). *Public Policy and Research Institute of Zimbabwe*. PPRIZ. https://ppriz.africa/

Qiang, X. (2019). The road to digital Unfreedom: President Xi's surveillance state. *Journal of Democracy, 30*(1), 53–67. https://doi.org/10.1353/JOD.2019.0004

Roberts, T., & Mare, A. (Eds.). (2025). *Digital surveillance in Africa: Power, agency, and rights*. Zed Books.

Roberts, T., Gitahi, J., Allam, P., Oboh, L., Oladapo, A., Appiah-Adjei, G., Galal, A., Kainja, J., Phiri, S., Abraham, K., Skelton, S. K., & Sheombar, A. (2023). *Mapping the supply of surveillance technologies to Africa Nigeria country report*. Opendocs. https://doi.org/10.19088/IDS.2023.027.

Romaniuk, S. N., & Marton, P. (2023). *The Palgrave encyclopedia of global security studies*. Palgrave Macmillan. https://doi.org/10.1007/978-3-319-74319-6

Shahbaz, A. (2018). *The rise of digital authoritarianism*. FreedomHouse. https://freedomhouse.org/report/freedom-net/2018/rise-digital-authoritarianism

Sheombar, A., & Skelton, S. K. (2023). Follow the surveillance: A Breadcrumb Trail of surveillance technology exports to Africa. In *IFIP Advances in Information and Communication Technology, 696 AICT* (pp. 241–261). Springer. https://doi.org/10.1007/978-3-031-50154-8_19

Tan, Y., Dallas, M., Farrell, H., & Newman, A. (2025). Driven to self-reliance: Technological interdependence and the Chinese innovation ecosystem. *International Studies Quarterly, 69*(2), sqaf017. https://doi.org/10.1093/isq/sqaf017

The Economist (2022). *China is helping Zimbabwe to build a surveillance state: Oppressive regimes stick together*. The Economist.

Travers, L. (2024). *Algorithmic coloniality? The case of Chinese artificial intelligence technology and Zimbabwean surveillance*. 15(2).

Voo, J. (2022, March 20). *Will China become the first cyber superpower?* The National Interest. https://nationalinterest.org/blog/techland-when-great-power-competition-meets-digital-world/will-china-become-first-cyber

Mbongeni Nhliziyo is a PhD student at the University of Fort Hare. He holds a Master of Science Degree in Public Policy and Development Management from Lupane State University. Mbongeni is also a research fellow at the Public Policy and Research Institute of Zimbabwe (PPRIZ), a leading organisation focused on democracy and governance advocacy. This institute aims to revitalise the role of public intellectuals in Zimbabwe's public sphere. Mbongeni's research and teaching interests include public policy, China-Africa relations, geopolitics, African agency, and Africa's development trajectory. He has published peer-reviewed articles on Zimbabwe's relations with China and the USA, the Chinese Model and its implications for democracy in Africa, China's infrastructure-for-resources model in Africa, and African agency.

Chapter 5
China, Security, the Spread of Remote Surveillance Models and the Construction of the "Panoptic State" in Cameroon

Auxence Augustin KOA

Abstract Auxence Augustin KOA analyses the way in which the discourses, practices, interactions and tensions surrounding Huawei's Cameroon Intelligent City Project and ZTE's National Emergency Telecommunications Network are helping to transform the State figure in Cameroon. The irruption of Chinese remote surveillance models discussed in this chapter is as much the product of mimetic practice as it is the result of Cameroon's quest for Chinese security standards. As well as examining the way the conformism of these security models fuels the friction surrounding their internalisation, this chapter also highlights the way in which this internalisation expresses the State's quest for a monopoly on surveillance and legitimate control of its territory, and therefore the reinforcement of the panoptic character of security governance.

Introduction

Six months after the release of the Moulin Founier family, kidnapped in the locality of Dabanga, in the far north region of Cameroon by the Nigerian Salafist jihadist group Boko Haramon, Thursday, 18 April 2013, the Minister for the Economy, Planning and Territorial Development and the Export Import Bank of China signed on 29 October 2013, a financing agreement for a project relating to the construction by the Chinese company Zhongxing Telecommunication Equipment Co. Ltd. (ZTE) of a National Emergency Telecommunications Network. One year later, on the night of Friday, 16 May 2014, Boko haram attacked again.

This time, it was a Chinese workers' camp in Waza in the same region, killing one Chinese worker and taking several hostages. The hostages included 10 Chinese employees of Sinohydro Co. Ltd., who were working on the rehabilitation of the Mora-Dabanga-Koussérisection of Cameroon's National Highway N°1

A. A. KOA (✉)
Political Science, University of Bertoua, Bertoua, Cameroon

G. Moyo (ed.), *An Anatomy of AI Surveillance in Africa*, Studies in Digital Politics and Governance, https://doi.org/10.1007/978-3-032-04269-9_5

(www.nouvelobs.com, 2014). While searches for their release were underway, a pilot phase of an intelligent video surveillance system was launched on 07 August 2014, in the towns of Yaoundé, Douala, Garoua-Boulai, Kye Ossi, Waza and Kousseri, part of the "Cameroon Intelligent City Project"; that pilot phase, carried out by Huaweiin corporates certain aspects of the components of the project launched a year earlier by ZTE (Koa, 2020).

After reiterating his country's commitment to help Cameroon in the fight against this sect and all other forms of terrorism and insecurities, Mr. Wo Ruidi, Chinese Ambassador to Cameroon at the time, praised the efforts made by the Head of State to secure the release of the Chinese hostages. On 12 October 2014, the Presidency of the Republic of Cameroon issued a press release announcing the release of the 10 Chinese hostages. Three years later, on 5 January 2017, the contract for the implementation of the National Emergency Telecommunications Network was signed by the Chinese company, ZTE, following authorisation of the competitive tendering procedure obtained on 19 December 2016. Six months later, on 19 June 2017, Cameroon's Ministry of the Economy, Planning and Development of the Territory signed a commercial loan agreement for 83,561,538.46 US dollars, or 45.9 billion CFA francs, with the Bank of China, for the partial financing of phase one of the Cameroon Intelligent City Project (www.prc.cm, 2018).

Such an opening of our chapter, with the abductions of the French Family Moulin Fournier and the Chinese workers in the space of a year, in the same region, as well as the almost simultaneous implementation of two remote surveillance systems by Chinese operators, while allowing us to specify the social conditions that underpin the formulation of our category of the panoptic State, enable us to analyse in a specific context, the way in which the reasons, enunciations, repercussions, contradictions and adjustments at work around the "Chinese models of remote surveillance" (Feldstein, 2019) contribute to the renewal of the State's figure in Cameroon. It is therefore a question for us of extending the perspectives of analysis and research on the diffusion of remote surveillance models centred on the decolonial reasons, the competitions of which they are the object and the global ambitions of the Chinese supplier (Feldstein S., 2019; Artigas, 2019; Mozur, 2019; Zhou, 2020; Sheena, 2020; Nyoni, 2021; Weber, 2021; Jili B., 2022). Similarly, our study also aims to use the case of Cameroon to enrich analytical perspectives focusing on the motivations and sovereign ambitions of African receivers of these remote monitoring models (Jili B., 2020, 2022, 2023; Eyenga, 2021; Wounba, 2021; Muthuri, 2025; Skelton, 2025). It, therefore, intends to complement the reflections on the reconfiguration, risks, tensions, effects, constraints and inertia generated by these systems in Africa (Jili B., 2025; Baraka, 2021; Nyoni, 2022; Bell, 2024; Zhang, 2020).

Our analytical approach, which is intended to be "grounded" (Strauss, 1967), is based on the Foucauldian and Weberian grids of "governmentality" (Foucault, 2004) and State "legitimacy" (Weber M., 1995). It is, therefore, backed not only on the use of scientific literature on the subject of Chinese telemonitoring models in Africa and Cameroon but also on factual data collection associated with the need of direct observations (in public places, crossroads, markets, administrative institutions, residences of public authorities in cities such as Yaoundé, Garoua-Boulai, Bertoua, Kribi, Kye-Ossi and Sangmélima). Furthermore, our analysis is also made on the basis of qualitative surveys based on ''comprehensive interviews'' (kaufmann, 2016) with five non-commissioned officers, senior officers and civil servants from the General Delegation of the National Security, the Gendarmerie and the Army, certain managers of Huawei, as well as the Directorate General of Public Contracts Control at the Ministry of Public Contracts, Ministry of Public Contracts's representative in the control and monitoring of the National Emergency Telecommunications Network project. We also use press articles, police magazines and documents such as the National Emergency Telecommunications Network implementation project.

The aim here is to gain a better interpretation and, above all, a better understanding of the way in which the narratives, facts, situations, discourses and practices that frame these new devices express their particularities in Cameroon. Thus, having set out the reasons for the emergence of these remote surveillance models in Cameroon, it is appropriate to indicate how the strategic situation underlying their emergence in Cameroon makes it possible to grasp the tensions and frictions that exist around their internalisation before highlighting how such internalisation expresses the quest for monopolies in Cameroon. Finally, the analysis looks beyond the thesis of mimicry to examine the conformism of these systems in Cameroon. It is worth highlighting here the way in which such an overtaking leads to a renewal of terminology, which seeks to take account of the specific issues linked to the transformation of the figure and security governance of the State in Cameroon.

The Rise of Chinese Telemonitoring Models and Mimetic Practices of Security in Cameroon

The advent of Chinese telemonitoring models in Cameroon lies at the crossroads of very specific international and internal circumstances. Internationally, remote surveillance is, first and foremost, the repercussion of a genuine "crisis of international leadership" (Chen et al., 2018). The exhaustion and shortcomings of Western-American international leadership are now allowing a new style of international leadership to emerge. In this respect, the Belt and Road Initiative (BRI), and above all, its technological dimension, expresses China's desire to gradually assume greater international responsibility by making up for the lack of technology infrastructure in African countries. While this "Chinese techno rising" operates in the energy, telecoms, education and agriculture sectors, security is now the fast-growing area of specialisation for these technology companies (Koa, 2015).

In fact, from 2001 onwards, and more decisively between 2011 and 2013, their national expertise will be asserting itself well beyond China's borders to invest in Africa (White Paper, 2013). This was confirmed by the Transform Africa summit held in Kigali, Rwanda, from 28 to 31 October 2013. This led to the drafting of the Smart Africa manifesto approved by all the heads of State and government of the

African Union at the 22nd ordinary session of the Assembly of the African Union in Addis Ababa on 30 and 31 January, 2014 (Wounba, 2021). Furthermore, the affirmation of the competence of Chinese technology companies in the field of remote monitoring is also apparent in the 2015 Johannesburg Declaration (FOCAC Focac, 2015). This is even clearer in the publication of the white paper by Huawei in 2016 and in the Huawei exhibition held in Nairobi, Kenya, on 14 and 15 October 2016.

It is even more apparent in the Huawei Summit on the Secure City in Africa, which will follow on 17 October 2016 (Huawei, 2016). We can see then that the "globalisation of Chinese technology companies" in this field will gradually go hand in hand with the expansion of the popularisation of its security models and practices in Africa (Barre, 2016). This overlap will help to align China's global ambitions not only with the expansion of the market for its technology companies but also with the security interests of its African countries, which now perceive attacks on China's interests as a threat to their own national security (FOCAC Focac, 2018). Furthermore, by often providing preferential loans for the supply of these devices, China is seeking to establish itself as a global benchmark in remote surveillance technology and to ensure, to the detriment of the United States, that its security standards are normalised (AI Global Surveillance Technology, 2019).

Internally, the emergence of remote surveillance is primarily a manifestation of Cameroon's "developmentalist ambition" (Bobo, 2018). This ambition is therefore characterised by the return of the concept of "emergence" to the governmental agenda of the State of Cameroon (Péclard, 2020). This return, which began in the 2000s, aims to make infrastructure a priority and the adoption of development programmes an essential means of achieving it. Indeed, it was under the Heavily Indebted Poor Countries Initiative that the Cameroonian government set the ambitious target of achieving emergence by 2035 (Khan-Mohammad, 2020).

Cameroon's developmentalist approach, which coincides with China's increased commitment, will therefore be based on exploiting not only the financial but also the technological potential of the Chinese partner. This is linked not only to China's pre-eminence in the field but also to the belief in the "quasi-magical virtues" (Jili, 2022) of these technologies in strengthening the security of States. The advent of remote surveillance also reflects the desire of the State of Cameroon to provide guarantees of safety and security during sporting competitions. Indeed, the implementation by the Chinese company, Huawei, of the Cameroon Intelligent City Project has "…greatly contributed to the security coverage of major official events, in particular the 2016 African Women's Cup of Nations, the 2020 African Championship of Nations and the 2021 African Cup of Nations…" (Nzié, 2024).

Cameroon's desire to maximise the chances of safety and security during sporting competitions can be seen in the signing, on 2 September 2019, as a prelude to the organisation of the 2020 African Championship of Nations and the 2021 African Cup of Nations, with Huawei of a contract for the supply, configuration and commissioning of fourth-generation video surveillance equipment at various sites selected for these two sporting events. Similarly, the performative nature of the discourse in the media, framing Huawei's remote surveillance system at the time of the competitions will reveal the way in which, between 2016 and 2021, it will participate in the co-construction, on the eve of the 2020 African Championship of Nations and the 2021 African Cup of Nations, of forms of branding, aimed at making the urban centres chosen to host these competitions appear to be ideal, viable and safe cities.

In the end, the rise of remote surveillance is the result of the desire of the State of Cameroon to find solutions to deal with repeated attacks on its territory. Indeed, it was with the approximations and inaccuracies due to strategic intelligence on the subject of the kidnapping of Chinese workers in Dabangain May 2014, that the idea of a remote surveillance system based on the Chinese model took shape in the minds of Cameroon's political-military and political-strategic elite. In fact, as an official of the Territorial Security Directorate admits (half-heartedly):

> "...the Chinese didn't like the fact that we had so little, if any, information about the death and kidnapping of their nationals (...) and neither did we. (...) especially as the wife of an important member of the government had also been kidnapped at the same time (...) perhaps, that is why they subsequently stepped up their security assistance (...)" (GDNS1, 2021).

Among the many forms of support that Cameroon was to receive from China were ZTE's National Emergency Telecommunications Network and Cameroon's Intelligent City Project, proposed by Huawei. These two remote surveillance models will therefore constitute the new "devices" (Deleuze, 1989; Foucault, 1975) through which the State of Cameroon will seek to establish, and even increase, the control and the domination of its territorial and social space through surveillance.

If it was for Cameroon a question of "setting the course and truly projecting itself towards modernity by opting for a nationwide video surveillance system", then the advent of Chinese remote surveillance technologies must be seen as a Cameroonian quest for a certain standard of security (Nzié, 2024, p. 43). The quest for a standard of security as an element in the normalisation and internalisation of these models in Cameroon can be seen in the words of an official from the General Delegation for National Security, according to whom:

> "(...) it was urgent for Cameroon to equip itself with an intelligent video surveillance system (...) the first concern was to adapt to the times and the other was to enable our services to react quickly and anticipate threats ..."(GDNS2, 2021).

In this light, the ambition, which will require the State of Cameroon to adapt its security apparatus to the current trend, corresponds to a genuine civilisation of its surveillance customs and practices by China. Indeed, by revealing the way in which security, conceived from the outside, is being brought in to secure the inside, it becomes very clear that the deployment of remote surveillance in Cameroon is a "mimetic practice" of security (Eyenga, 2021). In this way, the traffic implied by this mimetic process is characterised by the use of external technologies that have proved their worth and then, removed from their environment, to fit in Cameroon. These mimetic practices of security measures must be seen as legitimising strategies, which aims to build an image and status for China as a key partner in the fight against terrorism and insecurity in Cameroon. This is part of a game in which China's role in the field of security in Cameroon is based on a relationship of meaning with Western Europe, and above all, the United States.

Chinese Surveillance Systems, Presidentialism and Controversial Internalisation

It would seem appropriate to take an interest in the fact that the internalisation process of Chinese remote surveillance systems in Cameroon is shaped by controversy and disagreement. The disputed operationalisation of ZTE's National Emergency Telecommunications Network project, therefore, offers a glimpse of the impossible harmony that exists between Chinese operators on the one hand and Cameroonian institutional players on the other, around the positions and incomes that remote surveillance will generate in Cameroon. This tension can be explained by the way in which the technical and pragmatic materialisation of the project will be hampered by a politico-financial and "politico-administrative imbroglio" around which a battle of influence and interests is crystallising between Chinese operators and Cameroonian institutional players over the content and direction of this project (Nkam, 2016).

On closer examination, it is the granting to the government of Cameroon of a donation worth 7.3 billion FCFA for the construction of Emergency Transmission Centres, which will become National Emergency Operations Centres in Douala and Yaoundé, that divides. Indeed, on the 21st of June 2016, the Ministry of the Economy, Planning and Development of the Territory referred the matter to the Ministry of Public Works for a technical opinion on the construction of the two centres. After analysis, the Minister of Public Works concluded that the total cost of the work had been overestimated. Despite these clearly formulated reservations and observations, the Minister of the Economy, Planning and Development of the Territory, nonetheless, gave the go-ahead for work to begin on 2 September 2016.

The Minister of Post and Telecommunications was also critical of the fact that virtually all of the equipment imported for the project is already in storage at the port of Douala, and that some of it has already been installed, even though a reconfiguration of the project by the Presidency of the Republic had been formulated. In addition, she expressed reservations about the inclusion of the e-police component in the project, on the grounds that this component, which did not fall within its sphere of activity, was already the subject, on very high instructions from the Head of State, of particularly advanced negotiations between the General Delegation of National Security and Huawei, with a view to the nationwide installation of a video surveillance system that will offer the defence and security forces a range of services, including the e-police system. This is in line with the statement made by this Ministry of Post and Telecommunications official:

> "(...) It was indeed up to the Minister of Post and Telecommunications to notify ZTE of the order to start work. However, while the process is still underway and a reconfiguration of the project had been suggested by the presidential secretariat, we have been told that almost all of the equipment imported for the project is already in storage at the port of Douala, and that some of it is already on its way to Yaoundé (...)" (MINPOSTEL1, 2022).

It appears that, the disputed and controversial operationalisation of the National Emergency Telecommunications Network is a sufficient reminder that the process of securing the territory of Cameroon through the implementation of remote surveillance works through a triple logic of power struggles, personal interests and institutional competitions. It then appears that the National Emergency Telecommunications Network works through an inextricable tangle of actors, roles, influence, contextual adjustments of meaning, interests and rationalities. Moreover, the words of this manager illustrate this image sufficiently when he states that:

> "(...) That National Emergency Telecommunications Network affair is very complicated, my friend (...) it's even like a mafia (...) there were big interests behind it who sided with one side. If it's ZTE that implements first, that means it too should have exclusivity but, alas, that wasn't the case. (...) It goes without saying that there were things going on behind the scenes. (...) It's as if people in high places wanted to prove certain things to others ..." (MINMAP1, 2021).

It also appears that the disputed and controversial operationalisation of the National Emergency Telecommunications Network has put the relationship between ZTE and Huawei in a context of mimetic rivalry. Although ZTE was the first Chinese service provider chosen to carry out the project, it is clear that suspicions of espionage, unfair competition, and, above all, a battle of interests and influence between high-ranking players, led to the project being re-awarded to Huawei as this head of Huawei Technologies Co., Cam. Ltd. stated:

> "It was ZTE that won the contract and carried out the first phase (...), a bit like a test phase! This corresponds to the construction of the famous Emergency Transmission Centres (...) at this point, the project is not yet called National Emergency Telecommunications Network. However, when it comes to negotiating the large-scale deployment of the project, the technology proposed by ZTE will suffer from compliance problems. Furthermore, given that part of the project fell within the reserved domain of defence secrecy, we couldn't take the risk; we had to make the right choice of partner and technologies. That's why we came in with a better technical and financial offer to (...) snatch the project from ZTE's hands. (...). Of course, even if ZTE had very high-level guarantees, objectively speaking, there was no question of taking on this technology. We were the ideal partner (...) So we're going to roll out our offer independently, not only by renaming it, but also by including some additions (border areas) and starting from scratch, right from the beginning, without taking account of ZTE's initial roll-out. (...) That's why, in some places, you get an impression of too much, because you have two towers, two different pieces of equipment that nevertheless play the same role and fulfil the same functions ..." (HUAWEI1, 2021).

On looking, at the beginning of the reconfiguration of the National Emergency Telecommunications Network Project: is the Presidency of the Republic of Cameroon. More precisely, it is the General Secretary of the Presidency of the Republic that drives the redefinition, reorientation, restructuring and control of the dynamics of development projects in Cameroon. The General Secretary of the Presidency of the Republic, as the main matrix for the internalisation of Chinese remote surveillance systems in Cameroon, can therefore be seen in reference to the very high instructions of the Head of State that the General Delegation of the National Security mentions to justify the reassignment of the project to Huawei. Moreover, such a matrix can also be seen in the way in which the absences of the Minister General Secretary at the Presidency of the Republic of Cameroon from the inaugurations on the 8 June and the 13 July 2022, of the National Emergency Operations Centers at Bepanda in Douala and Ekounou in Yaoundé, stand in contrast to his appearances as the personal representative of the Head of State at the inaugurations on the 22nd of August 2019 and the 15th of June 2023, of the National Video Surveillance Command Centers of Etoudi in Yaoundé and Bepanda in Douala (Investir au cameroun, 2022).

On analysis, the emergence of remote surveillance systems reveals the way in which presidentialism appears to be a way of exclusively internalising Chinese technical and technological services and achievements in the field of security. This is also a good illustration of the way in which the power games and interests that are being played out, at the national level, around the rhetoric of the Chinese security offer in Cameroon. It also opens a window onto how the exorbitant political–financial alliance (which takes the form of shareholding), and which is dependent on the favourable treatment and affinity enjoyed by the Chinese technology companies involved in the implementation of remote surveillance systems in Cameroon, raises fresh questions about the logic of the procedural dilemma that marks out their implementation contract.

This is to say that contracts for the implementation of remote surveillance projects in Cameroon are no beauty contests. Everything is locked upstream. That's where the stakes are. In other words, Chinese technology companies are using a combination of political patronage and institutional mothering to establish a position of strong credibility and affinity, enabling them to make useful connections with Cameroon's main institutional operators. In this light, the behind-the-scenes political and financial formatting, the backroom dealings, within the framework of the National Emergency Telecommunications Network, first on behalf of ZTE and then within the framework of Cameroon's intelligent city project on behalf of Huawei, were aimed at exploiting the resources of their respective domains with a view to integrating and influencing Cameroon's State institutions. Incidentally, the National Emergency Telecommunications Network's knitted and quarrelled schema reveals that, the process of securing Cameroonian space through remote surveillance works to install conditions of (privileged) contractualisation for the benefit of Chinese operators. Our aim here is to highlight a perspective on contracting that is well appreciated by Jean Pierre Gaudin: "public action contracts" (Gaudin, 2007). This is because everything becomes blurred and opaque when it comes to detailed procedures, debates and partnership management.

The Quest for Monopolies and the Construction of the Omnivoyance Power of the State

The inclusion of Cameroon's surveillance apparatus in the register of what it is like elsewhere, or even what it is like in China, marks the intersection of legitimate quests for monopolies. First, that of a legitimate vision of one's space. If "power is correlated with a capacity to see and to dominate the gaze" (Foucault, 1975, p. 14), it would appear that the adoption of remote surveillance in Cameroon is a clear expression of the State's desire not only to increase but also to extend surveillance to the very edges of its territory. From this perspective, the use of Chinese remote surveillance systems is also an expression of Cameroon's quest for monopolies in risk and threat surveillance.

By observing and exploiting ZTE's National Emergency Telecommunications Network implementation project, the territorial breakdown of surveillance cameras reveals the way in which Cameroonian territory is surrounded and meshed by a surveillance cable network. The surveillance complex created by this cable network, which runs counter to conventional surveillance methods, is set up inside the country like a continuous, sinusoidal capillary system and at the borders like an ocular fence, erected to provide a better view and surveillance of the flows of people and goods passing through these peripheral locations and environments, which for a long time have been insufficiently scrutinised. The aim here is therefore twofold: (1) to break with the narratives of porosity that have long framed these Cameroonian border areas and (2) to break away from the foreign narratives of risk and peril that have long prevailed in Cameroon and return to those of safety and security, especially after the 2014 kidnapping of the Chinese and the 2013 kidnapping of the Moulin–Fournier family.

Furthermore, the deployment of Chinese remote surveillance systems in Cameroon corresponds to the legitimate quest for territorial control. In fact, both the National Emergency Telecommunications Network and Cameroon's Intelligent City Project are devices that mark the desire of the State of Cameroon to build and establish a close relationship with its territory. With these systems, territorial control is balanced between the centrality of control, "telecentrality" and the closeness of controlled peripheries, "teleproximity" (November, 2002, pp. 35-36). It is as if the territory, or almost the whole of it, is now visible from two central points (Yaoundé and Douala). Here, people are substituted for cameras. They are "auxiliaries of vision" (Virilio, 1988, p. 125) who, from the periphery, monitor, scan, capture and transmit fragments, pieces of vision, of remote images of the territory to command and emergency centres which receive, process and arrange them like a giant jigsaw puzzle or a fly's eye to form a global vision.

Indeed, whether within the framework of Cameroon's Intelligent City Project with the National Video Surveillance Command Centres of Etoudi in Yaoundé or Bepanda in Douala; or again, as part of the National Emergency Telecommunications Network with the National Emergency Operations Centres at Ekounou in Yaoundé and Bepanda in Douala, the fly's eye or jigsaw puzzle effect seen through large walls filled with screens transmitting images of what is happening in the distance, symbolises, to a certain extent, this dialectic of telecentrality and teleproximity that is so highly valued by November. From this perspective, the Chinese remote surveillance systems organise the sovereign Cameroonian security and safety administrations in charge of operating them, as kind of watchful shepherds capable of keeping an eye on everything and everyone. What's more, they give these administrations a new power: the "power of omnivoyance" (Virilio, 1988, p. 77). This power derives from the delegation (to the cameras) of the function of looking, watching, seeing and perceiving, a function usually assigned to police officers and gendarmes, whose gaze is now focused not on the surrounding environment, but on the control screens.

Towards a Panoptic State

We need to go beyond the thesis of the mimicry of remote surveillance systems in Cameroon and question their conformism. This is only possible if we understand the internal dynamics of the Cameroonian panoptic State. In Cameroon, the first thing that strikes you is the way in which the deployment of Cameroon's Intelligent City Project and the National Emergency Telecommunications Network embraces the institutional and decision-making centralisation that characterises the State of Cameroon. On observation, the deployment of surveillance systems goes hand in hand with the centralisation of State authority. This is done according to a sense of authority modelled on the a "centralisation of decision-making" of the current politico-administrative system of territorial organisation of power and government. It is in this sense that Yaoundé and Douala rightly appear as "both centralised and centralist poles" (Owona Nguini, 2001), housing the National Video Surveillance Command Centres of Cameroon's Intelligent City Project and the National Emergency Operations Centres of the National Emergency Telecommunications Network in Cameroon.

What is most striking is the layout and naming of National Video Surveillance Command Centres of Cameroon's and National Emergency Operations Centres. These follow a sense of authority modelled on an "organisational militarisation" reminiscent of the Cameroon army (Owona Nguini, 2018). Thus, the "geostrategic dipole" (Owona Nguini, 2001) that are the urban centres of Yaoundé and Douala, associated with the recurrent appearance of the terms (centre) or (command) to designate National Video Surveillance Command Centres of Cameroon's and National Emergency Operations Centres, do indeed reflect whithout leading to a certain dystopia, the crypto-authoritarian enunciation and orientation that characterises Chinese security models in Cameroon. Here, National Video Surveillance Command Centres of Cameroon and National Emergency Operations Centres, as infrastructural nodes and focal points for equipment and decisions relating to remote surveillance, reveal the way in which these models in Cameroon, adapt to the natural order of things.

In other words, their acclimatisation cannot make sense outside of any centralist and authoritarian State "imprinting" (Konrad, 1970). In this sense, it is the institutions and the governing elite that benefit. In other words, whether within the framework of the National Emergency Telecommunications Network or even Cameroon's Intelligent City Project, the work of breaking down the cameras is part of a spatial enterprise of legitimate and sovereign territorialisation of security, which runs on the rails of the State's administrative infrastructures. The result is an ordering and classification of spaces and sites to be monitored and controlled. From this perspective, the high density of surveillance cameras in the administrative city centres of regional capitals, in border towns and in the administrative and residential districts where the ruling elite live, reveals the sensitivity and importance of these places and environments that need to be protected and monitored.

As a result, Chinese video surveillance systems are captured and brought back into the deterrent, sovereignist fold of the State apparatus and the cameras, like the buildings of the gendarmerie or police units, are integrated into the relief, the security landscape of the places of State power. Here, security and authority of the State are now embodied by the presence of cameras whose lenses are focused not just on the surrounding environment or even places where risks are imminent, but also on administrative buildings, public spaces and the homes of the ruling elite. We can, therefore, see that the operating and orientation frameworks of remote surveillance become ambiguous, as they are situated halfway between the stated and vaunted security functions and their concealed disciplinary orientations. In this sense, the naming of the National Video Surveillance Command Centres of Cameroon's as well as the strategic territorial breakdown of surveillance cameras in Cameroon, come under the logic of "sissia" (Owona Nguini, 2018), understood in the Mboo language from Moungo in the Littoral region of Cameroon as a logic of dissuasion and constraint, making it possible to keep an eye on all forms of threat that would weigh primarily on the interests of the State. This logic is expressed in this implicit way: what must be monitored, protected and controlled as a priority is "the bliss of the State" (Foucault, 2004). At the top of this bliss stand the territorial integrity and State institutions.

Conclusion

The idea of the panoptic, which Foucault borrows from Bentham and from which we draw the lines of our category of the panoptic State, illustrates the way in which, under the influence of remote surveillance technologies from China, the African State is today being transformed into what we choose to call: The Panoptic State. In a context where the control exercised over its territory is increasingly relative, more and more limited and blurred as it is applied and extended to the periphery, the remote surveillance complex offered by Chinese models is renegotiating its relationship with its space. In this way, the African panoptic State is, first and foremost, a state in search of internal sovereignty. It is then as much the repercussion of an influence and contingency linked to Chinese neo-liberal globalisation as the local expression of a quest for self-determination characterised by its desire to legitimise its authority and deal with emergencies of all kinds. In the end, two things stand out in Cameroon's case: First, the way in which its controversial operationalisation confirms our hypothesis about the conformism of Chinese security models in Cameroon and updates our category of the panoptic State, since the interchinese competition around that project, combined with the battle of interests between Cameroonian actors relating as much to (exclusive) control of resources as to the monopoly of labelling and the legitimate choice of technologies linked to the project, contributes to reinforcing the panoptic character of the State in Cameroon. Second, the operationalisation of the National Emergency Telecommunications Network, albeit shaky, is not useless. On the contrary, it generates additional utility effects. By continuing with its contract as it stands, ZTE will incidentally generate a second video surveillance system in Cameroon: the Cameroon Intelligent City Project of Huawei. What we want to say here is that the quarrel over the project, which will lead to the retention of the video surveillance component in ZTE's project, is hardly a waste, still less a waste. Quite the contrary. Thanks to this duplication of vision generated by this other video surveillance system, the ability of Cameroon's security and safety authorities to manipulate tools and instruments enabling them to support and extend the depth of vision, to direct and focus the gaze in given directions, and to control is increased tenfold, amplified and accentuated. This is part of the strengthening of the State's power of omnivoyance, which now stems from the widening of its field of vision and the multiplicity of viewpoints from which its security and safety administrations now benefit.

References

Artigas, A. (2019). Beneath the surface of the Safe City : surveillance in the times of Chinese supremacy ? *Centre d'études européennes et de politique comparée, Working Paper N°01*, 45. Récupéré sur -

Baraka. (2021, June 1). "The Failed Promise of Kenya's Smart City. (R. o. World, Éd.) https://restofworld.org/2021/the-failed-promise-of-kenyas-smart-city

Barre, G. (2016). *BARRE Geneviève, Quand les entreprises chinoises se mondialisent: Haier, Huawei et TCL.* Paris: Éditions Collection.

Bobo, A. G. (2018). Ambition développementaliste, état stationnaire et extraversion au Cameroun de Paul BIYA. Le projet de construction du port autonome de Kribi. pp. 29–51. https://doi.org/10.3917/polaf.150.0029

Chen & al, ". (2018). Facilitative Leadership and China's New Role in the World . Vol. 3, No. 1. (C. P. (ESCI), Éd.) https://Récupérésurhairestrategique.pantheonsorbonne.fr/themes/2018/chinas-return-central-stage-towards-new-facilitative-leadership

Eyenga, M. (2021). Les nouveaux yeux de l'État ? L'introduction de la télésurveillance dans l'espace public à Yaoundé. *Dans Cahiers d'études africaines, 4* (244), 753–776. https://doi.org/10.4000/etudesafricaines.35559

Feldstein. (2019, Septembre). The Global Expansion of AI Surveillance". *Carnegie Endowment for International Peace*, p. 42.

Feldstein, S. (2019, Septembre 17). The Global Expansion of AI Surveillance. *Carnegie Endowment for International Peace*, p. 42. https://carnegieendowment.org/research/2019/09/the-global-expansion-of-ai-surveillance?lang=en

Focac. (2015). *the declaration of the Johannesburg summit of the forum on China-Africa cooperation,*. Focac. Consulté le 12 03, 2021, sur http://news.xinhuanet.com/English/china/2013-08/29/c_132673093_3.htm

Focac. (2018, 09 12). Consulté le 11 20, 2021, sur China-Africa Cooperation Beijing Action Plan: http://www.focac.org/eng/zywx_1/zywj/201809/t20180912_7933578.htm,

Foucault, M. (1975). *Surveiller et punir: naissance de la prison*. Paris: Gallimard.

Foucault, M. (2004). *Sécurité, territoire, population (1977–1978)*. Paris: Seuil/Gallimard.

Gaudin, J. P. (2007). *Gouverner par contrat*. Paris: Presses de Sciences Po. doi:https://doi.org/10.3917/scpo.gaudi.2007.01

GDNS1, O. o. (2021, Novembre 27). (A. Koa, Intervieweur) Bertoua, Cameroun.

GDNS2, O. O. (2021, Mai 16). (A. Koa, Intervieweur) Yaoundé, Cameroun .

Huawei. (2016, June 17). Huawei Hosts Safe City Summit in Africa to Showcase Industry Best Practice. Consulté le 12 03, 2021, sur https://www.huawei.com/us/news/2016/10/safe-city-summit-africa

HUAWEI1, C. O. (2021, Mars 16). Huawei Technologies Cameroon's Company. (A. Koa, Intervieweur) Douala, Cameroun.

Investir au cameroun. (2022, July 14). Consulté le 11 05, 2024, sur investiraucameroun.

Jili. (2022, October). China's Surveillance Ecosystem & The Global Spread of Its Tools. https://www.atlanticcouncil.org/in-depth-research-reports/issue-brief/chinese-surveillance-ecosystem-and-the-global-spread-of-its-tools/

Jili. (2022). Jili, B. (2022). Chinese ICT and Smart City Initiatives in Kenya. Asia Policy. https://www.atlanticcouncil.org/in-depth-research-reports/issue-brief/what-is-driving-the-adoption-of-chinese-surveillance-technology-in-africa/

Jili. (2023, May 15). What is driving the adoption of Chinese surveillance technology in Africa? (I. B. May, Éd.) Récupéré sur https://www.atlanticcouncil.org/in-depth-research-reports/issue-brief/what-is-driving-the-adoption-of-chinese-surveillance-technology-in-africa/

Jili, B. (2020, June 30). Chinese Surveillance Tools in Africa. *China, Law, Development Oxford Project ., 2019*(8). Récupéré sur https://cld.web.ox.ac.uk/file/678231

Jili, B. (2022, October 17). China's surveillance ecosystem and the global spread of its tools. Récupéré sur https://www.atlanticcouncil.org/in-depth-research-reports/issue-brief/chinese-surveillance-ecosystem-and-the-global-spread-of-its-tools/

Jili, B. (2022, july). Chinese ICT and Smart City Initiatives in Kenya. Asia Policy, 17(3), 40–50. Asia Policy, 17(3), p. 11. Récupéré sur https://www.jstor.org/stable/27227216

Jili, B. (2023, May 15). What is driving the adoption of Chinese surveillance technology in Africa? Récupéré sur https://www.atlanticcouncil.org/in-depth-research-reports/issue-brief/what-is-driving-the-adoption-of-chinese-surveillance-technology-in-africa/

Jili, B. (2025, May 30). Africanising Chinese surveillance technology. https://doi.org/10.59425/eabc.1748599200

kaufmann, J. C. (2016). *L'entretien Compréhensif*. Arman Colin. https://doi.org/10.3917/arco.kaufm.2016.01

Khan-Mohammad, G. A. (2020). Industrie et développement au Cameroun : les dynamiques d'un État dans l'« émergence ». *Critique internationale, 4* (89), pp. 53–74. https://doi.org/10.3917/crii.089.0056

Koa, A. (2015, Octobre). L'offensive technologique chinoise au Cameroun. *Master's Research thesis*. (University of Yaoundé II Soa, Éd.) Yaoundé.

Koa, A. (2020, Août). Le Centre National de Commandement de la vidéosurveillance, un dispositif stratégique de la Délégation Générale à la Sûreté Nationale, qui a pour objectif de surveiller afin de mieux sécuriser l'ensemble du territoire national. *Servir*(23), pp. 48–49.

Konrad, L. (1970). Studies in Animal and Human Behaviour. Volume 1. *Harvard University Press.*, p. 430.

MINMAP1, O. o. (2021, 10 3). Ministry of Public Contracts Interview. (A. Koa, Intervieweur) Yaoundé, Cameroun.

MINPOSTEL1, O. o. (2022, January 09). Ministry of Post and Telecommunications Interview. (A. Koa, Intervieweur) Yaoundé , Cameroun.

Mozur, P. J. (2019, Avril 14). Made in China, Exported to the World: The Surveillance State,. New York. Récupéré sur https://www.nytimes.com/2019/04/24/technology/ecuador-surveillance-cameras-police-government.html

Muthuri, J. G. (2025, Janvier). Panoptic real-time surveillance in Kenya. https://doi.org/10.5040/9781350422117.ch-

Nkam, H. (2016, 11 14). Cameroun - Imbroglio : Le marché des caméras de surveillance divise le gouvernement. *Actu-Cameroun*. https://actucameroun.com/2016/11/14/cameroun-imbroglio-le-marche-des-camerasde-surveillance-divise-le-governement/

November, V. K. (2002). Risques sous surveillance : une analyse géographique de l'utilisation de la vidéosurveillance. *Revue Internationale d'Ethique Sociale et Gouvernementale, 4*(2). https://doi.org/10.4000/ethiquepublique.

Nyoni, T. (2021). The geopolitical implications of Huawei in Zimbabwe: A critical analysis. (G. J. Studies, Éd.) *Global Journal of African Studies, 1*(4), pp. 23–37. https://doi.org/10.1080/23257929.2021.1880569

Nyoni, T. (2022). State surveillance in Zimbabwe: An analysis of trends and implications. *African Journal of Human Rights, 2*(6), 45–61. https://doi.org/10.1080/23311992.2022.1971465

Nzié, N. (2024, Mai). Le système de videosuveillance: un renfort technologique pour le maintien de l'ordre et le denouement des enquêtes judiciaires. *Servir*(31), p. 43. Récupéré sur https://www.dgsn.cm/wp-content/uploads/2024/05/servir-31-bon.pdf

Owona Nguini, M. E. (2001, Avril-Juin). Stratégies géopolitiques et géoéconomiques d'accès à la révolution informationnelle au Cameroun : Analyses de l'existant et approches prospectives. *Enjeux*, 7, pp. 20–25.

Owona Nguini, M. E. (2018). Gouvernement perpétuel » et démocratisation janusienne au Cameroun (1990-2018) . *Politique africaine, 150*(2), pp. 97–114. https://doi.org/10.3917/polaf.150.0097

Peace, C. E. (2019). AI Global Surveillance Technology. Consulté le 12 03, 2021, sur Carnegie Endowment For International Peace: https://carnegieendowment.org/features/ai-global-surveillance-technology?lang=en

Péclard, A. K.-M. (2020). États d'émergence. Le gouvernement de la croissance et du développment en Afrique. *Critique internationale, 4*(89), pp. 9–27. https://doi.org/10.3917/crii.089.0012

Sheena, G. (2020, Avril 28). dealing with demand for china's global surveillance exports. *Global China*, p. 16.

Skelton, S. &. (2025). Who supplies digital surveillance technologies to African governments? (Z. Books, Éd.) London.

Strauss, B. G. (1967). *The Discovery of Grounded Theory: Strategies for Qualitative Research.* (Adeline, Éd.) Chicago.

Virilio, P. (1988). *La machine de vision*. Galilée.

Weber, K. &. (2021, August 3). China's Surveillance State: A Global Project. https://www.top10vpn.com/research/huawei-china-surveillance-state/

Weber, M. (1995). *Economy and Society. 1. Les catégories de la sociologie* (Vol. 1). (A. series, Éd.) Paris: Pocke

White Paper, C. S. (2013). *China-Africa Economic and Trade Cooperation.* sur http://news.xinhuanet.com/English/china/2013-08/29/c_132673093_3.htm

Wounba, F. T. (2021, September-October). Smart City in Cameroon. *International Journal of Applied Science and Research, 4*(5), 389–412.

www.nouvelobs.com. (2014, Mai 17). Cameroun: Un Chinois tué, dix autres enlevés par Boko Haram. Récupéré sur https://www.nouvelobs.com/monde/20140517.OBS7521/cameroun-un-chinois-tue-dix-autres-enleves-par-boko-haram.html

www.prc.cm. (2013). Libération de la famille MOULIN-FOURNIER : la France dit « merci » au Président Paul BIYA. Yaoundé, Centre, Cameroun. https://www.prc.cm/fr/actualites/61-audiences/112-liberation-de-la-famille-moulin-fournier-la-france-dit-merci-au-president-paul-biya

www.prc.cm. (2018, Juin-Juillet). https://www.prc.cm/en/multimedia/documents/6625-tdr-bulletin-n-52

Zhang, K. (2020). The dual nature of Chinese technology in Africa: Opportunities and risks. *African Journal of International Relations, 3*(26), 256–274. doi:https://doi.org/10.1177/1464884918763247

Zhou, Y. (2020). The international implications of China's technology exports. *Chinese Journal of International Politics*, 115–137. doi:https://doi.org/10.1093/cjip/poaa002

Auxence Augustin KOA teaches political science, geopolitics, forest policy, wildlife, and environmental legislation of the Congo Basin in the Political Science Department of the Faculty of Legal and Political Sciences and in the Governance and Forest Policy Department of the Higher Institute of Agriculture, Wood, Water Resources and the Environment at the University of Bertoua, Cameroon. He is also a permanent researcher at the Paul Ango Ela Foundation for Central Africa's Geopolitics in Cameroon (PAEF), the Observatoire Chine-Afrique Francophone (OCAF), and the Unité de Recherche en Politique et en Science Sociale (URPOSSOC) at the University of Dschang. He is also a China-Central Africa expert in the CAIAC Local Network Chapter (SAF-CERDIA-RECAF) and a member of the chinese-in-africaafricans-in-china network. His research focuses mainly on China going global, Chinese local dynamics and renewable energy issues and clean technology infrastructure in the Global South. He has published, among others, "Quand la Chine pénètre en Brousse; géopolitique locale des investissements chinois affectant les terres forestières au Cameroun", In Enjeux n°54, 1er semestre, Yaoundé, 2021, pp. 119–156.

Chapter 6
Chinese-Funded Surveillance Systems in Zimbabwe: Socio-Economic, Political and Ethical Implications

Nevison Shumba and Bekimpilo Moyo Nhlabano

Abstract This chapter critically examines Chinese-funded surveillance and CCTV systems in Zimbabwe's urban areas, emphasising their dual role in enhancing public safety and threatening national sovereignty. While aiding crime prevention, these systems raise concerns about human rights violations, corruption and foreign influence. Using Panopticism theory and interviews with law enforcement agents, civil society, politicians and community members, the chapter exposes misuse of surveillance tools, including bribery and political targeting. Chinese involvement raises fears over access to sensitive data and manipulation of domestic policy. Drawing from findings in South Africa and beyond, the chapter emphasises the need for reform. It calls for transparent procurement, strong human rights protection and regulatory frameworks to curb dependence on foreign technology. African nations are urged to balance technological benefits with ethical governance and the protection of sovereignty.

Introduction

In recent years, surveillance systems, particularly Closed-Circuit Television (CCTV), have become a cornerstone of urban security worldwide. These systems, designed to monitor public spaces and deter crime, have been heralded for their effectiveness in improving safety and enhancing law enforcement capabilities (Fussey, 2020). CCTV systems are widely used in cities across the globe, with proponents citing their role in reducing crime rates, enhancing emergency responses and contributing to the development of smart cities where technology helps to improve urban living (Norris & Armstrong, 2018). However, while CCTV systems contribute to safety and security, they also raise significant concerns regarding

N. Shumba (✉) · B. M. Nhlabano
Development Studies, Lupane State University, Lupane, Zimbabwe
e-mail: nshumba@lsu.ac.zw; bnhlabano@lsu.ac.zw

G. Moyo (ed.), *An Anatomy of AI Surveillance in Africa*, Studies in Digital Politics and Governance, https://doi.org/10.1007/978-3-032-04269-9_6

privacy, civil liberties and governance, particularly in contexts where the systems are deployed with minimal transparency and accountability (Lyon, 2018a; Zuboff, 2019).

The use of surveillance systems, especially in politically sensitive countries like the Democratic Republic of Congo, Sudan and Burundi, presents a double-edged sword. McLuhan & McLuhan (2020) point out that these systems offer undeniable benefits in crime deterrence and urban management, while on the other hand, they have pervasive implications for human rights, state accountability and corruption. The pervasive reach of surveillance technologies can lead to the violation of privacy rights, especially when they are not subject to strict regulatory frameworks. In many instances, CCTV systems have been exploited for political control, with authorities using surveillance to monitor, suppress and target the opposition's activities. Furthermore, the increasing involvement of foreign actors, such as China, in financing and providing surveillance technologies raises concerns about external influence on domestic sovereignty and security.

Chinese investments in surveillance systems across Africa have sparked debate about the potential risks of foreign actors accessing sensitive data, which could compromise national security and sovereignty (Shin, 2021). In the case of Zimbabwe, the rapid expansion of Chinese-funded CCTV and surveillance systems has elicited a dichotomous response, generating both optimism regarding enhanced national security and apprehension concerning potential infringements on personal privacy and civil liberties. The expansion marks China's growing geopolitical footprint in Africa. Examples of Chinese-funded CCTV and surveillance systems include the 2018 Zimbabwe Smart Sustainable Cities Initiative for policing, which was rolled out in Harare and Bulawayo, the TelOne Huawei partnership for two data centres, which were funded by China's Axim Bank to the tune of US$98 million. The data centres will have state-of-the-art pan, tilt and zoom cameras with 290-degree view angles and 20X optical zoom lenses and night vision with high definition, inbuilt microphones and motion detection (Matiashe, 2024). The government of Zimbabwe also signed a US$71 million deal to install facial recognition in public spaces with Cloud Walk Technologies Company and Hikvision Technology Company, which are both Chinese entities (ADF, 2023). The Zimbabwean government agreed to provide training grounds for dark-complexioned facial recognition artificial intelligence.

While these systems are marketed as tools for enhancing national security and urban modernisation, their deployment has raised concerns about human rights violations, particularly related to the invasion of citizens' privacy, and the potential for state-sponsored surveillance of political opponents (Cummings, 2021). There are serious concerns about human rights infringement and they are subject to misuse by law enforcement agencies that operate or monitor them. Regrettably, China is helping Zimbabwe to create an environment that suppresses and suffocates the voices of dissent and freedom of expression. Travers (2024) notes that as a global leader in surveillance governance, China is now exporting its model to Africa. Zimbabwe's history of using surveillance to silence dissent during the Mugabe regime has been renewed and accelerated recently (ADF, 2023).

Building on studies conducted in Johannesburg, South Africa, this chapter illustrates how these surveillance tools violate civil rights and contribute to corruption, influencing domestic policies and dependence on foreign technology, ultimately undermining national sovereignty. Employing the Panopticism theory, the chapter incorporates extensive interviews with a varied array of stakeholders, including law enforcement agents, Chinese-employed local technicians, civil society advocates, political actors, local government officials and community members. This discourse contributes to ongoing debates regarding Chinese investments in surveillance systems in Zimbabwe.

This chapter contributes to the ongoing debate on the balance between technological advancements, human rights protections and national sovereignty in African states and cities. The debate is particularly in light of China's growing influence on Africa's security infrastructure. Most pressing, however, is the intensifying concern that China's expanding footprint in Africa may facilitate unauthorised access to sensitive state security information, while also exerting a profound impact on the continent's political landscape. Most of the studies focused on crime prevention with the use of CCTV and none were researched on their effects on socio-economic, political and how they fuel corruption by those who monitor them. This necessitated this chapter to explore how these technologies fuel corruption where they are used.

The chapter employs qualitative research to investigate the socio-economic, political and ethical implications of Chinese-funded CCTV and surveillance systems in Zimbabwe. In-depth interviews were conducted with stakeholders. Participants were interviewed about the potential contribution of corruption to the procurement, installation, operation and servicing of CCTV systems in the country. They include bribery, awarding of tenders to senior government officials, misuse of surveillance data and financial incentives for law enforcement or political actors. The study explored complex dynamics surrounding surveillance systems, including corruption, human rights violations and foreign influence. Purposive sampling was used to select participants, mostly relevant to the research questions, including 37 individuals who have been victims of surveillance systems. Interviews allowed flexibility in addressing sensitive themes like privacy violations, political control and role of surveillance in supporting or challenging state governance. The study also examined concerns about foreign influence and national sovereignty stemming from Chinese involvement in Zimbabwe's surveillance infrastructure.

Thematic analysis was used to interpret data collected during interviews, identifying patterns related to corruption in procurement and operation phases, misuse of surveillance data and financial incentives for political actors. The analysis was guided by Panopticism theory to assess how surveillance systems reinforce socio-political control and ethical dilemmas. Ethical measures were prioritised due to the sensitive nature of the study, ensuring participant anonymity and confidentiality through informed consent and secure data storage. The findings highlight critical issues such as the authoritarian use of surveillance technology for political manipulation and repression, raising concerns about privacy rights and Zimbabwe's dependence on Chinese technology without adequate legal safeguards. This chapter critically analyses the socio-economic, political and ethical implications of

Chinese-funded CCTV and surveillance systems in Zimbabwe. Specifically, it seeks to explore the dynamics of surveillance technologies in Zimbabwe's governance framework, focusing on how these systems affect privacy rights, contribute to corruption and influence political power structures. The chapter, therefore, intends to find strategies to balance the need to enhance public safety using surveillance technologies, at the same time safeguarding the right to personal privacy.

China and Smart Cities Agenda in Africa

China's growing involvement in Africa's infrastructure projects, particularly in surveillance technology, has sparked significant debate regarding its socio-political implications (Gros, 2021). As part of the Belt and Road Initiative (BRI), China has invested heavily in security infrastructures, including CCTV systems, across the African continent (Gros, 2021). Chinese firms, such as Huawei, have played a role in surveillance technologies in African countries, offering advanced systems at competitive prices. While these investments are often framed as a means of enhancing security and promoting economic development, they raise concerns about China's influence over African governance and its potential access to sensitive data (Shin, 2021).

Passalaoqua and Polito (2024) note that the increasing Chinese presence in the African surveillance technology market is due to an "authoritarian bias". They mention that states with authoritarian tendencies often turn to China. Notably, the Zimbabwe government is a proponent of this technology crackdown on its opponents. However, critics argue that Chinese involvement in the country's surveillance infrastructure could compromise national sovereignty, as the data collected by these systems may be shared with the Chinese government or used for purposes other than intended (Cummings, 2021). The potential for China to use its involvement in African surveillance projects to expand its geopolitical influence is a key concern, as it could lead to increased external control over domestic affairs (Shin, 2021). The concept of smart cities has gained traction across Africa, with several countries seeking to integrate digital technologies, including surveillance systems, into their urban planning and management strategies (Tshabalala & Simutowe, 2020). CCTV use to monitor public spaces, manage traffic and improve service delivery has reduced congestion, thereby enhancing urban governance. However, the integration of surveillance systems into these smart city frameworks raises concerns about the concentration of power in the hands of a few entities and the potential for misuse of surveillance data. In Zimbabwe, the push for smart city development has led to the installation of Chinese-funded CCTV systems in some parts of Bulawayo and Harare. While these systems are intended to improve urban management and security, their integration into smart city initiatives may exacerbate concerns about surveillance overreach, the erosion of privacy and the consolidation of political power in the hands of the ruling elite (Zhou, 2020). The challenge lies in ensuring that the benefits of smart city technologies do not come at the expense of fundamental human rights and democratic freedoms.

Effectiveness of CCTV and Urban Safety, Security and Crime Prevention

Despite notable socio-economic, political and ethical concerns, surveillance systems continue to be adopted globally. The Global South has also exhibited an appetite to exploit the opportunities arising from these technological initiatives. This chapter examines existing studies on the effectiveness of CCTV in urban settings; its socio-economic, political; and ethical implications, and how it aids corruption, with a focus on Zimbabwe. The Panopticism theory is the key theoretical framework that was applied for a better understanding of the dynamics of surveillance and power within the context of Chinese-funded CCTV and surveillance systems in Zimbabwe. The framework offers valuable insights into the mechanisms of control, corruption and accountability that arise from the deployment of surveillance systems in Zimbabwe, particularly regarding Chinese investments. The concept of Panopticism was introduced by Foucault (1975), who underscores the role of surveillance in exerting power over individuals. Foucault argues that surveillance is not merely about watching but is deeply tied to power relations that shape individuals' behaviours and societal norms. Panopticism describes a system where individuals are continuously observed, creating a sense of permanent visibility that induces self-discipline and conformity (Foucault, 1975).

Foucault's theory of surveillance is based on the Panopticon, a prison design where a central watchtower allows a single guard to observe all prisoners without being seen. This system, Foucault argues, instils a sense of permanent observation, even if surveillance is not actively occurring, making individuals behave as if they are constantly being watched. The power dynamics at play in such a system extend beyond simple monitoring and become a means of controlling and disciplining individuals by shaping their behaviour through fear of surveillance. In the context of Chinese-funded CCTV systems in Zimbabwe, Panopticism offers an understanding of how surveillance is used as a tool of control, particularly in urban spaces where the state monitors and regulates the behaviours of its citizens.

The installation of CCTV cameras across public spaces in Zimbabwe creates a similar sense of constant surveillance, which compels citizens to conform to the expectations set by the state and law enforcement authorities. This process is especially relevant in authoritarian contexts, where surveillance is often employed to control political opposition, manage public dissent and suppress civil liberties (Lyon, 2018a). In Zimbabwe, the deployment of surveillance systems funded by China may aggravate these power dynamics. Foucault's theory highlights how surveillance can be a mechanism of social control, particularly when combined with the political power of authoritarian regimes. The presence of Chinese stakeholders in the operation and monitoring of these systems may further complicate these dynamics, raising concerns about foreign influence on national sovereignty and the potential for manipulating surveillance data to target political rivals or suppress dissent (Zhou, 2020). It is important to recognise that China's behaviour in this context is not unique, as other major world powers such as the United States have also been implicated in similar activities.

CCTV systems are commonly touted as effective tools in enhancing urban safety and reducing crime rates. Welsh and Farrington (2009a) observed that CCTV installations in public spaces, particularly in high-crime areas, can deter criminal activities such as theft and violent crime. Welsh and Farrington (2009a) further argue that CCTV offers a deterrent effect by increasing the perceived risk of being caught, thus influencing potential offenders to reconsider criminal activities. The crime deterrence effect was also raised by Goold (2004), who reported that in London, a 20% decrease in street crime was observed following extensive CCTV installations. In the African context, the impact of CCTV systems has been similarly noted. A study by Marquette (2018) found that CCTV cameras deployed in South African urban areas led to a reduction in property crimes and increased the efficiency of law enforcement in crime detection. It seems studies conducted by both Goold (2004) and Marquette (2018) concluded that these technologies affect the reduction of crime, especially in central business districts. However, critics argue that CCTV systems are not a panacea for crime prevention and may shift the focus away from addressing the root causes of crime, such as socio-economic inequality and unemployment (Goold, 2004).

While CCTV cameras in cities such as Harare are part of a broader effort to enhance urban safety, concerns persist about their effectiveness in combating crime. Additionally, issues such as corruption can undermine the potential benefits of these technologies (Zhou, 2020). Lyon (2018a) argues that surveillance technologies, including CCTV, can lead to an invasive culture of constant monitoring, which undermines individual freedoms and personal privacy. As surveillance expands, citizens are increasingly subjected to surveillance without their consent, and their movements, behaviours and interactions are constantly monitored. This raises concerns about the balance between public safety and personal privacy. The fear of surveillance overreach and potential misuse of data by authorities calls for transparent and accountable policies surrounding the adoption of CCTV surveillance.

CCTV surveillance technologies contribute to an improved public perception of safety. A study conducted by Gray et al. (2011) established that individuals in areas where CCTV cameras are installed feel safe and are more likely to report crimes, for example, in Mombasa in Kenya and Cape Town in South Africa. This safety perception is very important as it promotes social cohesion and enhances community engagement. Ironically, knowing that you are in the scope of active CCTV cameras influences how people behave. People will behave in a manner that is consistent with social norms. This reduces the commission of crime in such areas and the public's fear of crime. However, scholars such as Tilley (2008) indicated that the presence of active CCTV cameras may activate a "false sense of security" as it does not always correspond with actual crime reduction. The capacity of CCTV to prevent crime is overestimated and criminals are sometimes aware of that. Criminals may also have better means to circumvent these technologies. A disturbing concern is that the agents who monitor and service the system may also be tempted to abuse their access to the system and become syndicates with criminals. For instance, in 2020, a Zimbabwe opposition member of parliament Joana Mamombe, and two youth activists, Cecilia Chimbiri and Netsai Marova, were intercepted on their mobile phones and tracked using their mobile phone location (Matiashe, 2024). The trio was abducted, sexually abused and tortured by state agents (Matiashe, 2024). To further buttress the notion of abuse of CCTV and surveillance systems, in 2021, President Mnangagwa officially commissioned the National Data Centre, which was built by the Chinese, and in his opening remarks boasted that "the government can track where people walk, who they talk to, and even where they sleep" (ADF, 2023). This is a testament to the fears raised by the rights activists that the system may be abused by the state and its agents to infringe on human rights. There is a high possibility of abuse of office by the individuals who monitor and service the CCTV system for their own gain.

In authoritarian regimes, the deployment of CCTV systems can aggravate these concerns by enabling the state to monitor political opponents and civil society actors. For instance, in Zimbabwe, there have been reports of surveillance systems being used to track and monitor opposition political activities (Cummings, 2021). This kind of state surveillance undermines citizens' ability to freely express political dissent without fear of retribution. Similarly, surveillance systems funded and managed by foreign actors, such as China, present a dilemma, especially about foreign governments accessing sensitive national data (Shin, 2021). Several scholars (Lyon, 2018b; Plaut, 2019; Cummings, 2021; ADF, 2023; Travers, 2024) have painted a grim picture of CCTV implications in Zimbabwe and the gloom emanates from CCTV's effects on human rights. However, the actual dynamics and their implications on corruption, governance accountability and compromising security are missing from academic discussions. This chapter, therefore, explores these ramifications from an intellectual perspective and makes practical recommendations to address the identified challenges.

The existing literature provides valuable arguments that support the adoption of CCTV surveillance technologies. A systematic review and meta-analysis conducted by Welsh and Farrington (2002, 2008, 2009b) established that CCTV surveillance significantly reduces crime by at least 16%. This was also supported by a review by Alexandrie (2017), who reviewed seven randomised and natural experiments on CCTV and established a 24% crime reduction. However, there is insufficient literature on the best practices for the implementation and maintenance of these technologies to enhance their overall effectiveness. This, therefore, warrants further investigation to determine effective means to implement CCTV surveillance tools and best practices in their maintenance and servicing. Furthermore, the implications of surveillance technology and its impact on civil liberties call for thorough exploration and critical analysis. There is very limited research that addresses the balance between security and privacy and its potential consequences for marginalised communities. There is also limited literature on abuse of office by those operating these systems for personal gain; hence, this study conducts a thorough exploration of the implications of surveillance on civil liberties and corruption.

Implications of Surveillance Systems in Zimbabwe

The operation of CCTV systems can be susceptible to corruption. Law enforcement officers who monitor CCTV and surveillance systems may be tempted to extort individuals caught on camera. Section 174 (1)(a) of Zimbabwe Criminal Law (Codification and Reform) Act Chapter 9.23, (2004) states that 'If one does anything which he knows is contrary to or inconsistent with his duty as a public officer with the intent of conferring an undue or illegal benefit on someone else or of unfairly or illegally prejudicing someone else, shall be guilty of criminal abuse of duty'. Notably, with this clear law in place, convictions are a challenge in Zimbabwe, especially when one has money to bribe both law enforcement agents and court officials. CCTV systems have also been associated with corruption, particularly in the procurement and operation phases.

In many African countries, the procurement process for surveillance systems often lacks transparency, which can lead to corrupt practices such as kickbacks and inflated contracts (Njiru, 2019). For instance, in Thailand, the government is reported to have lost Bt400 million (US$ 11.7 million) due to corruption and procurement irregularities for the CCVT system for the "Safe Schools Project" (Raj Shekhar, 2025). The Ministry of Education was meant to install CCTV systems at every school for at least 1000 schools with the hope of strengthening the security of students and school staff. According to the contract, each system at the school was expected to have 16 cameras, but on the ground, the contractors fixed only six cameras per system (Raj Shekhar, 2025). The investigations also revealed that the cameras were inflated and charged Bt31,000-00 each, a price which was wayward from the market value of the cameras, which was Bt4,000-00. In a similar and more recent case in India, Health Minister, Satyender Jain, is facing corruption charges in connection with a US$673 million CCTV installation project in Delhi (Raj Shekhar, 2025). The minister is alleged to have accepted a bribe of US$8.3 million.

CCTV and surveillance projects are large-scale projects that must go through proper bidding and tender processes. However, many times these processes are overshadowed by the political elite who always ensure that the tenders are awarded to their close ties or are awarded on the heels of a khaki envelope. Tender processes in Zimbabwe are fraught with numerous irregularities and that has promoted entrepreneurship in which some people are now thriving on winning tenders for services that they will never deliver. There are accusations of some business tycoons being offered tenders through unorthodox means to supply services that never materialised even after having received full funding for the tender. The Gwanda solar project scandal is a vivid example involving Intratrek Company, which was awarded a US$172.8 million tender to supply a solar power plant amid power challenges in the town (Harris, 2024). Despite having received the full amount to supply the system, the project failed and nothing was supplied. The project was meant to generate 100 megawatts for the national grid and alleviate power challenges facing the city. Until today, Gwanda town is still battling with power shortages amid increasing demand for the utility from both the domestic and the mining sectors.

In Zimbabwe, concerns have been raised about the lack of accountability in the procurement processes related to Chinese-funded surveillance technologies. This issue is compounded by weak governance structures, which increase the vulnerability of such projects to manipulation by both local officials and foreign investors (Zhou, 2020). Furthermore, law enforcement officers who monitor these systems may misuse their power, engaging in bribery or extorting money from individuals caught on camera (Liu & Zhang, 2020). The lack of proper oversight and the concentration of surveillance power in the hands of a few actors often linked to political elites can exacerbate these issues, undermining the effectiveness of CCTV systems in fostering public safety.

The analysis of the implications of Chinese-funded CCTV and surveillance systems in Zimbabwe reveals concerns related to exploitation by law enforcement agencies, privacy violations, political manipulation and the risks posed by foreign involvement, particularly by Chinese stakeholders in surveillance operations. One of the most notable implications is the exploitation of CCTV systems by law enforcement agents for personal gain. At least 80% of law enforcement agents demand monetary rewards from individuals caught violating the law, such as traffic offenders or petty criminals, to avoid legal repercussions or reduce penalties. Members of the public usually do not want the inconvenience of being taken to the police station for further interrogation and they usually volunteer to pay bribes to circumvent the inconvenience.

Law enforcement participants confessed that if one is caught on camera doing something wrong, the law enforcement agents can use the footage to their advantage. Offenders sometimes offer money to avoid prosecution or pay fines. Fines in Zimbabwe are generally high and this gives law enforcement agents leverage to extort bribes from the offenders who may volunteer to pay less than a gazetted fine. Findings revealed that corruption is prevalent at Zimbabwe's border posts, where law enforcement officials often solicit bribes of approximately US$100 per vehicle. With the potential to process over 40 vehicles per shift, this can result in law enforcement agents receiving substantial amounts exceeding US$ 3500-00 daily. The amount may double during holidays or in the festive season. Border post-deployment is a contentious issue and everyone has got vested interest in this deployment. It is not easy to be deployed on such a deployment. This explains why such deployments are mostly characterised by relatives and girlfriends of senior officials. If one is not connected to a senior official, one has to pay a bribe to be assigned to the border post. Furthermore, those deployed tend not to take time off or leave, as they aim to capitalise on potential earnings.

The abuse of the CCTV system is also evident in law enforcement agents who are involved in traffic enforcement duties in Zimbabwe. Law enforcement agents capture footage of those who proceed against red robots and make follow-ups at their residential premises, showing them video clips of their conduct. This confirms the notion raised by Langa (2024), who observed that CCTV surveillance may be misused by those who monitor it. The culture of silence and impunity within law enforcement organisations promotes reluctance among officials to pursue investigations or make arrests of their subordinates. It is very difficult for the superiors to enforce discipline on their juniors, especially when the superiors are beneficiaries of their junior members' corrupt spoils. Instead of holding their junior members accountable for their corrupt activities, the senior officials tend to work in cahoots with junior members and alert them whenever efforts are being made to arrest them. This perpetuates a cycle of corruption, where those who would normally be held accountable for wrongdoing are instead protected by their connections and alliances. This conforms to Sachs (2021), who suggests that CCTV systems, when not carefully regulated, can become tools of corruption.

The practice of demanding money in exchange for clemency was reported as widespread, indicating a systemic issue with accountability in the law enforcement sector (Baud & Synder, 2018). Corruption in Zimbabwe has been institutionalised as those who are mandated to take measures to address corruption are also receiving the proceeds of corruption from their subordinates. This makes it very difficult to deal decisively with corruption in the country. The impact of CCTV surveillance on privacy and civil liberties is a thorny issue with members of the public and civil society actors. The public and civil society are concerned about the intrusion of CCTV on their privacy, particularly in urban spaces where CCTV cameras are increasingly prevalent. The right to privacy is a constitutional right that must be protected and assured by the state. The advent of CCTV sponsored by the Chinese government as a tool for governance has seen many African governments encroaching on the right to privacy. While the system is marketed as a means to ensure safety, the people feel that they are constantly monitored and this compromises their freedom of expression and association. Critics of Chinese surveillance technologies allege that African states adopted these technologies as a means to entrench their authoritarian control, suppress dissent and surveillance of opposition groups, journalists and minority groups (Sakarombe et al., 2025).

The secretive procurement processes surrounding the acquisition of CCTV systems contribute to public mistrust. In Zimbabwe, government officials are unable or unwilling to provide clear details on the surveillance procurement process, including the criteria used for selecting Chinese firms. This lack of transparency exacerbates concerns about corruption and nepotism within the procurement system. The tender bidding process for the CCTV systems is unclear, is made behind closed doors, and is done by the central government. This supports the argument that impervious procurement procedures are fertile ground for corruption and foreign influence. In Zimbabwe, as in many other African nations, the secretive nature of public procurement processes undermines public trust in the government and the legitimacy of foreign investments (Moyo, 2020). The lack of oversight and accountability in these processes allows for both political and financial manipulation.

In addition, when members of the general public are constantly being monitored, especially without their consent, they feel uneasy and uncomfortable. One would expect to see a reduced crime rate in the cities where surveillance systems are installed everywhere. Ironically, cases of corruption are an order of the day, especially at passport offices, despite surveillance systems being in place. This is a clear sign that the surveillance system is not meant to protect the aspirations of the public but rather to instill fear. Incidents of armed robberies are happening in broad daylight in the city centreand a vivid example is a case of US$4 million armed robbery at Eco-Bank in Bulawayo. The robbery happened in clear view of the cameras and one would expect that the criminals would be intercepted or brought to book in the earliest possible time if the system is meant for public safety. But things do not go as expected by the public. This, therefore, seems to concretise the notion that law enforcement agents may be tempted to form a syndicate with criminals.

Sections 51 and 57 of the Zimbabwe Constitution Amendment (No. 20) (2013) have provisions for the right to human dignity and the right to privacy, respectively. The enshrined constitutional rights of civil liberties are violated by the surveillance systems installed in public spaces without public consultation and input. The widespread use of CCTV, particularly in public spaces, poses significant ethical questions about the balance between ensuring safety and preserving individual freedoms (Lyon, 2018b). These observations are consistent with global debates on surveillance, where privacy rights are often compromised in the name of security (Zuboff, 2019). Additionally, one wonders why public sector officials receive bribes in front of these systems. It is conclusive, therefore, that these public officials work in cahoots with both CCTV monitors and those operating the front.

The chapter also explored the use of surveillance systems by the ruling political elite to target political rivals and suppress dissent. Several respondents, including opposition political leaders, claimed that CCTV systems were strategically placed in areas where political protests or opposition gatherings were likely to occur. However, it should be noted that these systems work quite well in democratic countries where the rule of law prevails. There are many cases in which CCTV is technology-assisted, especially privately owned CCTV cameras. A case in point is the abduction of an opposition activist, Tawanda Muchehiwa, in 2020, in which a privately owned CCTV managed to capture the incident, leading to an outcry and eventually the release of the kidnapped victim.

In countries like Zimbabwe, surveillance systems are exploited by the political elite for their political advantage. The systems serve as a tool for political control by monitoring and recording opposition movements, potentially leading to political repression. The use of surveillance for political purposes is not unique to Zimbabwe; similar trends have been observed in other countries where governments use technological surveillance to stifle political opposition (Binns, 2021). Scholars such as Gorden Moyo echoed similar sentiments, mentioning that Chinese digital technologies provide authoritarian governments with tools to spy on the opposition and dissenting voices (Langa, 2024). This is further compromised by the poor regulatory environment in the digital space, which then attracts unwanted digital surveillance that subverts human rights. Chinese surveillance technologies have been weaponized by states to spy on their citizens (Moyo, 2020 in Langa, 2024). The case of Bobi Wine, the Ugandan Singer and opposition leader, bears witness to the abuse of surveillance technologies by state agents to violate human rights. The state of

Uganda used Chinese surveillance technologies to decrypt Bobi's communications and intercept his communications. These technologies can be analogised to honey with stings; they are always packaged with hidden costs. Despite its misuse, CCTV remains critical in the fight against crime in cities, as noted by Welsh and Farrington (2008, 2009a).

The involvement of Chinese stakeholders in the operation of Zimbabwe's CCTV systems is yet another concern in an authoritarian country. Chinese companies involved in installing and maintaining surveillance systems have access to sensitive data. Several civil society actors argue that this could pose risks to Zimbabwe's national sovereignty. These Chinese companies have access to information about state security, government activities and even private citizens. This jeopardizes state security and its autonomy both in its domestic and international affairs. Critics of Chinese surveillance technologies are raising concerns against data colonialism by China, where biometric data and digital dependencies create neo-imperial control structures (Warner & Ajibade, 2024). The case of Zimbabwe's Cloud Walkpartnership, which sends biometric data to China for facial recognition algorithm development, poses a potential risk for data colonialism. Warner and Ajibade (2024) noted that in Kenya, there were widespread reports that Chinese hackers invaded key ministries and state institutions, and they were focusing on information related to Kenya's debt to China. It is also reported that the African Union headquarters is bugged by China (Warner & Ajibade, 2024), and everything that happens within the headquarters is communicated to China. Therefore, China is deploying surveillance technologies to African states as a means to constantly monitor them and possibly influence their foreign policy. The technologies work in the best interest of China rather than benefiting the recipient countries.

Chinese firms have been linked to various surveillance projects across Africa, and questions have been raised about the potential for data exploitation and foreign interference in national affairs (Pilling, 2020). For instance, a smart city project in Addis Ababa, Ethiopia, in 2018, by Chinese Telecom giant ZTE, which aimed to improve urban management and transportation systems, was misused by ZTE to facilitate a back door into the system, allowing Chinese authorities to access data remotely (Johnson, 2020). While Chinese involvement brings significant investment, it also opens avenues for the transfer of sensitive data to foreign actors, thus compromising the nation's control over its critical infrastructure (Ngugi, 2022). Furthermore, the employment dynamics surrounding the operation and maintenance of this equipment are noteworthy. Specifically, it is the Chinese personnel who are responsible for ensuring its functionality and upkeep, which poses a significant challenge to local job seekers.

Chinese tech companies like Huawei and ZTE give low-interest loans, offering an opportunity for infrastructural development. However, Warner and Ajibade (2024) argue that these loans are non-concessional and are costly to repay. This can culminate in debt-trap diplomacy as African states may fail to repay the loans and are forced to cede strategic assets or lose their policy autonomy to China (Nhlabano Moyo & Shumba, 2025; Warner & Ajibade, 2024). The ongoing debt crisis in

Zimbabwe is likely to persist as the lack of domestic employment opportunities perpetuates economic instability and exacerbates the country's financial woes.

Generally, the smart cities initiative in Zimbabwe has gathered widespread public mistrust of both the government and the Chinese-funded surveillance systems. Members of the public and civil society are sceptical regarding the true motivations behind the installation of CCTV cameras. This mistrust is further compounded by the lack of transparency in how data collected through surveillance is used or shared. There is a strong sentiment among citizens that the CCTV systems are part of a broader surveillance state aimed at controlling the population rather than enhancing security. The chapter illustrated the complex and multifaceted implications of Chinese-funded CCTV and surveillance systems in Zimbabwe. While the systems may offer potential benefits in terms of security and crime prevention, their misuse by law enforcement for personal gain, human rights infringements, suppression of dissent, national security threats and serious fears of debt. The involvement of Chinese companies introduces significant risks to national sovereignty, particularly regarding the potential for foreign access to sensitive data. Furthermore, the secretive procurement processes surrounding the deployment of these systems have deepened public mistrust and fuelled worries about corruption. These findings suggest the need for greater transparency, accountability and regulation in the use of surveillance technologies in Zimbabwe.

Looking Ahead

To mitigate the potential negative impacts of surveillance technologies, particularly CCTV systems in Zimbabwe, several reforms and recommendations are proposed. These measures aim to ensure that surveillance systems align with international human rights standards such as freedom of assembly and expression as per the United Nations article 6316/1966. These measures enhance transparency, accountability and national security. Zimbabwe should adopt laws in alignment with international standards, such as the International Covenant on Civil and Political Rights (ICCPR), which safeguards privacy. This includes limiting the collection, use and storage of personal data through clear legal frameworks, implementing data minimisation principles and establishing data retention policies with regular audits. An independent oversight body should be created to ensure surveillance practices respect privacy rights. Surveillance should not suppress freedom of expression or political activism. Clear transparency procedures should ensure public awareness of how surveillance technologies are used, particularly in political contexts, to protect individuals participating in protests from intimidation.

The procurement process for surveillance systems should be open, competitive and involve clear evaluation criteria. Independent oversight should ensure fairness and reduce corruption risks. Contracts should be publicly accessible, and regular audits of the procurement and surveillance systems should be conducted by third-party agencies. Public officials involved in procurement must declare any conflicts of interest, especially in dealings with foreign companies. A whistle-blower protection bill should also be enacted into law to ensure reports of corruption are addressed without compromising the safety of those who report corruption. Officials and companies must be held accountable for any misuse of surveillance systems for personal or political gain and hence an independent body must be at the forefront to enforce these. Zimbabwe should establish comprehensive data protection laws to govern how personal data is collected and used by surveillance systems. These laws should ensure that sensitive data is not shared with foreign entities without proper oversight or consent, particularly in the context of foreign involvement by companies like those from China. A national cybersecurity strategy should be implemented to protect data from foreign cyber threats, particularly if surveillance systems are operated by foreign companies. The operation and maintenance of critical infrastructure should be under local control, with strong oversight mechanisms in place.

Government departments such as the Ministries of Justice, Information, and Technology should collaborate to regulate surveillance systems. Civil society organisations and human rights groups should be involved in monitoring and advocating for citizens' rights during the deployment of surveillance technologies. Zimbabwe should engage with international organisations like the United Nations and the African Union to develop standards for surveillance technologies. Additionally, Zimbabwe should negotiate agreements with foreign stakeholders, including China, to protect national sovereignty and data security. Implementing these reforms ensures compliance with international human rights standards, enhances transparency and accountability in procurement processes and introduces policy frameworks to limit external influence on critical infrastructure. Zimbabwe can better safeguard citizens' rights while benefiting from technological advancements. A co-ordinated approach that includes collaboration among government agencies, civil society and international stakeholders is essential for ensuring that surveillance systems are used ethically and effectively.

Conclusion

This chapter examined the complexities surrounding the deployment of surveillance technologies in Zimbabwe, highlighting both the benefits and risks they pose to human rights, governance and national sovereignty. While surveillance systems such as CCTV can enhance security and aid in development, they also raise worries about misuse for political gain, corruption and violations of privacy. The chapter concludes that CCTV systems present a dual challenge, as they can reduce crime but are vulnerable to misuse by law enforcement and political elites, compromising privacy and civil liberties. The chapter identified major concerns, including the role of surveillance systems in enabling corruption, violation of human rights, particularly privacy rights and the involvement of foreign entities in managing Zimbabwe's surveillance infrastructure. To address these challenges, the chapter recommends establishing clear regulations in line with international human rights standards, introducing robust national data protection laws and ensuring independent oversight and transparency in procurement processes. Ultimately, balancing technological progress with the protection of human rights and national sovereignty is crucial to ensure that these advancements contribute to a fair and just society.

References

ADF. (2023). *Zimbabwe turns to Chinese technology to expand surveillance of citizens*. African Defence Forum.

Alexandrie, G. (2017). Surveillance cameras and crime: A review of randomized and natural experiments. *Journal of Scandinavian Studies in Criminology and Crime Prevention, 18*(2), 210–222.

Baud, I., & Synder, D. (2018). Corruption in urban surveillance. *African Studies Review, 61*(2), 85–106. https://doi.org/10.1017/asr.2018. Accessed on 11/11/24

Binns, J. (2021). Political repression through technology: Surveillance in Africa. *Journal of African Politics, 49*(3), 112–130. https://doi.org/10.1016/j.jafpol.2020.12.007. Accessed on 13/11/24

Constitution of the Republic of Zimbabwe Amendment (No. 20) 2013, Harare.

Cummings, D. (2021). The growing influence of China in African governance: Implications for sovereignty and privacy. *Journal of African Political Economy, 48*(2), 112–129. https://doi.org/10.1080/01436597.2021.1883457. Accessed on 12/01/25

Foucault, M. (1975). *Discipline and punish: The birth of the prison*. Vintage Books.

Fussey, P. (2020). The ethics of surveillance technologies in urban spaces: Privacy concerns in the age of CCTV. *Surveillance Studies, 12*(4), 322–338. https://doi.org/10.1080/14741599.2020.1830786. Accessed on 15/02/25

Goold, B. (2004). Surveillance, counter-terrorism, and comparative constitutionalism: The role of CCTV in urban spaces. *International Journal of Constitutional Law, 2*(4), 77–94. https://doi.org/10.1093/icon/2.4.77. Accessed on 02/01/25

Gray, E., Farrington, D. P., & Medina, J. (2011). The impact of CCTV on crime and public safety: A review of the evidence. *Journal of Criminal Justice, 39*(4), 1–10.

Gros, J. (2021). China's belt and road initiative in Africa: Implications for the continent's governance and security. *African Security Review, 30*(3), 233–249. https://doi.org/10.1080/10246029.2021.1903467. Accessed on 11/01/25

Harris, L. B. (2024). *Stalled Gwanda solar project raises concerns: Parly visit exposes lack of progress*. CITE.

Johnson, K. (2020). *China's 'Smart City' ambitions in Africa raise concerns*. Financial Times Addis Ababa.

Langa, V. (2024). *Rice of Chinese surveillance tech in Africa: Development or Espionage?* https://www.theafricareport.com//354469//rise-of-chinese-surveillance-tech-in-africa-development-or-espionage/. Accessed on 08/04/25.

Liu, C., & Zhang, X. (2020). Corruption and the misuse of surveillance systems in China: A case study of law enforcement officers. *Asian Journal of Political Science, 28*(2), 175–189. https://doi.org/10.1080/02185377.2020.1805639. Accessed on 13/02/25

Lyon, D. (2018a). *The culture of surveillance: Watching as a way of life*. Polity Press.

Lyon, D. (2018b). *The surveillance society: A critical introduction*. Sage Publications.

Marquette, H. (2018). Surveillance and governance: The use of CCTV in crime prevention in South Africa. *African Security Review, 27*(2), 142–157. https://doi.org/10.1080/10246029.2018.1497627. Accessed on 23/01/25

Matiashe, F. S. (2024). *Zimbabwe: Digital rights activists fear misuse of surveillance cameras in Bulawayo*. The Africa Report.

McLuhan, M., & McLuhan, E. (2020). *Understanding media: The extensions of man*. MIT Press.

Moyo, J. (2020). Transparency and corruption in African public procurement. *Public Procurement Journal, 35*(4), 211–229. https://doi.org/10.1080/1366967X.2020.1740103. Accessed on 11/01/25

Ngugi, I. (2022). Chinese influence in Africa: The case of surveillance technologies. *Global Affairs Journal, 14*(2), 27–40. https://doi.org/10.1080/20421338.2022.1827392. Accessed on 10/11/24

Nhlabano Moyo, B., & Shumba, N. (2025). Entwined in debt: China-Zimbabwe relations and socio-economic implications. Zimbabwe. *Journal of Applied Research, 6*(Special Issue), 69–82.

Njiru, S. (2019). Transparency and corruption in the procurement of surveillance systems in Africa. *African Development Review, 31*(4), 424–439. https://doi.org/10.1111/1467-8268.12301 Accessed on 11/11/24

Norris, C., & Armstrong, G. (2018). The maximum surveillance society: The rise of CCTV and its impact on human rights. *Security Journal, 31*(1), 13–29. https://doi.org/10.1057/sj.2017.22. Accessed on 11/11/24

Passalaoqua, C., & Polito, C. (2024). *The Chinese supply of surveillance technology to Africa, working paper series SOG-WP7/2024, LUISS*. School of Government. https://sog.luis

Pilling, D. (2020). *Surveillance and state power in Africa: China's role*. The Guardian. https://www.theguardian.com/world/2020/jun/03/surveillance-china-africa-security. Accessed on 19/11/24.

Plaut, M. (2019). *Zimbabwe is trying to build a China style surveillance state*. Martin Plaut Blog, Vice Media. https://www.vice.com/en/article/zimbabwe-is-trying-to-build-a-china-style-surveillance-state/. Accessed on 20/02/25.

Raj Shekhar (2025). *ACB files FIR against Satyender Jain in CCTV "corruption" case, may seek custodial interrogation to unearth "larger conspiracy"*. The Times of India.

Sachs, N. (2021). Corruption and surveillance: A case study of African nations. *Journal of Political Science, 56*(1), 145–163. https://doi.org/10.1007/s12345-021-00237-x. Accessed on 01/12/24

Sakarombe, E., Chimwamurombe, F., Masuku, S. S., Mupanga, J., & Mutume, T. E. C. (2025). *The coloniality of Chinese surveillance technologies in Africa*. University of Zimbabwe.

Shin, W. (2021). Chinese technological influence in Africa: The case of surveillance systems. *Journal of International Politics, 58*(4), 540–560. https://doi.org/10.1080/00119911.2021.1855498. Accessed on 13/01/25

Tilley, N. (2008). The effectiveness of CCTV in reducing crime: A review of the evidence. *Crime Prevention and Community Safety, 10*(1), 1–12.

Travers, L. (2024). Algorithmic coloniality? The case of Chinese artificial intelligence technology & Zimbabwe surveillance. *Transience Journal, 15*(2) ISSN 2191-1150.

Tshabalala, P., & Simutowe, A. (2020). Smart cities in Africa: Opportunities and challenges of integrating surveillance systems. *Urban Studies Journal, 57*(5), 1235–1248. https://doi.org/10.1177/0042098019870493 Accessed on 19/02/25

Warner, J., & Ajibade, T. (2024). *China's smart cities in Africa: Should the United States be concerned?* Centre for Strategic and International Studies.

Welsh, B. C., & Farrington, D. P. (2002). *Crime prevention effects of closed-circuit television: A systematic review (No. 252)*. Home Office Research.

Welsh, B. C., & Farrington, D. P. (2008). Effect of closed-circuit television surveillance on crime. *Campbell Systematic Reviews, 17*, 1–73.

Welsh, B. C., & Farrington, D. P. (2009a). Public area CCTV and crime prevention: An updated systematic review and meta-analysis. *Justice Quarterly, 26*(4), 716–745.

Welsh, B., & Farrington, D. (2009b). Public area surveillance and crime prevention: A meta-analysis. *Criminology & Public Policy, 8*(1), 109–136. https://doi.org/10.1111/j.1745-9133.2009.00555.x. Accessed on 11/12/24

Zhou, M. (2020). CCTV and state control in Zimbabwe: Implications for privacy and human rights. *Surveillance Studies Journal, 12*(3), 298–314. https://doi.org/10.1177/2042134320916947. Accessed on 15/11/24

Zuboff, S. (2019). *The age of surveillance capitalism: The fight for a human future at the new frontier of power*. Public Affairs.

Nevison Shumba is a distinguished academic and researcher with a strong security background. He currently serves as a lecturer at Lupane State University as well as a part-time lecturer at the Zimbabwe Open University. His research focuses on the intersections of international relations, gender, population patterns, and governance, and he has contributed a book chapter on China-Zimbabwe relations and Chinese-funded surveillance systems in Zimbabwe. Email: nevisons@gmail.com.

Bekimpilo Moyo Nhlabano is a lecturer at Lupane State University, Zimbabwe, and is also a research fellow at the Public Policy and Research Institute of Zimbabwe. His research interests converge at international relations, governance, peace and security, and sustainable development. He has published a book chapter on China-Zimbabwe relations and articles on climate change, urban poverty, and Chinese-funded surveillance systems in Zimbabwe. https:orcid.org/ooo9-0008-3118-227X. Email: nhlabanobheki@gmail.com.

Chapter 7
The Potency of National Identity and Interest in the Penetration of Chinese Technologies in South Africa

Emmanuel Matambo

Abstract Emmanuel Matambo employs a constructivist framework to examine the role of national identity and interest in South Africa's embrace of Chinese technologies. Focusing on Huawei, Hikvision and smartphone manufacturers, he interprets South Africa's endorsement of Chinese technologies and postulates possible hazards which are partly based on Article 7 of China's National Intelligence Law, which enjoins all Chinese entities to aid the Chinese government's intelligence gathering. Matambo presents three main arguments: firstly, that the reception of Chinese technologies in South Africa has been positive and impervious to warnings by China's tech detractors; secondly, this embrace lies in South Africa and China's correlated identities and interests; and thirdly, Matambo urges vigilance on the part of South Africa as Article 7 of China's National Intelligence Law poses risks for the use of tech companies in South Africa for China's quest for political and social control.

Introduction

This chapter highlights the role of national identity and interest in South Africa's embrace of Chinese technologies. The first section presents a history that contextualises this embrace, followed by ongoing studies and debates about Chinese technologies. This will be done at two levels: showing the penetration of Chinese technologies, and the gaps in existing literature. The third section is an outline of constructivism, a prism through which the chapter interprets South Africa's reception of Chinese technologies. The fourth section focuses on the presence of Chinese tech entities in South Africa—Huawei, Hikvision and smartphone manufacturers. Finally, the chapter interprets South Africa's endorsement of Chinese technologies and postulates possible hazards that are partly based on Article 7 of China's National Intelligence Law, which enjoins all Chinese entities to aid the Chinese government's

E. Matambo (✉)
Centre for Africa-China Studies, University of Johannesburg, Johannesburg, South Africa
e-mail: ematambo@uj.ac.za

G. Moyo (ed.), *An Anatomy of AI Surveillance in Africa*, Studies in Digital Politics and Governance, https://doi.org/10.1007/978-3-032-04269-9_7

intelligence gathering. This justifies claims that Chinese tech entities are agents of the sprawling intelligence-gathering machinery of the Chinese government. Ineluctably, South Africa's reception of Chinese technologies is compared with the negative attitude of other countries, chiefly the United States of America. This clarifies how intersecting or divergent national identities and interests in the manner of constructivism explain why what one country considers a threat might not be considered as such by another. The chapter has three main arguments: firstly, that South Africa embraces Chinese technologies; secondly, this embrace lies in South Africa and China's intersubjective identities; and thirdly, Article 7 of China's National Intelligence Law poses risks for the use of tech companies in South Africa for China's quest for political control.

South Africa-China Relations: A Brief History

Apartheid South Africa had formal relations with Taiwan, while the People's Republic of China (PRC), which identified itself with the developing world (Third World was the expression in vogue at the time) and its struggles against colonial, settler and foreign domination, threw its support behind Africa's liberation movements. While initially in the mid-1950s—the PRC had interacted with the African National Congress (ANC) and the South African Communist Party (SACP), this changed in the 1960s when China was embroiled in ideological conflict with the Soviet Union, forcing liberation movements to pick sides. The SACP and the ANC had a long association with the Soviet Union, and so sided with it. China supported the Pan Africanist Congress (PAC) of South Africa, which had broken away from the ANC in 1959. Curiously, the PAC had left the ANC partly because it feared the corrosion of African nationalism by communism (Khumalo, 2020). However, the ideological differences between the PAC and PRC were overridden by China's preoccupation with limiting Soviet influence in the developing world. China's animosity with the ANC and SACP continued into the 1980s. It only thawed when the Sino-Soviet split was petering out. Oliver Tambo, who was president of the ANC at the time, visited China in 1983 as a sign of incipient reconciliation (Jiang, 2021).

After the election of the ANC as governing party in 1994, South Africa found itself in an awkward position, as it inherited formal relations with Taiwan. The following several years were characterised by what has been termed the two-Chinas dilemma. While Taiwan had relations with apartheid, it had made donations to the ANC's campaign for the 1994 elections. In addition, Taiwan after 1996 became a democracy, thereby assuming an identity that was in kilter with South Africa's own emerging credentials as a democracy. China came to the 1990s as a fast-growing economy that had squandered diplomatic goodwill when the government forcefully suppressed the pro-democracy movement at Tiananmen Square in 1989. Further complicating the issue was Hong Kong—one of South Africa's biggest trading partners, which was due to be returned to China in 1997 (Matambo, 2020). Mandela reportedly wanted to maintain relations with Taiwan, while formally recognising

China, an option that China could not allow. Eventually, pragmatism and the general trend of international diplomacy won the day, and South Africa established relations with China in 1998, at Taiwan's expense (Muresan & Naidu, 2021).

Since then, South Africa-China political, economic and social relations have grown exponentially. They have exchanged visits at the highest level. China's president—Xi Jinping—has completed four state visits (by 2025) to South Africa, which "underscores the importance which Xi attaches to South Africa, Africa and to BRICS and the Global South" (Fabricius, 2023). By August 2024, China was "South Africa's largest trading partner with bilateral trade standing at US$34 billion in 2023, made up of exports totalling US$12 billion and imports at US$22 billion" (Republic of South Africa, 2024). The impressive growth numbers are accompanied by a deep penetration of Chinese technologies in South Africa.

Chinese Technologies in (South) Africa

Science and technology were one part of the quartet of priorities that China focused on when it embarked on economic reforms in 1978. Called the four modernisations, the other three priorities were agriculture, industry and national defence (Mahoney, 2023). China's proliferating technologies provide 5G network towers, CCTV cameras and the construction of smart cities (Kwet, 2023). This penetration has raised concerns among China's opponents and competitors. Predictably, the United States leads the charge; numerous Chinese companies, including those that claim to be strictly commercial, have been placed on the list that comprises security threats from China (van der Westhuizen, 2024). The idea behind the classification is "that China fuses commercial and military technology" (Areddy 2025). China's National Intelligence Law (see below) somewhat makes this categorisation warranted.

The aspect of technology that has claimed most attention pertains to data harvesting and governance (O'Hara & Hall, 2018). In South Africa, the reception and rejection of Chinese technologies have mostly played out in the media space, though there is a growing academic focus, with some academics noting that southern African countries might emulate China's draconian surveillance practices (Munoriyarwa & Mare, 2023). South Africa is comparatively more digitalised than the rest of the African continent, even though its ICT index is just shy of 5 out of 10 on the ICT Development Index, coming at 92 out of 176 countries ranked. Unsurprisingly, "Africa has the lowest internet penetration rate globally" (Ayodele, 2024), which points to the limited levels of technology. According to the 2024 ICT Development Index, ICT development in Africa—which measures progress towards universal connectivity - stood at 50.3%, "by far the lowest among the [six] regions" studied (International Telecommunications Union, 2024). Access to mobile phones is at 84% while internet connection is at 53%. The numbers make obvious (South) Africa's eagerness and interest in attracting foreign technologies.

There are always concerns that as the ruling elite in South Africa becomes less popular and more polarised, they could use surveillance for their benefit and to the detriment of their critics (Duncan, 2018). Duncan has asserted that "China is using southern Africa as a surveillance commodity dumping ground, and exporting surveillance tools and practices *with no due diligence or real concern about how the countries they sell them to are using them*" (added emphasis) (Duncan, 2022, p. 5). Another concern has been that some of the Chinese providers of technology, for instance, Hikvision are susceptible to vulnerabilities that are "not only a threat to public safety, but can also place Internet services at risk" (Swart, 2019). Similar concerns—rather than "fears that Huawei will spy for China"—have been raised about Huawei (Swart, 2020). An interesting argument has been made by the South African Institute for International Affairs, that non-African scepticism of Huawei among the developed economies could make Africa "an early adopter of [Huawei's] 5G" (van Staden, 2020).

Concerns about Chinese technologies in Africa usually take the tenor of Biryabarema (2019) and Jili (2020), who highlight the concerns of authoritarian African governments using technologies to suppress dissent. Additional concerns have been raised about Chinese offering not only technologies but also training on how they are employed in surveillance activities (Apuzzo, Schmidt and Ng, 2018). Thus, Chinese technologies are interpreted in ways that favour mostly oppressive African regimes. However, less explored is how Chinese technologies could be used for the benefit of the Chinese government as it seeks to eliminate opposition to its rule, and to keep tabs on rivals and critics. South Africa is a relatively democratic country whose government cannot easily suppress the civil liberties of its citizens. Freedom House's Freedom in the World report rates South Africa as a free country on political rights, civil liberties and internet freedom (Freedom House, 2024). This freedom was mostly nurtured and supported by South Africa's strong democratic institutions that have played a seminal role in keeping the executive—led exclusively for the first 30 years (1994–2024) of South Africa's democracy by the African National Congress (ANC)—within constitutional parameters. This notwithstanding, the United States House of Representatives stated in February 2023 that "the increased Chinese presence in South Africa's technology sector has raised concerns that the ANC may be trying to copy the PRC's model of digitally aided authoritarian governance underpinned by cyber controls, social monitoring, and surveillance" (Congress.Gov, 2023). After the 2024 general election in South Africa, the ruling ANC lost its parliamentary majority of over 50% and was forced into a government of national unity with more than ten partners including the main opposition, the Democratic Alliance (DA). The DA's history of anti-China and anti-BRICS sentiment is well documented, and hence cannot acquiesce if the ANC tried to use Chinese technologies to spy on critics.

In 2022, Xi Jinping told the 20th National Congress of the Communist Party of China(CPC) that China "will expand science and technology exchanges and cooperation with other countries, cultivate an internationalised environment for research, and create an open and globally-competitive ecosystem" (Xi, 2022, p. 27). Africa, with its young population, could satisfy this expansion. South Africa's positive response has incurred American ire. In 2023, John James, a Republican Representative from Michigan, sponsored a resolution that expressed concerns about South Africa's use of Chinese technologies. Of specific concern was that Telkom, South Africa's partially State-owned telecoms operator, launched its 5G network throughout the country in October 2022 using Huawei Technologies (Congress.Gov, 2023). The resolution further urged that, if South African dithered on calls to be wary of Chinese technologies, then America should provide "a detailed account of positive economic results stemming from South Africa's inclusion in the African Growth and Opportunity Act [AGOA] and the United States-South Africa Trade and Investment Framework signed in 2012" (Congress.Gov, 2023). South Africa staved off the threats and duress by sending delegations to America to pacify concerned officials. In the meantime, Chinese technologies remained unabated. There is a paucity of academic attention on how African countries, South Africa in this case, have received Chinese technologies that could be used for China's domestic benefits. This leaves a lacuna in the academic space that this chapter intends to fill. This chapter argues, as the next section outlines, that South Africa and China are tied by certain historical, cultural and political contexts that cement their state-level relationship, thereby allowing the percolation of Chinese technologies even to ordinary South Africans. This social embeddedness of international relations forms the pith of constructivism.

Constructivism in International Relations

While realism and liberalism continue their dominance, constructivism is gaining modest traction as a prism for analysing the 'China in Africa' discourse (Shoba & Mlambo, 2024). As the name suggests, constructivism argues that international relations are constructed by manifold factors ranging from the subjective and intersubjective identities of actors, their geography (corporate identity), their interests and then the prevalent structure of international relations, which is not a predetermined structure, but one that has been created by practice. The term was coined by Nicholas Onuf in his book, *World of Our Making* (Onuf, 1989).More than rationalist theories acknowledged, constructivism highlights the importance of ideas, norms and social interactions (Becker, 2021) in dictating the nature of relations (Erbas, 2022).Thus, international relations are essentially social and as such do not exist impartially 'out there', impervious to human agency.

While rationalists argue that international relations happen in a realm of anarchy, constructivists argue that if this is the case, then "anarchy is what states make of it" (Wendt, 1992). Constructivism lifts international interaction from a Procrustean bed of rationalist theorists and places it on a case-by-case basis for state behaviour. Thus, depending on the players involved, the motives and methods of interaction are not necessarily the same. To put it in the context of this chapter, technological gains of one country might pose a threat to those who consider it a rival, competitor or foe. To its unfazed friends, however, its technological gains could be hailed as beneficial. The next section, talking about the reception of Chinese technologies in South

Africa, should be read from the background of how South Africa and China perceive each other.

The Reception of Chinese Technologies in South Africa

A caveat is apt: the positive reception of Chinese technologies needs nuance. While the government of South Africa has a positive view of China as a state and—ipso facto—its technologies, the same cannot be assumed of non-state actors and ordinary South Africans. While the affordability of Chinese phones and hard drives is convenient for ordinary citizens, at the level of China's state, South Africans have shown a preference for the United States, its politics and culture, compared to China, though they consider China as more respectful of South Africa's sovereignty. For instance, the accusation in 2023 by US Ambassador Ruben Brigety that South Africa was "supplying weapons to Russia despite its professed neutrality in the war in Ukraine" (Fihlani, 2023) seemed to have caught the South African government off guard, with the South African Communist Party—an alliance partner of the ANC—demanding the withdrawal of the ambassador (Mbolekwa, 2023). As the South African government claimed that no evidence had been rendered for the unexpected accusation, the implication was that Brigety's remarks had a subtext of American arrogance. This section will present how Huawei, Hikvision and Chinese smartphones have penetrated the South African market.

On its website, Huawei states the following:

> Founded in 1987, Huawei is a leading global provider of information and communications technology (ICT) infrastructure and smart devices. We have 207,000 employees and operate in over 170 countries and regions, serving more than three billion people around the world. We are committed to bringing digital to every person, home and organization for a fully connected, intelligent world (Huawei, 2024).

In South Africa, Huawei has both a branch office and a training centre. The latter, which partners with Mecer Inter-Ed, trains thousands of African students yearly. In October 2024, "MTN South Africa (hereinafter referred to as MTN SA) and Huawei [...] completed the world's first commercial deployment of the innovative SDB IBT 2D microwave solution in Johannesburg. This breakthrough solution leverages Super Dual Band (SDB) and two-dimensional intelligent beam tracking (IBT 2D) to prevent pole shaking from affecting link stability in dual-band scenarios" (Huawei, 2024). Huawei has the second biggest market share of smartphones in South Africa. "[W]ith an 18.89% mobile vendor market share," it is only behind Samsung's 49.08%, and ahead of Apple at 17.56% (Fraser, 2023). Rain, a South African company, enlisted Huawei equipment to launch its 5G data services in 2019 (van Staden, 2020).

David Shinn and Joshua Eisenman (2023: 129) have asserted that Huawei is China's designated "national champion" that works closely with the military and other state actors and their research institutes. It receives lines of credit from state banks and funding for research and development. This close association with state players has alarmed other countries. In 2018, Australia banned "Huawei from supplying 5G networks" (Hawes, 2022). When Huawei was put on the US's Entity List in May 2019, leaders of South Africa's biggest telecoms companies implored the South African president to refrain from showing hostility towards the tech giant, as this would cost the companies over R100 billion in infrastructure investment. South Africa has fiercely supported its adoption of Huawei technologies. President Cyril Ramaphosa said critics of Huawei's inroads in South Africa were jealous (Gavaza, 2019):

> The US has been unable to imagine a better future that goes beyond 4 plus one G, where they have been unable to imagine what 5G has to offer. They are clearly jealous that a Chinese company called Huawei has outstripped them and because they have been outstripped they must now punish that one company... We cannot afford to have our own economy be held back because there is this fight that the US is having and born out of their own jealousies (Hunter, 2019).

It can be inferred that South Africa takes umbrage at what it considers US bullying over which technologies a country could procure. In the words of an Africa-China specialist:

> As was the case during the Cold War, Western intentions over Africa should be scrutinised because they may not necessarily be for Africa's benefit. They could be gambits used to curtail the influence of America's foes. As South Africa appraises the pros and cons of engaging Huawei, it should keep these eventualities in mind (Monyae, 2020).

A similar argument has been made by those who assert that America's hostility to Huawei is not solely steeped in security and trade concerns, the return of protectionism or the sovereignty of intellectual property. America's concerns, the argument goes, stem from preventing China's development of alternative Information and Communication Technology (ICT) systems which could be beyond America's control (Farrell & Newman, 2023). Regardless of the changes of administrations in the United States, a leery foreign policy on China is constant. The Secure and Trusted Telecommunications Networks Act which banned "the Federal Communications Commission (FCC) from giving funds to U.S. telecom groups to purchase equipment from companies deemed threats" was a bipartisan decision, and it had Huawei as a specific target (Miller, 2020).

Hikvision "provide[s] integrated security solutions powered by AI technology to support end-users with new applications and possibilities for safety management and business intelligence" (Hikvision, n.d.). It also manufactures hard drives. It went public in 2010 and is listed on the SMEs Board at the Shenzhen Stock Exchange. Though the Chinese government has ensured that its controlling ownership (42%) of Hikvision is not highlighted, there is no ambiguity about this fact, as the China Electronic Technology Corporation Group (CETC), the founder of Hikvision, is an entity of the Chinese government. In 2018, Hikvision's Chen Zongnian joined the National People's Congress, thereby underlining the closeness between the Chinese government and its controlled video surveillance manufacturer (Honovich, 2018). In 2019, Hikvision was blacklisted in the United States "to punish Beijing for its treatment of Muslim minorities" (Shen & Horwitz, 2019). Reportedly, the company was supplying surveillance technology to the Xinjiang region, where scores of Uighur Muslims are said to be penned in detention camps.

Hikvision first opened a branch in South Africa in 2015, and received a fillip in 2019 when Vumacam, a video surveillance service provider, enlisted it for a project to connect 15,000 video surveillance cameras to provide all-round surveillance of Johannesburg (Swart, 2019). The 2023 US Resolution referred to above criticised the Vumacam deal and urged South Africa to "strengthen its political resilience to reject the Chinese Communist Party's authoritarian vision for South Africa; and [...] maintain its national sovereignty by reducing its reliance on Chinese companies in key sectors such as information and communication technology" (Congress. Gov, 2023). Vumacam, for its part, has asserted that it "only works with 'pre-vetted and approved' third-party vendors and has conducted a number of tests on products (including those provided by Hikvision) to ensure they are cyber safe and not easily hacked" (Allen & van Zyl, 2020). This notwithstanding, concerns persist with fears "that facial recognition cameras made by companies such as Hikvision [...] are collecting facial recognition data, which can then be used by the Chinese government" (Corfield, 2021). If Hikvision and Huawei have been dogged by relentless concerns, an issue that does not seem to court comparable controversy is the spread of Chinese smartphones in Africa.

Chinese mobile phones, mainly manufactured by Transsion Holdings, have proliferated in Africa, mainly due to their high quality at a comparatively lower cost than their competitors. This section does not include Huawei, as it was dealt with above, and its market share noted. Xiaomi, with a market share of 2.77% and Oppo with 2.62% are the fourth and fifth biggest smartphone providers in South Africa, behind Samsung, Huawei and Apple, respectively (Fraser, 2023). George Zhu, Transsion's founder, had worked in Africa for a mobile phone company. His experience left him convinced that selling prohibitively expensive phones—more appropriate for developed economies—was not germane for African consumers.

Interestingly, Transsion does not have a viable market in China. In this respect, it deviated from the Huawei and Xiaomi model that started at the home front before catering to the international market. Transsion is deliberate about its target market, which is "global emerging markets". While "[m]obile phones are its core products, [...] it also offers mobile Internet services based on a self-developed operating system" (Transsion Holdings n.d.). The most popular of Transsion's smartphones are TECNO, Itel and Infinix. Transsion has also been adept at working with United Nations institutions such as UNHCR and UN Economic Commission for Africa, collaborating on refugee aid activities and the acceleration of Africa's digital transformation. Since its penetration in Africa, "Transsion has left global players like Samsung and Apple trailing in its wake in a continent that's home to more than a billion people"(Marsh, 2018).In 2024, Transsion received a further boon when it was contracted as a partner for Africa's showpiece event, African Cup of Nations soccer tournament. Such inroads have helped Transsion to become a global player, despite concentrating on developing countries. The table below illustrates the top five companies involved in the manufacturing of smartphones (Table 7.1).

Table 7.1 IDC worldwide quarterly mobile phone tracker

Company	2024 Shipments	2024 Market Share	2023 Shipments	2023 Market Share	2024/2023 Growth
1. Apple	232.1	18.7%	234.3	20.1%	−0.9%
2. Samsung	223.4	18.0%	226.7	19.5%	−1.4%
3. Xiaomi	168.5	13.6%	146.0	12.5%	15.4%
4. Transsion*	106.9	8.6%	94.9	8.2%	12.7%
4. OPPO*	104.8	8.5%	103.4	8.9%	1.4%
Others	402.9	32.5%	358.9	30.8%	12.3%
Total	**1238.8**	**100.0%**	**1164.1**	**100.0%**	**6.4%**

It is noteworthy that three of the top five manufacturers are from China. In South Africa, Chinese-made phones are sold by South African telecoms companies. Vodacom, Cell C, MTN and Telkom are vendors for Oppo, Huawei and TECNO. Having noted the penetration of Chinese technologies—in providing internet, video surveillance and smartphones, the next section will outline the possible benefits and hazards of Chinese technologies and explain South Africa's reception of these technologies. Supposed national identities and interests—in deference to constructivist arguments—will be key in analysing South Africa's response to concerns about Chinese technologies.

China Technologies in South Africa: Benefits and Hazards

While Chinese technologies have undoubtedly increased access to the internet and cell phones, the attacks that they suffer emanate from many angles, including at the basic level of ownership. Huawei, for instance, is usually touted as a private company owned by a union and the company's founder, Ren Zhengfei. However, "if the ownership stake of the trade union committee is genuine, and if the trade union and its committee function as trade unions generally function in China, then Huawei may be deemed effectively state-owned" (Balding & Clarke, 2019). The proximity of Chinese tech companies to the state machinery points to the likely possibility that they do not act "on market imperatives alone" but that they also "serve China's foreign policy and national security strategies" (Khalil, 2020, p. 25). This ties in with the argument that "[f]or Beijing, exporting its information technology is not only about securing important new sources of revenue and data, but also generating greater strategic leverage vis- à- vis the West" (Polyakova & Meserole 2019, 6). In addition, the Chinese government sees in Huawei the embodiment of the "government's ambitions of escaping the middle-income trap by becoming a global tech leader" (van Staden, 2020).

China has thus been accused of using its technologies as a prong to its political and economic ambitions. It was no wonder that when it handed over the

Chinese-built African Union headquarters in Ethiopia, rumours surfaced that the institution was bugged (Kadiri & Tilouine, 2018), an allegation that China strenuously denied (Tiezzi, 2018). Former Chinese Ambassador to South Africa—Lin Songtian—convened a press conference to specifically rebut the accusations and argue that China's relationship with Africa was such that if it needed information, it would simply ask. Lin took aim at the West, accusing it of seeking to besmirch China's ties with Africa (Magubane, 2018). Ramaphosa's response to the Huawei saga points to the fact that China and South Africa are in tandem, although some South African writers have taken a cynical view of South Africa's positive view of China and its technologies. In a scathing critique of South Africa's close association with China (a country the authors argue South Africa shares little with) in lieu of India (with which it shares several characteristics and is also democracy), the authors conclude that if you give South Africa "a bit of attention, it stands for nothing and falls for everything" (Mills & Hartley, 2023).

The concerns raised in this chapter are aimed at China's legislation and the expectations that it foists on Chinese companies. The sampled literature has shown that more attention has been paid to how African governments can use Chinese technologies to target critics and opponents, while some literature noted immanent vulnerabilities of Chinese tech companies such as Huawei, while still more literature noted that American, Australian and European scepticism of Huawei technologies could help Africa to be an early adopter of latest technologies from Huawei (van Staden, 2020). None of this literature seems to take into serious cognisance the implications of China's legislation on tech companies. In its 2017 New Generation Artificial Intelligence Development Plan, China's State Council outlined the country's plans to be a world leader in artificial intelligence (AI) (Roberts et al., 2021). During the 28th Session of the Standing Committee of the Twelfth National People's Congress, China adopted the National Intelligence Law "for purposes of strengthening and guaranteeing national intelligence work and safeguarding national security and interests" (National Intelligence Law of the People's Republic of China, 2017). Article 7 of this law states that "an organisation or citizen shall support, assist and cooperate with the state intelligence work in accordance with the law, and keep confidential the national intelligence work it or he knows" (National Intelligence Law of the People's Republic of China, 2017).Under the same article, the state promises to "protect the individual or organisation that has supported, assisted in or cooperated in national intelligence work" (National Intelligence Law of the People's Republic of China, 2017). Article 14 states that the government "may require relevant organs, organisation and citizens to provide necessary support, assistance and cooperation".

Acquiescence to the state by Chinese tech companies may not be as controversial in China, as they are crucial to China's Digital Silk Road, launched in 2015 (Tugendhat & Voo, 2021). It is noteworthy that some private Chinese companies, Huawei included, have CPC branch committees, though some scholars have argued that these party committees have been more interested in the commercial success of firms rather than using the political heft of the governing party to dictate to firms (Dickson, 2008). Expectedly, the National Intelligence Law courted widespread criticism, with one detractor excoriating its "insidious and pervasive power" (Girad, 2019). Lydia Khalil has averred that having consolidated "digital authoritarianism" at the domestic front, "Chinese-engineered digital surveillance and tracking systems are now being exported around the globe in line with China's Cyber Superpower Strategy" (Khalil, 2020).

Chapter 2, Articles 17, 18 and 20 of China's 2021 Data Security Law, talk about state support for "industry associations, enterprises, education and research institutions, relevant specialised agencies, etc. in the fields such as data security related risk assessment, prevention, and disposal" (National People's Congress, 2021). There is also an argument that China sees what has hitherto been Western dominance of IT as "network hegemony" (Shinn & Eisenman, 2023, p. 305). Thus, countries such as South Africa could be unwitting players in China's intent to gnaw at Western dominance of IT infrastructure, and its intent to use technology as a weapon for surveillance. According to Freedom House, China was "the world's worst environment for internet freedom" (Freedom House, 2024). In 2024, for the first time, it was tied by another country, Myanmar, for this dubious distinction. These are concerns that are not domestic to China. They should also exercise the vigilance of countries such as South Africa that are using Chinese technologies with mounting enthusiasm. This recommendation, however, contends with arguments that say, even if South Africa were to want to be vigilant in using Chinese technologies, "narratives of development and cost/benefit considerations overshadow ... perceptions of security risk" (van der Westhuizen, 2024, p. 1).

It cannot be gainsaid that Chinese technologies are more affordable than their competitors and hence, at a practical level, appeal to an African market. China's importance to South Africa's economy is a powerful incentive in discouraging Pretoria from courses of action that could be construed as hostile to Beijing. This was the case in Brazil during Jair Bolsonaro's presidency, when the president's alignment with American hostility to Huawei was fought on the grounds of the sheer expense of replacing Huawei technologies, and the risks of antagonising an increasingly economically important China (van der Westhuizen, 2024). Coupled with these practical necessities are the identities and interests that South Africa, the developing world in general and China have constructed of each other. As members of BRICS, South Africa and China share the default identity of being champions of the developing world. To developing countries such as South Africa, China represents the success that the developing world should aspire to attain.

In a deeply polarised world, with the West withdrawing into an insular shell, China successfully presents itself as the new paragon of globalisation and its attendant global trade and technological transfer. American hostility to South Africa on issues such as South Africa's International Court of Justice case against Israel and America's hostility to South Africa's proposed land expropriation act stand in stark contrast to China's support for South Africa's international posture. China's claims of not interfering in the domestic affairs (e.g. South Africa's divisive land legislation proposal) of other nations solidify China's palatable identity as a country that is responsive to the history of an Africa whose affairs have been historically dictated to by foreign (read Western) powers. This ideological and contextual milieu forms the basis for employing constructivism as a theory through which South Africa's embrace of China and its technology could be understood. Because China has constructed an identity of a friendly nation, and presented interests that purport to champion the development and technological advancement of all and sundry with a bias towards the developing world, South Africa finds comfort in embracing Chinese technologies, the possible hazards notwithstanding.

Conclusion

Chinese technologies in South Africa have become ubiquitous. This trend is fraught with passionate debates with the South African government and China on the same side, ranged against detractors, such as the United States, the United Kingdom, Australia and even some South African writers. There are fears that rogue African governments could use Chinese technologies to spy on their citizens and to harass opposition politicians. Developed countries fear that China could use its technology to pilfer confidential data and to hunt down Chinese dissidents. South Africa has been singled out for warning by the United States, with threats that continued use of Chinese technologies might compel the United States to eject South Africa from the list of AGOA beneficiaries. Hitherto, South Africa has been unmoved, and Chinese technologies continue to find their way to the country. The chapter used constructivism to argue that South Africa and China present themselves as kindred countries, de facto leaders of their respective regions and the developing world in general, and that the identities and interests that emerge from these contexts leave South Africa with no reason to suspect that Chinese technologies in South Africa could be used for malevolent purposes. Finally, the chapter carries a cautionary note; that, while academic literature tends to focus on African use of Chinese technologies for sinister reasons, not much attention has been paid to China's use of technology for its own ends. The legislation that compels Chinese technological firms to cooperate with the government indicates the sway that the government has on tech companies. This clout could be used by Chinese companies to reach dissidents and critics scattered all over the world—including in South Africa.

References

Allen, K, & van Zyl, L. (2020). *Who's watching who? Biometric surveillance in Kenya and South Africa*. ENACT Africa. https://enactafrica.org/research/research-papers/whos-watching-who-biometric-surveillance-in-kenya-and-south-africa

Apuzzo, M., Schmidt, M.S. & Ng A. (2018) *Software installed on cheap Android phones sends user data to China*. Privacy International. https://privacyinternational.org/examples/2591/software-installed-cheap-android-phonessends-user-data-china

Areddy, J. T. (2025, January 7). *Pentagon labels more Chinese companies as military in nature*. WSJ. https://www.wsj.com/politics/national-security/pentagon-labels-more-chinese-companies-as-military-in-nature-bac351b5

Ayodele, O. (2024). Digital infrastructure: Creating the backbone for development. In S. Nkala & D. Monyae (Eds.), *The quest for unity* (1st ed., pp. 403–426). Routledge. https://doi.org/10.4324/9781003521334-24

Balding, C., & Clarke, D. C. (2019). *Who owns Huawei?* (SSRN Scholarly Paper No. 3372669). Social Science Research Network. https://doi.org/10.2139/ssrn.3372669

Becker, J. (2021). Speaking to the wall: Reconceptualizing the US–Mexico Border "Wall" from the perspective of a realist and constructivist theoretical framework in international relations. *Journal of Borderlands Studies, 36*(1), 17–29. https://doi.org/10.1080/08865655.2018.1482775

Biryabarema, E. (2019). *Uganda's cash-strapped cops spend $126 million on CCTV from Huawei*. Reuters. Retrieved April 24, 2025, from https://www.reuters.com/article/technology/ugandas-cash-strapped-cops-spend-126-million-on-cctv-from-huawei-idUSKCN1V50QL/

Corfield, G. (2021). *UK's surveillance camera commissioner grills Hikvision on China human rights abuses*. The Register. https://www.theregister.com/2021/08/20/hikvision_surveillance_camera_commissioner_uighur_controversy/

Dickson, B. J. (2008). *Wealth into power: The Communist Party's embrace of China's private sector* (1st ed.). Cambridge University Press. https://doi.org/10.1017/CBO9780511790706

Duncan, J. (2018). *Stopping the spies: Constructing and resisting the surveillance state in South Africa*. Wits University Press. https://doi.org/10.18772/12018062156

Duncan, J. (2022). *National Security Surveillance in Southern Africa: An anti-capitalist perspective* (1st ed.). Bloomsbury Publishing Plc. https://doi.org/10.5040/9780755640256

Erbas, I. (2022). Constructivist approach in foreign policy and in international relations. *Journal of Positive School Psychology, 6*(3), Article 3.

Fabricius, P. (2023, August 21). *Chinese President Xi Jinping makes rare trip abroad to touch many bases in SA*. Daily Maverick. Retrieved April 24, 2025, from https://www.dailymaverick.co.za/article/2023-08-21-chinese-president-xi-jinping-makes-rare-trip-abroad-to-touch-many-bases-in-south-africa/

Farrell, H., & Newman, A. (2023). *Underground empire: How America weaponized the world economy*. Henry Holt and Co.

Fihlani, P. (2023, May 11). *South Africa supplied arms to Russia—US ambassador Reuben Brigety*. BBC. https://www.bbc.com/news/world-africa-65563027

Fraser, L. (2023). *The most popular smartphone brands in South Africa*. Business Tech. https://businesstech.co.za/news/trending/676573/the-most-popular-smartphone-brands-in-south-africa/

Freedom House. (2024). *Freedom on the net 2024 digital*. Retrieved April 24, 2025, from https://freedomhouse.org/sites/default/files/2024-10/FREEDOM-ON-THE-NET-2024-DIGITAL-BOOKLET.pdf

Gavaza, M. (2019). *Cyril Ramaphosa backs Huawei amid US-China trade tussle*. BusinessLIVE. Retrieved April 24, 2025, from https://www.businesslive.co.za/bd/national/2019-07-05-cyril-ramaphosa-backs-huawei-amid-us-china-trade-tussle/

Girad, B. (2019). *The real danger of China's national intelligence law*. The Diplomat. https://thediplomat.com/2019/02/the-real-danger-of-chinas-national-intelligence-law/

Hawes, C. (2022, August 18). *Huawei: Critically assessing the 5G ban and commonly cited risks*. https://www.uts.edu.au/news/2022/08/huawei-critically-assessing-5g-ban-and-commonly-cited-risks

Hikvision. (n.d.). *Hikvision Chairman Joins China National Government (NPC)*. Retrieved April 24, 2025, from https://ipvm.com/reports/hikvision-npc

Honovich. (2018). *Hikvision company profile*. Hikvision. http://www.hikvision.com/africa/about-us/company-profile/

Huawei. (2024). *MTN SA and Huawei launch world's first commercial SDB IBT 2D microwave deployment*. Huawei. https://www.huawei.com/en/news/2024/10/mtn-sdb-ibt

Hunter, Q. (2019 July). 'We can't be held back by US jealousy,' says Ramaphosa on Huawei sanctions. *Times Live*, 5.

International Telecommunications Union. (2024). The ICT Development Index 2024: *Measuring digital development*. file:///C:/Users/Latitude%20E5470/Downloads/d-ind-ict_mdd-2024-3-pdf-e.pdf

James, J. (2023, February 21). *H.Res.145—118th Congress (2023-2024): Opposing the Republic of South Africa's hosting of military exercises with the People's Republic of China and the Russian Federation, and calling on the Biden administration to conduct a thorough review of the United States-South Africa relationship.* (2023-02-21) [Legislation]. https://www.congress.gov/bill/118th-congress/house-resolution/145

Jiang, L. (2021). South Africa–China relations of seven decades (1949–2019): Review and reflection. In C. Alden & Y.-S. Wu (Eds.), *South Africa–China relations* (pp. 65–81). Springer. https://doi.org/10.1007/978-3-030-54768-4_4

Jili, B. (2020). *The spread of surveillance technology in Africa stirs security concerns*. Africa Center for Strategic Studies. https://www.academia.edu/44692188/The_Spread_of_Surveillance_Technology_in_Africa_Stirs_Security_Concerns

Khalil, L. (2020). *Digital authoritarianism, China and COVID*. Low Institute. https://www.lowy-institute.org/publications/digital-authoritarianism-china-covid

Kadiri, G., & Tilouine, J. (2018). "A Addis Abeba, le siège de l'Union africaine espionné par Pékin." Le Monde, January 26. https://www.lemonde.fr/afrique/article/2018/01/26/a-addisa-beba-le-siege-de-l-union-africaine-espionnepar-les-chinois_5247521_3212.html

Khumalo, T. S. (2020). *From UPoqo to APLA: The Pan Africanist Congress (PAC) and its armed struggle: 1960–1982* [University of Pretoria]. https://repository.up.ac.za

Kwet, M. (2023). Surveillance in South Africa: From skin branding to digital colonialism. In M. Kwet (Ed.), *The Cambridge handbook of race and surveillance* (1st ed., pp. 97–122). Cambridge University Press. https://doi.org/10.1017/9781108241304.006

Magubane, K. (2018). *China 'had no need to spy' on AU headquarters*. Business Day. https://www.businesslive.co.za/

Mahoney, J. G. (2023). China's rise as an advanced technological Society and the rise of digital orientalism. *Journal of Chinese Political Science, 28*(1), 1–24. https://doi.org/10.1007/s11366-022-09817-z

Marsh, J. (2018, October 10). *The Chinese phone giant that beat Apple to Africa*. CNN. https://www.cnn.com/2018/10/10/tech/tecno-phones-africa/index.html

Matambo, E. (2019). *Constructing China's identity in Zambian politics: A tale of expediency and resignation*. https://ujcontent.uj.ac.za/esploro/outputs/journalArticle/Constructing-Chinas-identity-in-Zambian-politics/9913116907691

Matambo, E. (2020). South Africa-China relations: A constructivist perspective. *Strategic Review for Southern Africa, 42*(2). https://doi.org/10.35293/srsa.v42i2.74

Mbolekwa, S. (2023). *SACP wants ambassador Brigety recalled after Lady R probe finds no evidence of his claims*. https://www.sowetanlive.co.za/

Miller, M. (2020). *Senate unanimously approves bill to ban purchase of Huawei equipment with federal funds*. The Hill. https://thehill.com/

Mills, G., & Hartley, R. (2023). *SA's strange obsession with China is proof that it's a cheap date*. Hartley,

Monyae, D. (2020). *Is Huawei any different to other tech giants, or are we just getting caught up in Trump's mud-slinging?* Daily Maverick. https://www.dailymaverick.co.za/

Munoriyarwa, A., & Mare, A. (2023). Digital surveillance in southern Africa: Policies, politics and practices, 1–220). Springer. https://doi.org/10.1007/978-3-031-16636-5/COVER.

Muresan, A., & Naidu, S. (2021). Chinese and south African labour relations: An analysis. In C. Alden & Y.-S. Wu (Eds.), *South Africa–China relations* (pp. 199–220). Springer. https://doi.org/10.1007/978-3-030-54768-4_10

National Intelligence Law of the People's Republic. (2017). *NationalIntelligenceLaw*. https://cs.brown.edu/courses/csci1800/sources/2017_PRC_NationalIntelligenceLaw.pdf

National People's Congress. (2021). *Data Security Law of the People's Republic of China*. https://www.npc.gov.cn/englishnpc/c2759/c23934/202112/t20211209_385109.html

O'Hara, K., & Hall, W. (2018). *Four internets: The geopolitics of digital governance*. 206.

Onuf, N. (1989). World of our Making. *Rules and Rule in Social Theory and International Relations*. London: Routledge

Polyakova, A., & Meserole, C. (2019). *Exporting digital authoritarianism: The Russian and Chinese models* (Demoracy and disorder) [policy brief]. https://www.brookings.edu/

Republic of South Africa. (2024). Statement on the Cabinet Meeting of 21 August 2024. https://dirco.gov.za/statement-on-the-cabinet-meeting-of-21-august-2024/

Roberts, H., Cowls, J., Morley, J., Taddeo, M., Wang, V., & Floridi, L. (2021). The Chinese approach to artificial intelligence: An analysis of policy, ethics, and regulation. *AI & SOCIETY, 36*(1), 59–77. https://doi.org/10.1007/s00146-020-00992-2

Shen, S., & Horwitz, J. (2019). *China's Hikvision sees only limited impact from U.S. blacklisting*. Reuters. https://www.reuters.com/

Shinn, D. H., & Eisenman, J. (2023). *China's relations with Africa: A new era of strategic engagement*. (p. 504 Pages). Columbia University Press.

Shoba, M., & Mlambo, V. H. (2024). A constructivist analysis of the bilateral relations between South Africa and China. *Cogent Social Sciences, 10*(1), 2321699. https://doi.org/10.1080/23311886.2024.2321699

Swart, H. (2019). *Visual surveillance and weak cyber security, Part One: When cameras get dangerous*. Daily Maverick. https://www.dailymaverick.co.za/article/2019-06-13-visual-surveillance-and-weak-cyber-security-part-one-when-cameras-get-dangerous/

Swart, H. (2020). *Are South Africans safe with Huawei? (Part 2): A different kind of virus*. Daily Maverick. Retrieved April 24, 2025, from https://www.dailymaverick.co.za/article/2020-06-10-are-south-africans-safe-with-huawei-part-2-a-different-kind-of-virus/

Tiezzi, S. (2018). *If China bugged the AU headquarters, what African countries should be worried?* The Diplomat. https://thediplomat.com/2018/01/if-china-bugged-the-au-headquarters-what-african-countries-should-be-worried/

Tugendhat, H., & Voo, J. (2021). *China's Digital Silk Road in Africa and the future of internet governance* (Policy Brief, No. 60/2021). https://www.econstor.eu/bitstream/10419/248239/1/sais-cari-pb60.pdf

van der Westhuizen, J. V. D. (2024). Huawei or the US way? Why Brazil and South Africa did not securitize 5G. *Revista Brasileira de Política Internacional, 67*(2), e016. https://doi.org/10.1590/0034-732202400216

van Staden, C. (2020). *Africa could be the winner as the US attempts to stifle Huawei*. South African Institute of International Affairs. https://saiia.org.za/research/africa-could-be-the-winner-as-the-us-attempts-to-stifle-huawei/

Wendt, A. (1992). Anarchy is what states make of it: The social construction of power politics. *International Organization, 46*(2), 391–425. https://doi.org/10.1017/S0020818300027764

Xi, J. (2022). *The 20th National Congress of the Communist Party of China*. https://english.www.gov.cn/2022special/20thcpccongress/

Emmanuel Matambo (PhD) is the Research Director at the Centre for Africa-China Studies (CACS) at the University of Johannesburg in South Africa. He holds a PhD in Political Science from the University of KwaZulu-Natal (UKZN). From October 2018 to September 2019, he was retained as a postdoctoral research fellow. He has held fellowship positions at the Africa Program at the Woodrow Wilson International Center for Scholars and the Atlantic Council's Millennium Leadership Program in Washington, DC, USA. He has been involved in training Belgian and American diplomats posted to Southern Africa. In October 2023, Dr. Matambo was appointed as a research fellow for the Public Policy and Research Institute of Zimbabwe, focusing on the likely impact of China and Africa-China relations on African democracy.

Chapter 8
China's Surveillance Technology and Civil Liberties in West and Southern Africa

Lucy Anning

Abstract China's surveillance technology is reshaping governance and civil liberties in Western and Southern Africa under the guise of diplomatic and developmental ties. This chapter critically examines how the proliferation of these tools erodes civil rights, deepens state control, and exploits weak regulatory frameworks in Ghana, Nigeria, Côte d'Ivoire, Zambia, and Zimbabwe. Employing a qualitative approach, it unpacks the intersection of digital diplomacy, political influence, and technological imperialism. By exposing China's strategic "gaze," the study highlights urgent ethical and sovereignty concerns, offering a compelling analysis of the region's vulnerability to external tech dominance in the evolving digital age.

Introduction

China has emerged as a global leader in technological innovation, particularly in surveillance technology—which encompasses tools for monitoring, data collection, and security enforcement (Scarpi & Pantano, 2024). China has developed sophisticated surveillance systems, including facial recognition cameras, internet monitoring tools, and biometric databases. These technologies have not only strengthened its domestic security but have also positioned the country as a major exporter of surveillance infrastructure, influencing governance and security models worldwide (Heeks et al., 2024). A key driver of this expansion is China's foreign policy strategy, notably the Belt and Road Initiative (BRI), which promotes economic and technological partnerships across Africa.

In Western and Southern Africa, Chinese surveillance technologies are embedded in smart city projects and public security networks, ostensibly designed to address crime, terrorism, and infrastructural gaps. The deployment of surveillance technologies has raised pressing concerns about privacy, human rights, and democratic governance (Sáenz & García, 2024). Huawei's "Safe City" and ZTE's "Smart

---

L. Anning (✉)
Center for Africa-China Studies, University of Johannesburg, Johannesburg, South Africa

G. Moyo (ed.), *An Anatomy of AI Surveillance in Africa*, Studies in Digital Politics and Governance, https://doi.org/10.1007/978-3-032-04269-9_8

City" initiatives exemplify this trend. While these systems enhance security and digital infrastructure, they also introduce risks of mass surveillance, data exploitation, and political control, especially in countries with weak regulatory frameworks (Gagliardone, 2020; Jili, 2023). Governments in South Africa, Kenya, and Zimbabwe, for instance, have been accused of using such technologies to monitor political opponents, journalists, and activists, thereby suppressing dissent and restricting freedoms of expression and assembly (Li, 2020; Jili, 2023). The lack of transparent oversight further exacerbates the risk of personal data misuse, weakening democratic institutions (Gagliardone, 2020).

Beyond individual freedoms, the widespread use of surveillance tools has broader implications for governance. The study findings of Sheombar and Skelton (2023) identify that in transitional democracies with fragile institutional checks, surveillance strengthens executive power, reducing government accountability. The omnipresence of monitoring technologies creates a climate of fear, discouraging civic engagement and fostering self-censorship among citizens and media organisations (Li, 2020). As China's influence grows, Gurram (2024) and Melber et al. (2023) show that African governments are increasingly adopting these technologies with minimal oversight, aligning themselves with a global model that prioritises state control over individual liberties (Gagliardone, 2020).

This chapter critically examines China's role in shaping Africa's surveillance landscape through an extensive literature review. Drawing from over 400 academic sources, 30 high-impact studies were analysed using interdisciplinary perspectives from political science, technology, and governance. The research explores the intersection of surveillance, regulatory challenges, and civil liberties across case studies in Ghana, Nigeria, Côte d'Ivoire, Zambia, and Zimbabwe. By expounding on the complex realities of China's "gaze," this chapter provides a vital lens for understanding the evolving relationship between technology, governance, and human rights in Africa's digital age.

Effects of Chinese Surveillance on Democracy, Civil Liberties, and Governance

Chinese surveillance technologies have gained significant traction across Africa, reshaping governance structures and raising critical questions about their impact on civil liberties and democratic norms. Through initiatives such as Huawei's "Safe City" and ZTE's "Smart City" projects, these tools have been marketed as solutions for urban safety and infrastructure challenges. However, their adoption has highlighted serious risks, especially in nations lacking robust regulatory frameworks, where their use has often led to human rights violations and authoritarian practices.

The increasing adoption of Chinese surveillance technologies across Africa, including facial recognition cameras, biometric systems, and internet monitoring platforms, has raised significant concerns about privacy, political freedoms, and democratic integrity. Initially introduced to address public security, these tools are often repurposed for political surveillance, as seen in Kenya and Uganda, where they have been used to track political opposition and suppress dissent, undermining freedoms of assembly and expression (Li, 2020; Gagliardone, 2020). The absence of robust institutional safeguards and public consultations exacerbates the risks of misuse, allowing these technologies to strengthen authoritarian power structures.

China's "no-strings-attached" approach to partnerships facilitates the rapid deployment of these surveillance tools without necessitating governance reforms (Jili, 2023). While appealing to African governments seeking security enhancements, this model often consolidates state control, hindering transparency and accountability. In countries like Ethiopia, digital infrastructure investments have improved public security, but the lack of regulatory oversight allows for the misuse of surveillance systems to suppress political opposition and maintain authoritarian rule (Chang, 2023; Heeks et al., 2024).

Chinese surveillance technology has fundamentally altered electoral integrity in fragile democracies like Zimbabwe and Nigeria. Advanced facial recognition and digital monitoring tools enable governments to track political opponents, journalists, and activists, creating an atmosphere of fear that discourages dissent (Li, 2020). Voter intimidation escalates as authorities use surveillance data to target opposition strongholds, manipulate voter rolls, and suppress turnout (Gagliardone, 2020). Additionally, mass data collection allows regimes to predict and counter opposition strategies, tilting elections in favour of incumbents. This digital control not only weakens electoral transparency but also entrenches autocratic rule, eroding democratic participation.

Despite the risks, Jili (2023) opines that African states exercise agency in adopting Chinese surveillance technologies, prioritising security and development needs. However, international actors play a crucial role in ensuring this technological expansion aligns with democratic values. Organisations like the UN, AU, and human rights watchdogs can advocate for stronger data protection laws and ethical AI governance. Western allies and development agencies should promote transparency by conditioning tech investments on accountability measures. Additionally, global regulatory bodies must establish frameworks to prevent digital authoritarianism, ensuring surveillance tools enhance security without eroding civil liberties (Mannan, 2025). This balance safeguards democracy in Africa's digital future.

Emerging evidence also questions the effectiveness of Chinese surveillance technologies in achieving their stated objectives. Acharya et al. (2025) highlight implementation gaps, where these tools fail to deliver promised outcomes due to chaotic deployment and insufficient local expertise. These limitations underscore the need for more robust oversight mechanisms to ensure responsible use. Gravett suggests leveraging existing international and regional human rights frameworks to counter abuses, advocating for civil society involvement in promoting transparency and accountability.

The intersection of Chinese surveillance technologies, governance, and civil liberties in Africa presents a complex dynamic. While these tools address critical infrastructure and security needs, their unchecked deployment threatens to entrench authoritarian practices and erode democratic norms, and to balance these risks and opportunities, African states must prioritise regulatory frameworks, international human rights standards, and the protection of civil liberties.

Chinese Surveillance in Southern Africa

South Africa occupies a complex position in the global surveillance ecosystem, simultaneously serving as an importer, financier, and exporter of surveillance technologies (Ibekwe et al., 2024). This dual role reflects its strategic aspirations, leveraging both Western and Chinese technological advancements to enhance domestic security while extending influence across the Global South. Historically rooted in apartheid-era intelligence networks, the country's surveillance infrastructure has evolved into a mid-tier global player, blending local expertise with foreign innovations.

The adoption of Chinese surveillance technologies, particularly from Huawei and Zhongxing Telecommunication Equipment Corporation (ZTE), is driven by the promise of enhanced public safety, urban management, and digital infrastructure. Through initiatives like Smart City and Safe City projects, these technologies streamline security operations, optimising traffic control, law enforcement, and emergency response. However, this integration raises critical concerns regarding data sovereignty, mass surveillance, and potential state overreach. South Africa's reliance on Chinese surveillance tools risks embedding external technological dependencies, reinforcing asymmetrical power dynamics that mirror broader geopolitical struggles (Duncan, 2018). Thus, while these technologies offer efficiency, they necessitate stringent regulatory frameworks to safeguard civil liberties and prevent democratic backsliding. However, these advancements pose significant risks to civil liberties, democratic integrity, and governance, highlighting the urgent need for robust regulatory frameworks to address these challenges in the digital age (Cloete, 2024).

The adoption of Chinese surveillance technologies in South Africa, including facial recognition systems, CCTV networks, biometric tools, and real-time monitoring, has revolutionised public security and urban management through initiatives like Huawei's Safe City and ZTE's Smart City solutions. While these technologies promise benefits such as enhanced crime monitoring and improved public services, they raise serious concerns about privacy and civil liberties.

Gravett highlights the troubling implications of "digital neocolonialism," where Chinese technologies not only introduce advanced systems but also propagate authoritarian governance models. In South Africa, these systems could be exploited to track journalists and activists, stifle freedom of expression, and discourage public participation. The resulting surveillance infrastructure poses a chilling effect, leading to self-censorship and jeopardising the country's democratic foundations and citizens' fundamental freedoms.

The integration of Chinese surveillance technologies in South Africa presents a dual-edged reality in enhancing urban management while threatening privacy, sovereignty, and democratic integrity. Although legal safeguards like the Protection of Personal Information Act (POPIA) exist, weak enforcement leaves room for potential abuses, including unauthorised data access by foreign entities, particularly China (Sekalala et al., 2023). The absence of stringent regulatory oversight compounds governance challenges, enabling mass surveillance under the guise of security. Marketed as modernisation tools, these technologies consolidate state power, reducing transparency and accountability. Left unchecked, they risk eroding institutional independence and fostering authoritarian tendencies (Gagliardone, 2020), ultimately undermining democratic governance.

These technologies also pose a threat to democratic processes by enabling state surveillance of opposition leaders and activists, particularly during elections. This undermines political pluralism, distorts power dynamics, and threatens the principles of free and fair democracy (Li, 2020). As state surveillance normalises, it risks influencing election outcomes and suppressing dissent. South Africa's increasing reliance on Chinese surveillance technologies could lead to greater dependence on China, compromising its political autonomy and sovereignty. This trend mirrors broader patterns across Africa, where countries align more closely with Chinese geopolitical interests, undermining governance and human rights (Kang, 2025).

Though these technologies promise short-term improvements in urban security and management, they threaten civil liberties, democracy, and sovereignty. The lack of regulatory oversight and the potential for state misuse may infringe on privacy, freedom of expression, and political participation. To safeguard its democratic values, South Africa must strengthen its legal frameworks, improve oversight, and remain cautious about the geopolitical and sovereignty risks posed by increasing dependence on Chinese technology.

The increasing use of Chinese surveillance technology in Southern Africa, particularly in countries like Zambia, provides a compelling case for understanding the broader implications on civil liberties, democracy, and governance (Heeks et al., 2024). In the assertion of Mendez and Estrada (2024), the deployment of surveillance infrastructure, primarily through partnerships with Chinese tech giants like Huawei and ZTE, offers potential urban and security benefits. However, it also raises concerns about political freedoms and human rights. Zambia's experience with Chinese surveillance systems illustrates the intersection of technological development and the erosion of individual rights, a phenomenon observable across Africa (Ndhlovu, 2024).

In Zambia, Chinese surveillance systems have been implemented under the guise of enhancing urban planning and security (Shempela et al., 2024). Notably, projects like Huawei's Safe City initiative involve the installation of biometric technologies, facial recognition, and advanced CCTV networks (Da Vinha, 2024). These tools are promoted as solutions for managing crime, traffic, and public safety. However, as Majerowicz and de Carvalho (2024) warn, the implementation of such technologies without proper safeguards can lead to abuses, particularly in regions with weaker democratic frameworks and regulatory systems. While these systems can increase public safety, there is a significant risk of them being misused to infringe upon civil liberties.

A major concern surrounding the use of Chinese surveillance technology in Zambia is its impact on privacy and freedom of expression. Technologies such as biometric identification and facial recognition collect vast amounts of personal data, which could be used to monitor individuals' movements and activities. In countries with fragile political environments, such technologies present a risk to activists, journalists, and political dissidents. According to Wernick et al. (2024), the widespread use of Chinese surveillance technology in Africa mirrors patterns seen in authoritarian regimes, where these tools are used to suppress opposition and control public discourse. Although Zambia's political system is relatively stable, the potential for surveillance overreach still poses a threat to political freedoms and individual privacy.

This risk is further exacerbated by Zambia's insufficient legal framework to regulate these technologies. Although Zambia has made progress with data protection laws, the enforcement of these regulations remains inconsistent. Without strong legal oversight, citizens are vulnerable to the misuse of their personal data by both state actors and private companies. The lack of proper regulation and accountability opens the door for government agencies to misuse surveillance tools, particularly to monitor political opponents, thereby stifling dissent and limiting political freedoms. Öztürk (2025) suggests that the use of surveillance data for political purposes can lead to self-censorship, with citizens refraining from expressing political opinions out of fear of retaliation.

The introduction of Chinese surveillance technology also has significant implications for Zambia's democracy. While the country has maintained a relatively robust democratic system compared to other African nations, the expansion of mass surveillance could gradually undermine democratic processes. Jia (2024) argues that the deployment of surveillance technologies, especially those backed by authoritarian states like China, can increase the state's power over citizens and diminish democratic accountability. In Zambia, these technologies might give the government the ability to monitor and potentially influence elections by tracking the movements and activities of voters, candidates, and political activists. If used to target opposition groups or manipulate public opinion, surveillance tools could compromise the fairness of elections and weaken Zambia's democratic structures (Lin, 2024). Additionally, the impact of Chinese surveillance technologies on Zambia's governance cannot be overlooked. Chinese-backed surveillance tools are often framed as a way to enhance public safety, particularly in urban areas facing crime and social unrest (Pereira, 2024). However, this shift towards a security-centric model of governance may inadvertently deepen challenges related to governance and accountability in Zambia. As Chan et al. (2024) note, increased reliance on Chinese surveillance technology could heighten state control over citizens' lives, potentially leading to more authoritarian practices in a country that has traditionally valued democratic governance.

China's growing influence in Zambia's governance structure is another area of concern. Gravett refers to the export of Chinese surveillance technology as a form of "digital neocolonialism," wherein China gains substantial influence over African governments through the provision of technological tools for monitoring and controlling their populations. Zambia's increasing dependence on Chinese technology could limit its sovereignty, making it more difficult for the country to make independent decisions regarding governance and regulatory policies. This situation could have broader implications for African nations, where the influx of Chinese surveillance systems could promote authoritarian governance models at the expense of democratic ideals and individual freedoms.

In essence, Zambia's adoption of Chinese surveillance technology underscores a complex set of trade-offs between technological advancement and the erosion of civil liberties, democracy, and governance. While surveillance systems can offer benefits such as improved public safety and urban management, they also pose significant risks to privacy, political freedoms, and the democratic process. The lack of comprehensive legal protections, coupled with the potential for government misuse, calls into question the long-term impact of such technologies on individual rights. As Jili (2023) and Li (2020) suggest, the proliferation of Chinese surveillance tools in Africa may contribute to a global shift towards authoritarian governance, where state control overrides democratic participation. Therefore, Zambia must implement effective legal frameworks to ensure that these technologies are used responsibly, protecting civil liberties and preserving democratic values in the country.

The deployment of Chinese surveillance technology in Zimbabwe exemplifies how digital tools are leveraged to consolidate political power while simultaneously raising complex governance and sovereignty issues. Technologies such as facial recognition systems, AI-powered surveillance cameras, and biometric data collection tools, supplied by Chinese firms like CloudWalk Technology and Hangzhou Hikvision Digital Technology Co., Ltd., have redefined state control under the Zimbabwe African National Union-Patriotic Front (ZANU-PF) (Yingi & Benyera, 2024). While framed as modernisation efforts to enhance national security, these systems have played a decisive role in political repression.

A striking example of this surveillance apparatus in action occurred during the 2019 anti-government protests following the sharp rise in fuel prices. Protestors, journalists, and opposition figures were systematically tracked using facial recognition systems installed in Harare's central business district, leading to widespread arrests and intimidation (Munoriyarwa, 2022). Reports indicate that law enforcement officials accessed data from these systems to preemptively detain activists before planned demonstrations, creating a chilling effect on dissent (Gohdes, 2024). Similarly, opposition leader Nelson Chamisa and his campaign team reported being followed and monitored through state-controlled CCTV networks during the 2023 election period, further raising alarms about the erosion of democratic freedoms (Azinogo & Erasmus, 2025).

Beyond real-time surveillance, Zimbabwe's collaboration with CloudWalk Technology involves the collection and storage of biometric data, including fingerprints, iris scans, and facial images, in databases that are reportedly shared with Chinese authorities (Heeks et al., 2024). This data transfer is embedded within China's broader Digital Silk Road initiative, raising concerns about "data colonialism"—a phenomenon where digital infrastructure and data sovereignty are effectively controlled by external powers (Ozturk, 2025). The implications are profound: Zimbabwe not only loses control over its citizens' personal data but also risks external influence over its security infrastructure. The reliance on foreign entities for data processing and storage exacerbates national vulnerabilities, as sensitive information could be leveraged for political and economic purposes beyond Zimbabwe's borders (Bayrali & Jimale, 2025).

While these risks are significant, the adoption of surveillance technologies has not been without merit. Proponents argue that AI-driven monitoring has improved urban security, particularly in crime-prone areas. The Safe City project, implemented in Harare and Bulawayo with Huawei's support, has reportedly contributed to crime reduction through real-time tracking of criminal activities and automated emergency responses (Vava, 2014). Similarly, biometric verification has enhanced border security, curbing illegal crossings and smuggling (Curtis & Klaus, 2024). However, these gains are overshadowed by the potential for misuse, particularly in a state where political accountability remains weak. The unchecked proliferation of these surveillance technologies further blurs the line between military and civilian oversight. The Zimbabwean Defence Forces (ZDF) have increasingly integrated AI-powered surveillance tools into their operations, reinforcing their role in internal security matters that traditionally fall under civilian law enforcement (Munoriyarwa, 2022). This shift strengthens the executive branch's grip on power, allowing security agencies to operate with minimal oversight while stifling opposition activities (Bayrali & Jimale, 2025).

A lack of transparent legal frameworks exacerbates these risks. While Zimbabwe has data protection laws, enforcement remains sporadic, allowing state authorities to use surveillance data with impunity. Unlike the European Union's General Data Protection Regulation (GDPR), which imposes strict controls on data processing and transfer, Zimbabwe lacks independent oversight bodies capable of holding government agencies accountable for privacy violations (Soulé, 2025).

The broader geopolitical ramifications cannot be ignored. China's Digital Silk Road extends beyond Zimbabwe, fostering dependencies across Africa through digital infrastructure projects. As Beijing strengthens its foothold in the continent's digital economy, concerns over technological sovereignty intensify. Countries like Zimbabwe risk becoming entangled in digital dependencies that extend beyond hardware supply chains to encompass data governance, cybersecurity, and policy alignment with Chinese interests (Ozturk, 2025). This dynamic raises the question of whether technological partnerships are fostering genuine development or merely deepening external control over Africa's digital future.

To mitigate these threats, Zimbabwe must implement robust oversight mechanisms, ensuring surveillance technologies serve national security without encroaching on civil liberties. Strengthening data protection laws, establishing independent regulatory bodies, and mandating transparent public consultations before deploying surveillance tools are crucial steps (Curtis & Klaus, 2024). Furthermore, international actors, including human rights organisations and technology watchdogs, must engage with Zimbabwean policymakers to promote ethical AI use and prevent authoritarian entrenchment under the guise of technological advancement.

Without proactive governance reforms, Zimbabwe's reliance on Chinese surveillance technology risks deepening its authoritarian trajectory, suppressing political pluralism, and eroding fundamental freedoms. The challenge lies in harnessing digital innovations for societal benefit while safeguarding democratic values in an era where technology increasingly shapes governance and civil rights.

Chinese Surveillance in West Africa

The expansion of Chinese surveillance technology in Nigeria exemplifies the increasing adoption of advanced digital tools by states seeking to enhance governance capabilities and address security challenges. However, the integration of these technologies raises critical concerns about their implications for civil liberties, democracy, and governance. As part of China's broader Digital Silk Road initiative, Nigeria has embraced tools such as AI-powered surveillance cameras, facial recognition systems, and biometric data platforms. These technologies are framed as solutions for public safety and administrative efficiency, yet their deployment often reveals deeper governance and human rights challenges.

The introduction of Chinese surveillance technologies in Nigeria has sparked significant concerns about civil liberties, particularly the right to privacy enshrined in Section 37 of Nigeria's 1999 Constitution. These technologies, including those from Huawei and ZTE, facilitate mass surveillance, posing risks to privacy due to insufficient legal safeguards and weak enforcement of the Nigerian Data Protection Act. As noted by Salau (2024), surveillance of electronic communications by state agencies undermines constitutional protections, leaving citizens vulnerable to privacy violations without adequate accountability.

Financial incentives, such as concessional loans from Chinese institutions, have played a crucial role in expanding the adoption of these surveillance systems, prioritising state security over individual rights (Passalacqua & Polito, 2024). This fosters a trend of digital authoritarianism, concentrating state control while eroding transparency and accountability. Furthermore, weak regulatory structures have led to the militarisation of surveillance, reinforcing a culture of impunity and suppressing political dissent (Feldstein, 2019).

The pervasive use of surveillance technologies also impacts Nigeria's democracy, particularly in electoral processes. These systems have been used to monitor opposition and suppress voter turnout, undermining public trust in democratic institutions and skewing political discourse (Passalacqua & Polito, 2024). The geopolitical implications of China's Digital Silk Road initiative raise concerns about data sovereignty and external influence on Nigeria's policies (Feldstein, 2019). To mitigate these risks, stronger legal frameworks, rigorous enforcement, and public oversight are essential. Without these measures, reliance on surveillance technology could entrench authoritarianism and further harm Nigeria's democratic development (Salau, 2024).

The deployment of Chinese surveillance technology in Nigeria thus serves as a cautionary tale of the dual-edged nature of technological progress. While these tools have the potential to address pressing security and governance challenges, their misuse highlights the need for ethical considerations and robust safeguards. Ensuring that technology is used to enhance, rather than undermine, democratic values and civil liberties is critical to Nigeria's future as a democratic state.

The integration of Chinese surveillance technology into Ghana's digital ecosystem is a compelling facet of China's Digital Silk Road (DSR), raising critical concerns about civil liberties and governance. Nguyen et al. (2024) assert that while Ghana benefits from infrastructural advancements driven by Chinese firms such as Huawei and ZTE, the growing influence of these technologies in national security and political monitoring has sparked widespread debate. Concrete examples of government surveillance, allegations of espionage, and geopolitical consequences underscore the multifaceted impact of China's technological footprint in Ghana (Arnold, 2024). Ghana has historically been celebrated for its democratic resilience, yet recent reports suggest a shift towards increased surveillance, particularly targeting activists, journalists, and opposition figures. One of the most high-profile cases occurred in 2019 when Ghanaian investigative journalist Ahmed Hussein-Suale, a key figure in the renowned exposé on football corruption, was assassinated after his identity was publicly disclosed (Ameyaw-Brobbey, 2024). While no direct link to Chinese surveillance was established, the increasing adoption of AI-driven monitoring tools has raised concerns about the potential for state-backed tracking of dissenters. Similarly, reports emerged in 2022 about the Ghanaian government allegedly using surveillance technology to monitor activists protesting the controversial Agyapa Royalties deal (Kuyini Mohammed, 2023). Civil society organisations, including the Economic Fighters League, reported increased digital surveillance, with encrypted messages intercepted and movement patterns analysed. These developments echo broader concerns that Chinese-provided surveillance infrastructure, including facial recognition cameras and data analytics, might be leveraged for political suppression rather than security (Arnold, 2024).

China's investment in Ghana's digital infrastructure is not just an economic engagement but a strategic move within the DSR framework that redefines Ghana's geopolitical alignments (Teye et al., 2024). The rapid expansion of Chinese-backed projects such as Huawei's Safe City Initiative, which equips Ghanaian law enforcement with advanced surveillance tools, has undoubtedly drawn scrutiny from Western allies, particularly the United States. In 2019, the US Embassy in Ghana issued an advisory about cybersecurity risks associated with Chinese telecommunications infrastructure, hinting at potential espionage and data vulnerabilities (Schatz & Silvey, 2025). Ghana's reliance on Chinese technology has placed it at an intersection of geopolitical tensions. While the Ghanaian government publicly emphasises the economic advantages of these partnerships, some policymakers express concerns about alienating Western allies, who remain crucial trade and diplomatic partners. The African Union (AU), for instance, has warned against unchecked technological dependence, especially after reports surfaced in 2018 alleging that China had embedded spyware within the AU's headquarters in Addis Ababa, a building China constructed (Lubin, 2024).

Domestically, China's growing surveillance footprint has triggered debates within Ghanaian society, as civil rights organisations, including the Media Foundation for West Africa, as opined by Rojo (2024), have raised alarms over the opaque nature of Ghana's agreements with Chinese firms, questioning the implications for data sovereignty and privacy. In Parliament, opposition members have called for greater scrutiny over Chinese-backed security projects, arguing that these initiatives could be exploited for political leverage.

Moreover, the legal framework governing digital privacy in Ghana remains inadequate. The Data Protection Act of 2012, while a step in the right direction, lacks robust enforcement mechanisms to regulate the use of surveillance technologies. This legislative gap creates an environment where Chinese firms operate with minimal oversight, amplifying concerns about state-sponsored surveillance and potential misuse of biometric data (Achinivu, 2024). While Chinese surveillance technology has undeniably propelled Ghana's digital evolution, the associated risks necessitate urgent regulatory interventions. The country must adopt comprehensive data protection laws, establish independent oversight bodies, and ensure transparency in security-related technology agreements. Furthermore, diversifying technology partnerships by engaging both Western and African stakeholders can mitigate over-reliance on China and promote a balanced digital ecosystem.

As Ghana navigates the intersection of technological advancement and civil liberties, the challenge remains clear: How can the nation harness digital innovation without compromising its democratic values? The answer lies in robust governance, accountability, and an unwavering commitment to protecting the rights and freedoms of its citizens. Without these safeguards, the allure of economic growth through Chinese partnerships risks becoming a gateway to digital authoritarianism.

The integration of Chinese surveillance technology in Côte d'Ivoire has emerged as a defining feature of the country's urban security and governance strategy, reflecting broader trends across Africa under China's Digital Silk Road (DSR) initiative. With firms like Huawei and ZTE supplying AI-powered surveillance cameras, biometric systems, and facial recognition technology, the Ivorian government has embraced these tools as essential components of modernisation. Passalacqua and Polito (2024) highlight the framing of these technologies as catalysts for public safety and urban management, yet their deployment raises profound concerns about civil liberties, democratic governance, and national sovereignty.

A primary issue revolves around legal vulnerabilities and their implications for civil liberties. The absence of robust data protection laws and regulatory oversight exposes citizens to privacy violations and potential misuse of personal information. Surveillance tools continuously collect and store biometric data, often without public consent, heightening the risk of unauthorised access and exploitation. The lack of clear legal frameworks governing data storage and transfer leaves room for governmental overreach and opaque agreements with Chinese firms, further complicating issues of accountability (Passalacqua & Polito, 2024). These gaps in oversight do not merely threaten privacy but also serve as a mechanism for political suppression. As Feldstein (2019) observes, surveillance technologies in authoritarian-leaning states often double as instruments for monitoring political activists, journalists, and opposition figures. In Côte d'Ivoire, such concerns are validated by increased scrutiny of protesters and the stifling of political dissent. Fear of constant surveillance discourages civic engagement, leading to a gradual erosion of democratic participation.

Public perception of surveillance technology in Côte d'Ivoire presents a complex dynamic. While some citizens recognise its potential benefits for crime prevention and enhanced urban security, others express growing unease over its unchecked expansion. Public trust in these systems is largely shaped by their application—if surveillance is perceived as a means of improving safety, it garners cautious support. However, when used to silence opposition or unfairly target certain demographics, widespread resentment builds. According to a survey by Soussane and Ibourk (2024), many Ivorians feel caught between a desire for enhanced security and a fear of government overreach. The trade-off between national security and individual privacy remains a contentious issue, particularly given historical concerns about state surveillance being used as a political weapon. Transparency in how these systems are managed and ensuring independent oversight could improve public confidence in their intended purpose.

Examining Côte d'Ivoire's surveillance landscape within the broader West African context reveals similar patterns in neighbouring states. In Ghana, for instance, the government has partnered with Chinese firms to introduce biometric voter registration and AI-powered monitoring tools. While framed as efforts to enhance electoral integrity, critics warn of potential misuse for voter suppression and targeted surveillance of opposition groups (Salau, 2024). Nigeria, another regional powerhouse, has embraced Chinese digital infrastructure under its "Smart City" initiatives, but reports of state surveillance targeting activists raise concerns about a shift toward digital authoritarianism. Unlike Ghana, which has a relatively stronger regulatory environment, Côte d'Ivoire shares Nigeria's challenge of opaque governance structures that allow for the unchecked expansion of surveillance programmes. The lack of a unified West African legal framework governing surveillance technology means that each country navigates its challenges independently, often reinforcing governance imbalances rather than addressing them collectively (Passalacqua & Polito, 2024).

A particularly alarming implication of increased surveillance in Côte d'Ivoire is its impact on electoral processes. Surveillance tools can be leveraged to track political gatherings, intimidate opposition candidates, and suppress voter turnout. In the 2020 presidential elections, reports emerged of increased monitoring around opposition strongholds, raising fears of digital surveillance being weaponised for electoral advantage. The ability of the state to track and identify protesters in real-time discourages political activism, effectively restricting political participation. This aligns with global trends where digital surveillance is used to manipulate electoral outcomes by controlling political expression and limiting the ability of opposition groups to mobilise (Gohdes, 2024). The presence of surveillance technology near polling stations further exacerbates voter intimidation, subtly pressuring citizens to align with the ruling party's interests to avoid future targeting. Without strict oversight, Côte d'Ivoire risks normalising a governance model where elections are influenced not by free political discourse, but by state-controlled digital monitoring.

Beyond its national implications, Côte d'Ivoire's deepening reliance on Chinese surveillance technology raises geopolitical concerns. As part of the Digital Silk Road, these systems establish long-term dependencies on Chinese firms, increasing Beijing's strategic influence over Ivorian digital infrastructure (Salau, 2024). This reliance is not merely economic; it has sovereignty implications. The transfer of biometric data to China, often facilitated through ambiguous contracts, positions the Ivorian government in a precarious situation where it may lack full control over its citizens' most sensitive information (Ozturk, 2025). Scholars like Heeks et al. (2024) argue that this practice constitutes a form of "data colonialism", wherein national data sovereignty is eroded in favour of foreign control. The risks extend beyond privacy; if external actors possess access to critical databases, they wield significant power over national security, political stability, and economic intelligence.

While Chinese surveillance technology provides short-term benefits, including enhanced public safety and urban development, its long-term implications cannot be ignored. Addressing these risks requires immediate legal reforms, including the establishment of a comprehensive data protection framework, independent oversight mechanisms, and public transparency in surveillance agreements. Côte d'Ivoire must navigate a delicate balance between technological modernisation and safeguarding democratic values. Without stringent regulations, surveillance risks becoming a tool of political control rather than a mechanism for security and governance enhancement. By aligning its policies with broader regional efforts to regulate surveillance, Côte d'Ivoire can mitigate the pitfalls of unchecked digital monitoring while ensuring that security imperatives do not come at the cost of fundamental rights and freedoms. Table 8.1 presents a regional comparison.

The comparison of Chinese surveillance proliferation in Southern and Western Africa reveals a distinct intersection between the expansion of surveillance technologies (independent variable) and the erosion of civil liberties (dependent variable) as depicted in Table 8.1. In Southern Africa, surveillance is often deployed in authoritarian contexts, where its primary purpose is to enhance national security and political control, particularly targeting opposition and activists (Munoriyarwa, 2022). This has resulted in significant erosion of civil liberties, creating a climate of fear and suppressing political pluralism (Passalacqua & Polito, 2024). Conversely, in Western Africa, surveillance is framed as a tool for urban governance and crime prevention, although concerns about political monitoring remain (Millner et al., 2024; Iwuoha & Doevenspeck, 2023). Despite these differing uses, both regions experience significant civil liberties violations, driven by weak legal frameworks and a lack of public oversight (Feldstein, 2019). The proliferation of Chinese surveillance technologies in both regions deepens economic dependencies, increasing China's geopolitical influence while intensifying risks to privacy and individual freedoms (Salau, 2024).

Table 8.1 Comparison of Chinese surveillance in Western and Southern Africa

Aspect	Southern Africa (Zambia, Zimbabwe)	Western Africa (Ghana, Nigeria, Côte d'Ivoire)
Primary use of surveillance	Surveillance is often used in authoritarian contexts, with a focus on national security and political control, including monitoring political opposition, protests, and activists	Surveillance is primarily framed as a tool for urban governance, crime prevention, and improving public safety, though political monitoring is still a concern.
Civil liberties	Significant erosion of civil liberties, with surveillance tools used explicitly for political repression, creating a climate of fear (Passalacqua & Polito, 2024; Munoriyarwa, 2022)	Concerns about privacy violations and data misuse persist, particularly in the absence of strong data protection laws (Feldstein, 2019; Passalacqua & Polito, 2024).
Impact on democracy	The use of surveillance tools undermines political pluralism, discourages public engagement, and suppresses dissent (Munoriyarwa, 2022; Passalacqua & Polito, 2024)	Surveillance discourages public participation and fosters self-censorship, especially in politically sensitive contexts (Passalacqua & Polito, 2024).
Geopolitical dynamics	There is a close alignment with Chinese interests, where dependence on Chinese technology enhances China's influence in return for supporting authoritarian governance (Feldstein, 2019)	The adoption of Chinese technologies is often framed as mutually beneficial, with countries seeking modernisation and improved governance while becoming dependent on China (Passalacqua & Polito, 2024)
Surveillance for political control	Surveillance systems are heavily integrated into state security forces, monitoring and controlling opposition, particularly in politically charged environments (Munoriyarwa, 2022)	Surveillance systems, while mainly focused on public safety, are sometimes used to monitor political activities and protests, raising concerns about state overreach (Passalacqua & Polito, 2024)
Security concerns	The militarised use of surveillance technologies increases the risk of espionage and external influence, with less public oversight (Munoriyarwa, 2022; Salau, 2024)	Similar security concerns exist, especially regarding espionage risks and the influence of Chinese firms, but there are greater efforts for public oversight in some countries (Feldstein, 2019; Salau, 2024)
Economic and strategic interests	The reliance on Chinese surveillance technology deepens economic dependencies, allowing China to extend its influence, especially in isolated or politically unstable regimes (Feldstein, 2019)	Economic modernisation is often the driving force for adopting these technologies, creating dependencies on Chinese economic support while also embedding Chinese geopolitical interests (Passalacqua & Polito, 2024)
Legal and institutional frameworks	Weak legal frameworks and lack of oversight enable misuse of surveillance, contributing to a concentration of power in the state (Feldstein, 2019)	Legal frameworks are often underdeveloped, leaving citizens vulnerable to privacy violations, but some countries are beginning to implement stronger data protection laws (Passalacqua & Polito, 2024)

Source: Author's Own Construct, 2025

Conclusion

Beneath the Dragon's unblinking gaze, Western and Southern Africa's digital frontiers are no longer neutral spaces of progress but battlegrounds of power, surveillance, and silent subjugation. What was once framed as technological modernisation through China's *Smart City* and *Safe City* initiatives has morphed into an intricate web of biometric tracking, AI-powered monitoring, and mass data extraction. This transformation erodes democratic resilience, fostering fear-driven self-censorship while entrenching state control. Yet, the peril extends beyond borders—sensitive biometric data flows outward, deepening Africa's digital dependency and transforming nations into data colonies, where sovereignty is relinquished, and governance is steered by external interests. This unchecked expansion of surveillance infrastructure demands urgent countermeasures. African nations must move beyond passive adoption and reclaim digital autonomy through enforceable data protection laws, independent oversight mechanisms, and transparent regulatory frameworks. Without decisive intervention, the Dragon's gaze will not merely observe but dictate, ensuring that governance is shaped not by democratic will but by the cold calculus of perpetual surveillance and control.

References

Acharya, D. B., Kuppan, K., & Divya, B. (2025). Agentic AI: Autonomous intelligence for complex goals—A comprehensive survey. *IEEE Access, 13*, 18912–18936. https://doi.org/10.1109/ACCESS.2025.3532853

Achinivu, C. (2024). *Digital authoritarianism in Africa: Chinese strategy or African legacy* [University of Delaware]. https://www.proquest.com/

Ameyaw-Brobbey, T. (2024). The media in China–Africa public relations: Assessing China's attractiveness beyond economic development assistance. *Politics & Policy, 52*(3), 551–572. https://doi.org/10.1111/polp.12596

Arnold, S. (2024). Africa's roads to digital development: Paving the way for Chinese structural power in the ICT sector? *Review of International Political Economy, 31*(4), 1148–1172. https://doi.org/10.1080/09692290.2023.2297363

Azinogo, B. K., & Erasmus, L. J. (2025). Corporate governance challenges and their impact on public sector auditing in Africa: An exploration of effectiveness, accountability, and transparency. *Journal of Accounting, Finance and Auditing Studies, 11*(1), 1–14. https://doi.org/10.56578/jafas110101

Bayrali, O. G., & Jimale, A. (2025). COVID-19 pandemic in Somalia, South Africa and Zimbabwe: Why do leaders love COVID-19 precautions? In *COVID-19 and public policy* (Vol. 33, pp. 177–197). Emerald Publishing Limited. https://doi.org/10.1108/S1572-832320240000033012

Chan, M., Yi, J., & Kuznetsov, D. (2024). Government digital repression and political engagement: A cross-national multilevel analysis examining the roles of online surveillance and censorship. *The International Journal of Press/Politics, 29*(2), 371–393. https://doi.org/10.1177/19401612221117106

Chang, Y. Y. (2023). China beyond China, establishing a digital order with Chinese characteristics: China's growing discursive power and the Digital Silk Road. *Politics & Policy, 51*(2), 283–321. https://doi.org/10.1111/polp.12524

Cloete, F. (2024). Governing artificial intelligence (AI) and other technologies in the digital era. *Administratio Publica, 32*(1), 1–30. https://doi.org/10.10520/ejc-adminpub_v32_n1_a3

Curtis, S., & Klaus, I. (2024). *The belt and Road City: Geopolitics, urbanization, and China's search for a new international order*. Yale University Press.

Da Vinha, L. (2024). Smart for whom? Africa's smart cities and digital authoritarianism. *International Journal of Intelligence and CounterIntelligence, 37*(3), 941–959. https://doi.org/10.1080/08850607.2023.2284629

Duncan, J. (2018). *Stopping the spies: Constructing and resisting the surveillance state in South Africa*. Wits University Press.

Feldstein, S. (2019). The road to digital unfreedom: How artificial intelligence is reshaping repression. *Journal of Democracy, 30*(1), 40–52.

Gagliardone, I. (2020). *The impact of Chinese tech provision on civil liberties in Africa*. South African Institute of International Affairs. https://www.jstor.org/stable/resrep29588

Gohdes, A. R. (2024). *Repression in the digital age: Surveillance, censorship, and the dynamics of state violence*. Oxford University Press.

Gurram, A. (2024). Biometric (data) governance and digital surveillance: A comparative analysis of biopolitics in India and China. In T. Ø. Kuldova, H. O. I. Gundhus, & C. T. Wathne (Eds.), *Policing and intelligence in the global big data era, volume II: New global perspectives on the politics and ethics of knowledge* (pp. 287–315). Springer Nature. https://doi.org/10.1007/978-3-031-68298-8_11

Heeks, R., Ospina, A. V., Foster, C., Gao, P., Han, X., Jepson, N., Schindler, S., & Zhou, Q. (2024). China's digital expansion in the Global South: Systematic literature review and future research agenda. *The Information Society, 40*(2), 69–95. https://doi.org/10.1080/01972243.2024.2315875

Ibekwe, E., Etukudoh, E., Nwokediegwu, Z., Umoh, A., Adefemi, A., Ilojianya, V., & Magash, T. (2024). Energy security in the global context: A comprehensive review of geopolitical dynamics and policies. *Engineering Science & Technology Journal, 5*, 152–168. https://doi.org/10.51594/estj/v5i1.741

Iwuoha, V., & Doevenspeck, M. (2023). Dilemmas of 'biometric nationality': Migration control, biometric ID technology and political mobilisation of migrants in West Africa. *Territory, Politics, Governance, 13*, 1–26. https://doi.org/10.1080/21622671.2023.2205885

Jia, M. (2024). Authoritarian privacy. *The University of Chicago Law Review, 91*(3), 733–810.

Jili, B. (2023). *Africas-demand-for-an-adoption-of-Chinese-surveillance-technology* [issue brief may]. https://dfrlab.org/wp-content/uploads/sites/3/2023/05/Africas-Demand-for-an-Adoption-of-Chinese-Surveillance-Technology.pdf

Kang, X. (2025). Navigating tensions between authoritarian governance and human rights: Towards a business and human rights regime within China's dual-state context. *Nordic Journal of Human Rights, 43*(1), 19–39. https://doi.org/10.1080/18918131.2024.2415197

Li, H. (2020). *Human rights in the age of surveillance: China's expansion of technological and normative power* [New York University]. https://scholar.google.com/

Lin, B. (2024). Beyond authoritarianism and liberal democracy: Understanding China's artificial intelligence impact in Africa. *Information, Communication & Society, 27*(6), 1126–1141. https://doi.org/10.1080/1369118X.2023.2239322

Lubin, A. (2024). *Selling surveillance* (SSRN scholarly paper no. 4323985). Social Science Research Network. https://doi.org/10.2139/ssrn.4323985

Majerowicz, E., & de Carvalho, M. H. (2024). China's expansion into Brazilian digital surveillance markets. *The Information Society, 40*(2), 168–118.

Mannan, M. A. (2025). Surveillance and privacy: Examining the complex interplay between National Security and individual freedoms. In *Analyzing privacy and security difficulties in social media: New challenges and solutions* (pp. 465–486). IGI Global Scientific Publishing. https://doi.org/10.4018/979-8-3693-9491-5.ch019

Melber, H., Bjarnesen, J., Lanzano, C., & Mususa, P. (2023). Citizenship matters: Explorations into the citizen-state relationship in Africa. *Forum for Development Studies, 50*(1), 35–58. https://doi.org/10.1080/08039410.2022.2145992

Mendez, A., & Estrada, G. (2024). Geopolitical game-changer: China's expanding role in Latin America's defense, aerospace, and telecommunications. In A. Farhadi, M. Grzegorzewski, & A. J. Masys (Eds.), *The great power competition volume 6: The rise of China* (pp. 185–206). Springer Nature. https://doi.org/10.1007/978-3-031-70767-4_9

Millner, N., Newport, B., Sandbrook, C., & Simlai, T. (2024). Between monitoring and surveillance: Geographies of emerging drone technologies in contemporary conservation. *Progress in Environmental Geography, 3*(1), 17–39. https://doi.org/10.1177/27539687241229739

Mohammed, A. K. (2023). An evaluation of the quality of democracy of Ghana. *Democracy and Security, 19*(4), 347–388. https://doi.org/10.1080/17419166.2023.2220140

Munoriyarwa, A. (2022). The militarization of digital surveillance in post-coup Zimbabwe: 'Just don't tell them what we do'. *Security Dialogue, 53*(5), 456–474. https://doi.org/10.1177/09670106221118796

Ndhlovu, T. P. (2024). Food (in)security, the moral economy, and Ubuntu in South Africa: A Southern perspective. *Review of International Political Economy, 31*(1), 199–223. https://doi.org/10.1080/09692290.2022.2161110

Nguyen, D., Wang, B., & Mutsvairo, B. (2024). (Pragmatic) collaboration for progress or threat to autonomy? African news discourses about Chinese technology in Nigeria and Ghana. *Global Media and China, 9*(4), 469–490. https://doi.org/10.1177/20594364241232757

Öztürk, İ. (2025). Journal of populism studies article unveiling China's "transnational populism" and sharp power politics: The case of the belt and road initiative. *Journal of Populism Studies*, 1–28.

Passalacqua, C. C., & Polito, C. (2024). *Going beyond the authoritarian bias.*

Pereira, C. (2024). Africa's natural resources amid old and new Imperial relations: What implications for gender justice? *Feminist Africa, 5*(2), 14–41.

Rojo, J. V. (2024). China's technological footprint in Africa: A patent network analysis. *South African Journal of Business Management, 55*(1), 4331. https://doi.org/10.4102/sajbm.v55i1.4331

Sáenz, R., & García, C. (2024). *China's tech surveillance applications in Europe and Latin America: Analysing the impact on democratic governance*. European University Institute. https://doi.org/10.2870/097533

Salau, A. (2024). *Cybersecurity, state surveillance and the right to online privacy in Nigeria: A call for synergy of law and policy. 1.* https://doi.org/10.29053/ajpdp.v1i1.0008

Scarpi, D., & Pantano, E. (2024). "With great power comes great responsibility": Exploring the role of corporate digital responsibility (CDR) for artificial intelligence responsibility in retail service automation (AIRRSA). *Organizational Dynamics, 53*(2), 101030. https://doi.org/10.1016/j.orgdyn.2024.101030

Schatz, E., & Silvey, R. (2025). *Seeing China's belt and road.* Oxford University Press.

Sekalala, S., Rawson, B., & Andanda, P. (2023). A socio-legal critique of the commercialization of digital health in Sub-Saharan Africa. *Policy Studies, 0*(0), 1–21. https://doi.org/10.1080/01442872.2025.2451966

Shempela, D. M., Mudenda, S., Kasanga, M., Daka, V., Kangongwe, M. H., Kamayani, M., Sikalima, J., Yankonde, B., Kasonde, C. B., Nakazwe, R., Mwandila, A., Cham, F., Njuguna, M., Simwaka, B., Morrison, L., Chizimu, J. Y., Muma, J. B., Chilengi, R., & Sichinga, K. (2024). A situation analysis of the capacity of laboratories in Faith-Based Hospitals in Zambia to conduct surveillance of antimicrobial resistance: Opportunities to improve diagnostic stewardship. *Microorganisms, 12*(8), Article 8. https://doi.org/10.3390/microorganisms12081697

Sheombar, A., & Skelton, S. K. (2023). Follow the surveillance: A breadcrumb Trail of surveillance technology exports to Africa. In M. R. Jones, A. S. Mukherjee, D. Thapa, & Y. Zheng (Eds.), *After Latour: Globalisation, inequity and climate change* (pp. 241–261). Springer Nature. https://doi.org/10.1007/978-3-031-50154-8_19

Soulé, F. (2025). *Negotiating Africa's digital partnerships amid geopolitical competition* [special report]. The Centre for International Governance Innovation (CIGI).

Soussane, J. A., & Ibourk, A. (2024). Is the country's preparedness for epidemics and pandemics an FDI location factor? An empirical analysis using panel data. *Journal of Chinese Economic and Foreign Trade Studies, 18*(1), 24–43. https://doi.org/10.1108/JCEFTS-03-2024-0024

Teye, J., Wang, X., & Manzi, E. (2024). The role of auditing culture in sustainable mining practices: A review of Ghana's mining sector. *Journal of Infrastructure, Policy and Development, 8*, 5426. https://doi.org/10.24294/jipd.v8i8.5426

Vava, B. (2014). *All-weather friend? Chinese ICTs in Zimbabwe as general purpose technologies (GPTs)—University of Johannesburg* [University of Johannesburg]. https://ujcontent.uj.ac.za/esploro/outputs/doctoral/All-weather-friend-Chinese-ICTs-in-Zimbabwe/9942804107691

Wernick, A., Udoh, G., & Banzuzi, E. (2024). *Reimaging smart city transplants for the global south* (pp. 109–135). https://doi.org/10.4324/9781003395966-10

Yingi, E., & Benyera, E. (2024). The future of democracy in the digital era: Internet shutdowns, cyber laws and online surveillance in Zimbabwe. *Alternatives: Global, Local, Political*, 3043754241259878. https://doi.org/10.1177/03043754241259878

Lucy Anning (PhD) is a distinguished industrial economist, SME development strategist, and researcher whose multifaceted expertise shapes China-Africa relations. With 2 years of service under Ghana's Ministry of Finance, she now serves at the Centre for Africa-China Studies, University of Johannesburg, and as Chief Economist for the Pan African Chamber of Commerce in South Africa, representing the chamber at the AfCFTA Secretariat in Ghana. Recently appointed Southern Africa Coordinator for OSAESSDA, her roles emphasise economic, social, and cultural synergies across the continent. As the current Director of DevAfrica Institute, she bridges academic and practical domains, furthering her research with the University of Electronic Science and Technology of China. Dr. Anning, an award-winning leader in research and development in Africa, holds advanced degrees in industrial economics, quantitative economics, and economics with mathematics. Her dedication to fostering academic and diplomatic exchanges underscores her pivotal role in advancing China-Africa collaboration.

Chapter 9
Weaponisation of Digital Sovereignty in Africa

Gorden Moyo

Abstract One of the tragedies of Africa in this age of digital technologies and Artificial Intelligence (AI) is its reliance on externally owned and externally controlled technological epistemes, digital infrastructures, applications, algorithms, and platforms, among others. The continent's digital landscape is completely dominated by a small number of Silicon Valley-based tech giants, including Google/Alphabet, Apple, Facebook/Meta, Amazon, and Microsoft (GAFAM), among others. Apparently, these big tech corporations are currently involved in a fierce geo-economic battle for the 'digital soul' of Africa with the Chinese tech firms, such as Alibaba, Baidu, ByteDance, China Mobile, China Telecom, Hikvision, Huawei, Tencent, and ZTE (Zhongxing Telecommunication Equipment Corporation Limited). In this context, most of the digital data produced by Africa's over 590 million internet users are appropriated and sent to data centres owned and operated by both the United States and Chinese tech conglomerates. It is argued in this chapter that tech giants, regardless of whether they are American or Chinese-based, have developed intrusive, subversive, and covert mechanisms to extract data for their profit motives from Africa. This is where the concept of digital sovereignty comes into play, as it seeks to restore digital independence and data control to Africa and African peoples.

Introduction

One of the tragedies of Africa in this age of digital technologies and Artificial Intelligence (AI) is its reliance on externally owned and externally controlled technological epistemes, digital infrastructures, applications, algorithms, and platforms, among others. The continent's digital landscape is completely dominated by a small number of Silicon Valley-based tech giants, including Google/Alphabet, Apple,

G. Moyo (✉)
Fort Hare Institute for Social and Economic Research, University of Fort Hare, East London, South Africa

G. Moyo (ed.), *An Anatomy of AI Surveillance in Africa*, Studies in Digital Politics and Governance, https://doi.org/10.1007/978-3-032-04269-9_9

Facebook/Meta, Amazon, and Microsoft (GAFAM), among others. Apparently, these big tech corporations are currently involved in a fierce geoeconomic battle for the 'digital soul' of Africa with the Chinese tech firms, such as Alibaba, Baidu, ByteDance, China Mobile, China Telecom, Hikvision, Huawei, Tencent, and ZTE (Zhongxing Telecommunication Equipment Corporation Limited). In this context, most of the digital data produced by Africa's over 590 million internet users are appropriated and sent to data centres owned and operated by both the United States and Chinese tech conglomerates. It is argued in this chapter that tech giants, regardless of whether they are American or Chinese-based, have developed intrusive, subversive, and covert mechanisms to extract data for their profit motives from Africa. This is where the concept of digital sovereignty comes into play, as it seeks to restore digital independence and data control to Africa and African peoples.

African countries are not self-sufficient in terms of digital infrastructure, big data collection and analytics, data protection, and technological innovation and development. These are the main reasons why the idea of digital sovereignty has gained currency in recent years. The idea is to free the continent from the clutches of external digital domination, especially in terms of subsea fibre-cables, data centres, cloud storage, and software, and many more. Consequently, some African governments, including Ghana, Kenya, Nigeria, and South Africa, have been ratcheting up their efforts towards digital freedom by designing strategies, policies, and rules that seek to decolonise the hegemonic digital governance systems in their respective countries.

However, the pursuit of digital sovereignty is replete with concerns of weaponisation and instrumentalisation of digital technologies by authoritarian governments in Africa. There is an emerging body of evidence that demonstrates some worrying trends of mis-sovereignisation, instrumentalisation, and weaponisation of digital technologies across the content (see Calandro, 2025; Laibuta et al., 2024). To put this into perspective, the rise of digital sovereignty on the continent has been accompanied by an equal and opposite force of digital mis-sovereignisation that is undermining and compromising the freedoms and civil liberties of citizens in countries such as Cameroon, Chad, Egypt, Equatorial Guinea, Ethiopia, Gabon, Sao Tome and Principe, Tanzania, Togo, Uganda, Zambia and Zimbabwe. In these countries, digital technologies are used as tools and mechanisms to surveil, manipulate, censor, and control the populace, thereby undermining the citizens' freedom of expression and other civil liberties as well as fundamental human rights.

It is on the account of these emerging trends that this chapter sets out to unmask the contradictions of digital sovereignty in Africa. It explores the idea of digital sovereignty, while on the other hand, it explores the emerging practices of mis-sovereignisation, instrumentalisation, and weaponisation of digital sovereignty by some African governments. In doing so, the chapter discusses the duality of digital sovereignty, as both a form of resistance to foreign domination as well as a tool for reinforcing and justifying authoritarian governance practices in Africa (Pohle et al., 2024). The questions raised here are: What is digital sovereignty? Which aspects of digital sovereignty matter to African countries? To what extent are citizens' rights to privacy and freedom of expression at risk? And, what version of digital sovereignty is likely to prove beneficial for Africa? The chapter is based on qualitative research methods, including analysis of selected country policies, policy frameworks, policy briefs, and other works published in this field.

After providing a brief contextual overview of the concept of digital sovereignty, the chapter examines the importance of digital sovereignty to Africa's democratic development. It then goes further to address the trends of digital governance in the United States, the European Union, and China. It is these countries that dominate Africa with their global influence and technological power. This analysis is followed by a brief discussion on Africa's own approach to digital governance. The chapter also discusses the abuses of digital sovereignty as well as introduces the notion of digital agency as a potential solution to the problem of weaponisation of digital sovereignty in Africa. The chapter concludes with some remarks on the need for African governments to rethink digital sovereignty.

Contextualising Digital Sovereignty

Since the dawn of Africa's independence in the 1960s, African and Africanist scholars such as Achille Mbembe, Adebayo Adedeji, Adebayo Olukoshi, Amilca Cabral, Amina Mama, Archie Mafeje, Bade Omnimode, Bernard Ngubane, Charles Ubugre, Cheikh Anta Diop, Claude Ake, Dani Nabudare, Demba Dembele, Eshetu Chole, Fanta Cheru, George Nzongola-Ntalaja, Kwesi Prah, Mahmood Mamdani, Pauline Hountondji, Paul TiyambeZeleze, Peter Anyang' Nyong'o, Sabelo Ndlovu-Gatsheni, Sam Moyo, Thandika Mkandawire, Valentine Mudimbe and Walter Rodney (the roll call of the African luminaries is far longer than this) have been questioning the Euro-Western dominance of Africa in terms of finance, trade, investment, culture and knowledge among others (see Moyo, 2021). Today, there is an emerging group of scholars who are particularly concerned about Africa's place in the geo-technological hierarchies of power. These include Kwet (2019), Benyera (2021), and Mejias and Couldry (2024). In particular, these scholars and researchers argue that tech giants collect massive amounts of data about the users of digital platforms without their informed consent. This has some adverse implications on individuals' privacy, freedoms, civil liberties, human rights, national revenues/taxes, cybersecurity, and many more. The example of the Cambridge Analytica scandal in Kenya in 2013 and 2017 quickly comes to mind. The Cambridge Analytica scandal revealed that the political processes are vulnerable to the shenanigans of tech companies (Hendrickson & Galston, 2019).

To explore the emerging practice of digital sovereignty, I begin by deconstructing the concept of digital sovereignty. This concept was first etched in the canons of the Organisation of African Unity (OAU) in 1963. It remains as one of the pillars of the OAU predecessor, the African Union (AU). The concept is reified in Africa because of the continent's long history of external interference through slavery, colonisation, imperialism, neo-imperialism, globalism, and globalisation. Viewed from this background, African governments, scholars, academics, civil society and the general populace are so sensitive to the growing presence of the external actors in the economy, including the tech giants such as Google/Alphabet, Apple, Facebook/Meta, Amazon, Microsoft, Alibaba, Baidu, ByteDance, China Mobile, China Telecom, Hikvision, Huawei, Tencent and ZTE. These tech companies are now organically linked to people's homes, families, work, workouts, leisure, health and education, as well as financial transactions, among others.

Despite its widespread endorsement as an important imperative in digital governance, there is no collective understanding of the concept of digital sovereignty. To be clear, the term digital sovereignty is slippery, fluid, multi-perspectival, polyvalent, and highly contentious. Digital sovereignty also goes by the monikers data sovereignty, internet sovereignty, cyber sovereignty, digital freedom, digital autonomy, technological independence, and technology self-sufficiency. For the present discussion, digital sovereignty is defined as the capacity of the nation-state to exercise control over its digital asserts such as datasets, content, or digital infrastructures in pursuit of its national interests (Edler et al., 2020; Tokat, 2022; Akinyetun, 2023; Calandro, 2025; Venske, 2023; Soulé, 2024). Put differently, digital sovereignty is the capacity of a country to acquire the technologies it considers crucial for its well-being, development, dignity, self-sufficiency, self-management, self-assertion, and self-determination. Nonetheless, this chapter contends that digital sovereignty is a double-edged sword. It is a bulwark against foreign states and tech giants, while at the same time, it gives authoritarian governments the cover to control, manipulate, and repress their citizens, as will be explained anon.

For some decolonial thinkers, digital sovereignty is a concept that is ranged against Africa's digital domination, data colonialism, and digital imperialism. It is an idea that is predicated upon the rejection of external hegemony and the desire to reduce reliance on digital infrastructures and services of foreign providers, predominantly from the transatlantic states as well as from emerging economies, including China and Russia (Akinyetun, 2023). As explained, Africa's digital life is dominated by the Silicon Valley-based and Shenzhen-based tech giants, such as Google, Apple, Facebook/Meta, Amazon and Microsoft, Alibaba, Baidu, ByteDance, China Mobile, China Telecom, Hikvision, Huawei, Tencent, TikTok, and ZTE. Without adequate infrastructure, skills, and capital, African countries find themselves dangerously dependent on tech firms. In particular, these companies own and control digital infrastructures, software, apps, and Artificial Intelligence (AI), and other aspects of the digital ecosystem in Africa. In this way, they have an overwhelmingly disproportionate amount of power, influence, and domination over the global digital ecosystems, let alone African digital environments. As previously mentioned, digital infrastructures, including subsea fibre-optics, data centres, and software applications as well as algorithms, are provided by foreign companies that have their own profit motives, geoeconomic and geopolitical agendas (Okojie, 2023; Gavelle, 2024).

In response, African governments have been canvassing for internet sovereignty by putting in place policies, laws, and regulations for data localisation and construction of digital infrastructures. For example, the governments of Ethiopia, Ghana, Nigeria, Uganda, and South Africa have pursued an aggressive policy of building their own technological infrastructures, data centres, and data regulation policies, among others.

There is no doubt that digital sovereignty offers some benefits to African countries. These range from the possibilities for regulatory independence; preservation of distinctive languages, cultures, and traditions online; protection of privacy and sensitive information; consumer protection; and cyber security. Digital sovereignty also has the potential to stimulate economic growth and innovation by fostering an environment conducive to local start-ups and digital entrepreneurship (Chander & Sun, 2023). Ideally, digital sovereignty is critical to ensure the protection and rights of users, and to guarantee Africa's benefits from the economic and political value-adds of digital transformation. A typical example is that of the European Union, which has been enacting regulations and laws to protect its citizens and local companies from the darker side of digital technologies. Similarly, Africa can use digital sovereignty to enhance the full enjoyment of the fundamental rights to self-determination, and economic, social, and cultural development enshrined in Article 1 of the United Nations Charter, of the International Covenant on Civil and Political Rights, and, of the International Covenant on Economic, Social and Cultural Rights (Belli, 2024). In this way, digital sovereignty is a vital cog in the advancement of national security, crime prevention and investigation, law enforcement, economic stability and well-being, as well as public emergency and safety (Laibuta et al., 2024).

Unfortunately, digital sovereignty has been instrumentalised by some African governments, including those of Cameroon, Chad, Egypt, Equatorial Guinea, Ethiopia, Gabon, Sao Tome and Principe, Tanzania, Togo, Uganda, Zambia and Zimbabwe, to achieve some narrow political objectives of the ruling elite. It will be explained in the rest of this chapter that surveillance technologies such as mobile spyware, internet interception, communication surveillance, biometric ID data gathering, social media monitoring, facial recognition and car number plate identification are often used for mass citizen surveillance that results in harm (Laibuta et al., 2024).

Africa's Approach to Digital Sovereignty

African governments have been actively promoting digital sovereignty through policies and regulations aimed at reducing dependence on foreign technologies and promoting start-ups as well as indigenous innovation. However, several African countries have introduced digital governance frameworks that resemble those of China. To be clear, Beijing has deployed digital tools to enhance its control over its own population, including clamping down on political critics, disseminating propaganda and disinformation, as well as fostering economic exchange without respect for human rights and democratic principles. In this regard, China is accused of fast becoming a digital dictator; exploiting data from Africa for profit and corporate gain (Kumar, 2024). It is also accused ofexporting digital authoritarianism and promoting an illiberal political order in Africa and the rest of the Global South.

Broadly speaking, African countries are keen to govern their own digital spaces. Two major methods appear to be the mainstay of Africa's digital governance system: data localisation and data protection laws. Many African countries are currently pursuing data localisation. This simply means the data that is collected from Africans is increasingly hosted on servers based on the continent. This gives African governments control over critical data and data infrastructure. In other words, this approach prevents data from being accessed by foreigners who may jeopardise the security of the African states. Thus, several African states place the construction of data centres at the heart of their ambition for digital sovereignty. Today, there are approximately 155 data centres across Africa that support the continent's growing digital economy, and there are plans to increase these to around 700 in the next few years. Major data centres' construction projects are currently going on in Benin, Congo, Côted'Ivoire, Ghana, Nigeria, Senegal, South Africa, and Zimbabwe. However, there are concerns about equating data localisation to digital sovereignty in Africa. This is largely because the data centres are constructed with the help of external actors, and the technology used in these centres is controlled and owned by foreigners. In other words, the data centres are geographically located in Africa but epistemically residing in the Silicon Valley and Shenzhen-based tech firms, thereby turning the idea of digital sovereignty into a mockery.

The other road to digital sovereignty is through data protection laws. Some scholars contend that policymakers should regulate the power of tech giants, the use of personal data, fighting the spread of disinformation, and cybercrime, as well as strengthen fiscal oversight (Teevan & Shiferaw, 2022). The tech firms are violating the privacy of users, and cybercrimes have increased exponentially over the past few years in Africa. It is for this reason that data protection regulations have been touted as vital cogs in the internet sovereignty conundrum. However, currently, less than half of the African countries have adopted or drafted cyber security strategies, among them are Kenya (Data Protection Act), Nigeria, Rwanda (Law on Regulating the Protection of Personal Data and Privacy, Law on Regulation of Interception of Communications), South Africa, Tanzania (Personal Data Protection Act), and Uganda (The Regulation of Interception of Communication Act, Data Protection and Privacy Act). This means that nearly half of Africa's countries have no privacy rules (Teleanu & Kurbalija, 2022; Hoskins, 2023). Unfortunately, the said laws only serve to threaten to punish Big Tech companies if they breach data privacy regulations. And the penalty is only a few tens of thousands of dollars (Sheik, 2022). Moreover, the idea for regulation has been used to reaffirm the authority of the African state over its citizens rather than over the foreign tech companies. Most of the laws not only allow surveillance but also compel telecom providers to assist in communication interception, restrict encryption usage, demand the localisation of personal data, and bestow quasi-independent powers on the states and regulatory authorities (Laibuta et al., 2024). The next section takes a deep dive into the question of weaponisation of digital sovereignty in Africa.

Instrumentalisation of Digital Sovereignty

Although governments often call for digital sovereignty as a means to contain the many risks and harms, such as disinformation and cybercrime of the digital ecosystem, practically, digital sovereignty has exacerbated many harms, including centralisation of power, consolidation of authoritarianism, and human rights violations, among others. Digital sovereignty, as advanced by some African governments, is premised on a Westphalian understanding of sovereignty, which locates nation-states as the legitimate organs with legitimate control over digital technologies. Essentially, the argument is that surveillance is instrumental in creating strategies and responses for a state to protect itself from threats, such as internal strife, espionage, cyber-attacks and external threats, generally. African governments also argue that surveillance is essential for law enforcement, crime prevention, border control, and migration. Additionally, surveillance provides information for policy-making processes, especially in areas such as public health, education, transport, and agriculture (Laibuta et al., 2024). Notwithstanding the benefits of surveillance technologies, there is evidence that these same tools, in Africa, have been used against the citizens instead of foreign tech firms. Available evidence indicates that illiberal African states such as Egypt, Sudan, Tanzania, Togo, Uganda, and Zimbabwe have been manipulating digital technologies for their political ends. In some of these countries, journalists, government critics, civil society activists, and political opponents are closely monitored, and civil society space has been constricted.

Under the cover of digital sovereignty, some governments use spyware and or malware to track domestic political opponents with the same vigour as they pursue criminals and terrorists (Allen & Kelly, 2022). Information gathered during surveillance is then used for blackmail, harassment, or targeted arrests and detention, as happened with Bobi Wine, Uganda's presidential candidate in 2018. Thus, instead of protecting their countries from external control and influence, some African governments, including Cote d'Ivoire, Egypt, Eswatini, Kenya, Malawi, Morocco, Rwanda, Tanzania, Togo, Uganda, and Zimbabwe, have used their digital laws to harass and arrest citizens, activists and political opponents (Akinyetun, 2023; Passalacqua & Polito, 2024). At the same time, some of the countries like Tanzania and Togo have enacted regulations that have stifled political debate by enabling the unjustified detention, arrest and intimidation of opposition figures, independent journalists, and political and civil society activists (Allen & Kelly, 2022).

The rise of digital sovereignty has been associated with the rise of technologies of surveillance in Africa. Surveillance technologies, including CCTV, facial recognition technologies, iris scans, fingerprints, vehicle number plate recognition systems, digital ID systems, and DNA data, have been incorporated into the contemporary digital governance architecture in a number of African countries. Some of the countries have used vast amounts of money to acquire these mass surveillance technologies. For example, Nigeria, Ghana, Morocco, Malawi, and Zambia collectively spend over US$1 billion per year on surveillance technologies largely supplied by China, as well as by the United States of America, the United

Kingdom, the European Union and Israel (Roberts, 2023). Another example is that of the city of Kampala in Uganda, which procured surveillance technologies from Huawei worth US$126 million in 2019 (Passalacqua & Polito, 2024). These are massive amounts of public spending in countries where education, health care, and water are underfunded.

In spite of the massive amounts of public funds spent on surveillance technologies, available evidence indicates that Huawei's Safe City and ZTE's Smart City projects have not yet achieved their stated goals in Africa. For example, crime rates have increased in Nairobi and Mombasa in Kenya, and the levels of crime in Johannesburg in South Africa have not been significantly reduced by the installation of surveillance technologies (Passalacqua & Polito, 2024). In fact, many African cities are still far from being free from crime despite the installation of Chinese-sourced surveillance technologies. Ironically, the countries with surveillance systems have seen increased arrests, harassment, and clampdown on political dissent, instead. Precisely, surveillance practices affect individuals' privacy rights, their freedom of expression, freedom of the press, freedom of movement, political rights, right to health, right to education, rights against discrimination, right to dignity, and right to access to information (Laibuta et al., 2024).

What is even more ironic about some African governments is that, in pursuing their digital independence, they tend to become more digitally integrated into foreign firms, especially those from China. It is the Chinese companies, such as Huawei and Tencent, that are providing digital infrastructures, including 5G networks, subsea-fibre cables, data centres, and AI. While these are enabling the continent to delink from the Euro-Western control and influence, the whole approach tends to promote Chinese digital colonialism with its associated challenges of loss of sovereignty and economic dependence. In this sense, Africa is moving from one unhappy relationship to another unhappy relationship.

Towards Digital Agency

The idea of digital agency privileges the rights, priorities, and needs of both the sovereign governments and the individual citizens of the state (Belli, 2024; Kapur, 2024). At its core, the notion of digital agency recognises the role of various stakeholders, including communities, corporations, states, and supra-national bodies and many more, in ensuring digital sovereignty. To this extent, the idea of digital agency retains much of what is appealing about sovereignty, particularly its emphasis on freedom and autonomy, while frowning at the darker side of sovereignty, such as recentralisation tendencies. In short, the idea of digital agency privileges the digital rights, priorities, and needs not of the sovereign governments but also of the communities and individuals they purport to represent (Kapur, 2024).

It is encouraging that some countries are already making considerable progress to adopt citizen-centric cybersecurity policies. For example, South Africa's cybercrimes and personal data protection legislation makes purposeful attempts to establish rights-respecting standards for combating cybercrime. Similarly, civil society organisations in countries like Senegal and Kenya are also putting pressure on their respective governments to have digital governance that is respectful of the citizens' rights. This should be augmented by the enactment of transparency laws that will provide for clear disclosures and better transparency from tech companies and the population. By adopting citizen-centric digital policies, African governments will safeguard democracy, further peace, and rebuild public trust.

For digital sovereignty to be realised in Africa, it must be coordinated at the continental level through the adoption and enforcement of continent-wide regulations. To this extent, the African Union must work towards achieving a pan-African legal framework that will shape digital governance on the continent in accordance with the priorities of the AU Agenda 2063. Frameworks such as the African Union's Digital Transformation Strategy for Africa, the Convention on Cyber Security and Personal Data Protection, and the Malabo Convention, as well as the African Continental Free Trade Area (AfCFTA), represent a step in the right direction. In addition, the African Union needs to prioritise its own funding and capacity building in digital governance and cybersecurity. Currently, African countries depend on capacity building provided by external actors, leading to the lack of a harmonised approach and external dependence.

Overall, there is a compelling case for strengthening the accountability of executive oversight mechanisms, reducing the use of blunt tools of internet shutdowns and restrictions that cut off internet services or deter online speech and communications for large groups of people (Allen & Kelly, 2022). In the net, Africa's attempts to increase digital autonomy must be done in a balanced manner so that the rights of people are not infringed. To do so, African governments must balance the need to curb cybercrime, security, and freedom of their citizens.

Conclusion

It was argued that while digital sovereignty offers greater control over digital infrastructures and datasets, it can also be instrumentalised by those with power and influence who use it as cover for human rights violations and repression. The idea of digital sovereignty has opened the floodgates of surveillance technologies to Africa. As such, state surveillance is now pervasive across Africa, threatening people's fundamental rights and liberties, constitutionalism, the rule of law, and human rights. As such, it is not enough for African governments to invest in data infrastructure, enact data localisation policies, and promote local content creation while using all these against their citizens. The central proposition of this chapter is that African governments must engage in open and transparent dialogues with stakeholders, including civil society, tech companies, and citizens, in order to promote digital technologies for social and economic transformation. Finally, African governments must strive to overcome risks to digital sovereignty if the latter is to genuinely empower nation-states and citizens in this age of digital technologies and AI.

References

Akinyetun, T. S. (2023). *Digital sovereignty in Africa: The albatross of digital transformation and autonomy*.

Allen, N., & Kelly, C. L. (2022). Deluge of digital repression threatens African security. *Africa Centre for Strategic Studies, 4*.

Belli, L. (2024). *Building good digital sovereignty through digital public infrastructures and digital commons in India and Brazil* (SSRN Scholarly Paper No. 4966348). Social Science Research Network. https://doi.org/10.2139/ssrn.4966348

Benyera, E. (2021). *The fourth industrial revolution and the recolonisation of Africa: The Coloniality of data*. Taylor & Francis. https://doi.org/10.4324/9781003157731

Calandro, E. (2025). South African digital sovereignty at the crossroad of securitization and development. In M. Jiang & L. Belli (Eds.), *Digital sovereignty in the BRICS countries* (1st ed., pp. 81–102). Cambridge University Press. https://doi.org/10.1017/9781009531085.006

Chander, A., & Sun, H. (2023). *Digital sovereignty as double-edged sword*. http://hub.hku.hk/handle/10722/325928

Edler, J., Blind, K., Frietsch, R., Kimpeler, S., Kroll, H., Lerch, C., Reiss, T., Roth, F., Schubert, T., Schuler, J., & Walz, R. (2020). *Technology sovereignty: From demand to concept* (research report no. 02/2020). Perspectives—policy brief. https://doi.org/10.24406/publica-fhg-300409

Gavelle, J. (2024). *Challenges and issues of digital sovereignty in West Africa in 2024: From the principle of sovereignty to a strategic, adaptive, and resilient digital autonomy*.

Hendrickson, C., & Galston, W. A. (2019). *Big Tech threats: Making sense of the backlash against online platforms*. https://policycommons.net/artifacts/4141152/big-tech-threats/4950381/

Hoskins. (2023). *Decoding Meta's infrastructural turn in Africa: Access with strings*. Bot Populi. Retrieved April 26, 2025, from https://botpopuli.net/?post_type=post&p=7337

Kapur, A. (2024). *Does BigTech have too much power?* Awyer Monthly. https://www.lawyer-monthly.com/2020/10/does-bigtech-have-too-much-power/

Kumar, S. (2024). China's digital expansionism in Africa and the US counter-strategies. *Insight on Africa, 16*(2), 146–165. https://doi.org/10.1177/09750878231217957

Kwet, M. (2019). Digital colonialism: US empire and the new imperialism in the Global South. *Race & Class, 60*(4), 3–26. https://doi.org/10.1177/0306396818823172

Laibuta, M., Hove, K., Oloyede, R., & Salami, A. (2024). *The state of deployment of surveillance technologies in Africa* (Paradigm Initiative). Retrieved April 25, 2025, from https://paradigmhq.org/report/the-state-of-deployment-of-surveillance-technologies-in-africa/

Mejias, U. A., & Couldry, N. (2024). *Data grab: The new colonialism of big tech and how to fight back*. University of Chicago Press. https://www.degruyterbrill.com/document/doi/10.7208/chicago/9780226832319/html

Moyo, G. (2021). *African Agency, Finance and Developmental States,* Palgrave Macmillan: Switzerland

Okojie, D. (2023, November 16). *From data vulnerability to data sovereignty: Africa's path to digital security, By Dovish Okojie*. Premium Times. https://www.premiumtimesng.com/opinion/643796-from-data-vulnerability-to-data-sovereignty-africas-path-to-digital-security-by-dovish-okojie.html?tztc=1

Passalacqua, C. C., & Polito, C. (2024). *Going beyond the authoritarian bias*.

Pohle, J., Nanni, R., & Santaniello, M. (2024). Unthinking digital sovereignty: A critical reflection on origins, objectives, and practices. *Policy & Internet, 16*(4), 666–671. https://doi.org/10.1002/poi3.437

Roberts, T. (2023, November 1). *Some African governments are spending millions to spy on their citizens—stifling debate and damaging democracy*. The Conversation. http://theconversation.com/some-african-governments-are-spending-millions-to-spy-on-their-citizens-stifling-debate-and-damaging-democracy-215554

Sheik, M. (2022, April 8). *Africa's struggles in regulating Big Tech's data colonialism.* Daily Nation. https://nation.africa/kenya/blogs-opinion/blogs/-africa-s-struggles-in-regulating-big-tech-s-data-colonialism%2D%2D3776636

Soulé, F. (2024). *Digital sovereignty in Africa: Moving beyond local data ownership* (Policy Brief No. 185).

Teevan, C., & Shiferaw, L. T. (2022). *Digital geopolitics in Africa: Moving from strategy to action.* ECDPM. https://ecdpm.org/work/digital-geopolitics-africa-moving-strategy-action

Teleanu, S., & Kurbalija, J. (2022). *Strong digital voices from Africa: African digital foreign policy.* Diplo Foundation. https://www.diplomacy.edu/wp-content/uploads/2023/01/African-digital-foreign-policy_En.pdf

Tokat, Y. (2022, December 1). The Big Tech versus the Nation-States: Clash of economic interests and struggle to compete on a global scale. In *8th international conferences on economics and social sciences, Antalya, Turkiye.* https://www.researchgate.net/

Venske, T. (2023). Navigating digital sovereignty in Africa: A review of key challenges and constraints. *The Africa Governance Papers, 1*(4), Article 4. https://tagp.gga.org/index.php/system/article/view/51

Gorden Moyo (PhD) is currently a Research Fellow at the Fort Hare Institute for Social and Economic Research at the University of Fort Hare in South Africa; Fellow at the University of the Free State in South Africa; Senior Lecturer in the Faculty of Humanities and Social Sciences at Lupane State University in Zimbabwe; Director of the Public Policy and Research Institute of Zimbabwe (PPRIZ); Member of the Editorial Board of the Sabella Abidde Publishing House, University of Alabama (USA); Member of the Board of Trustees of the Mass Public Opinion Institute (MPOI); Associate Member of the International Society for Development and Sustainability (ISDS), Japan; President of the Development Studies Association of Zimbabwe (DeSAZ); Member of the Southern African Development Parliamentary Forum Technical Group on Public Financial Management; ex-Minister of State in the Prime Minister's Office, ex-Minister of State Enterprises and Parastatals, and former Member of Parliament of the Republic of Zimbabwe (2009–2013); and former British Council Facilitator of the Pan-African Leadership Programme in 19 countries across Africa, including Botswana, Cameroon, Eritrea, Ethiopia, eSwatini, Ghana, Kenya, Lesotho, Liberia, Malawi, Mauritius, Namibia, Nigeria, South Africa, Tanzania, Uganda, Zambia, and Zimbabwe. He is a Chevening Scholar whose primary research interests are in global finance, international economic relations, developmental states, public leadership, military commercialism, Africa-China relations, and African agency, among others. He has published several articles in peer-reviewed journals and several book chapters. His most recent books include African Agency, Finance, and Developmental States (Palgrave Macmillan, 2021); Making Politics in Zimbabwe's Second Republic: The Formative Project by Emmerson Mnangagwa (Springer, 2023), co-edited with Prof. Kirk Helliker; Africa in the Global Economy: Capital Outflows, Enablers and Decolonial Responses (Springer, 2024); and Global Storms and Africa in Global Politics: Contemporary Challenges and Decolonial Responses, co-edited with Sabelo J. Ndlovu-Gatsheni (Springer, 2025).

Chapter 10
The Forum on China-Africa Cooperation and Africa's Quest for Digital Transformation

Lucy Anning

Abstract Amid Africa's accelerating push for industrial advancement and digital transformation, the Forum on China-Africa Cooperation (FOCAC) emerges as a pivotal force, driving infrastructure expansion, technological diffusion, and economic integration. Embedded within this cooperation, however, is the strategic deployment of Chinese surveillance technologies, raising urgent questions about digital sovereignty, governance, and dependency. Drawing on qualitative analysis and regional case studies from Western and Southern Africa, the chapter critically unpacks the duality of FOCAC's promise and peril. It advocates for a reimagined African engagement that embraces innovation while safeguarding autonomy against techno-authoritarian entanglements and surveillance-induced vulnerabilities.

Introduction

The Forum on China-Africa Cooperation (FOCAC) has emerged as a defining force in reshaping Africa's industrial and digital landscapes. Since its inception, FOCAC has provided transformative opportunities, propelling large-scale infrastructure projects, manufacturing growth, and digital integration across the continent. However, alongside the promising prospects of these developments lies an underexplored dimension—the rising entanglement of Chinese surveillance technology with Africa's evolving digital frameworks. While FOCAC's financial and technological support has undeniably fuelled Africa's quest for industrial and digital transformation, it has simultaneously sparked intense debates on economic sovereignty, digital autonomy, and governance (Arnold, 2024a, b). As Africa seeks to harness these opportunities, a critical examination of the implications of Chinese surveillance systems is increasingly crucial.

Central to FOCAC's initiatives is industrialisation, a focus that Mamo (2024a, b) identifies as the engine behind many of Africa's development strategies. China has

L. Anning (✉)
Center for Africa-China Studies, University of Johannesburg, Johannesburg, South Africa

G. Moyo (ed.), *An Anatomy of AI Surveillance in Africa*, Studies in Digital Politics and Governance, https://doi.org/10.1007/978-3-032-04269-9_10

invested heavily in manufacturing hubs, industrial parks, and technology transfer mechanisms, which aim to diversify African economies beyond raw commodity exports and spur value-chain development. These investments are vital to Africa's long-term economic resilience, as they offer opportunities to bolster domestic manufacturing and enhance industrial output. However, the sustainability of these advancements hinges on Africa's ability to chart a path of industrial self-sufficiency, free from over-reliance on Chinese capital and strategic interests (Khan et al., 2024). The key question remains: Can Africa manage this industrial revolution without surrendering its autonomy to foreign interests?

Alongside industrial transformation, digital expansion has surfaced as another major pillar of FOCAC's engagement with African states. As noted by Cissé (2023), the integration of ICT infrastructure, digital finance, and e-commerce has played a pivotal role in enabling African economies to leapfrog traditional development stages. The digital revolution has empowered African nations to build resilient economies capable of competing in the global digital arena (Rambe, 2024). Yet, as FOCAC deepens its involvement, an evolving concern emerges: the increasing entrenchment of Chinese surveillance systems within Africa's digital infrastructure. Chinese companies, such as Huawei and ZTE, have become synonymous with the construction of smart cities, the implementation of cybersecurity solutions, and the establishment of digital identity systems across Africa. While these technologies enhance state capacity and promote efficient governance, they also pose a significant risk to civil liberties and digital sovereignty (Jiang, 2024).

The rise of Chinese surveillance technologies in Africa, embedded within these large-scale infrastructure projects, highlights a critical challenge. Many African governments have embraced these innovations without the implementation of stringent data protection frameworks. While these systems are marketed as efficient solutions for urban planning, security, and economic management, they also introduce the possibility of unchecked surveillance. The risk of embedding surveillance mechanisms into Africa's digital infrastructure, without proper regulatory oversight, raises concerns about privacy violations, data harvesting, and the potential for foreign influence over Africa's political and economic decision-making (Bond, 2024). As FOCAC's influence deepens, these concerns become more pronounced, suggesting the need for a comprehensive, strategic response to mitigate the risks of digital dependence.

To navigate this intricate landscape, African policymakers must find a delicate balance between harnessing the opportunities presented by FOCAC and mitigating the risks associated with its growing influence. The over-reliance on Chinese investment not only raises concerns about long-term economic self-sufficiency but also exacerbates vulnerabilities in governance structures. Africa's reliance on Chinese firms in key sectors, including technology, fuels concerns over monopolistic practices and the potential for China to leverage its technological dominance to influence African economies (Ngundu et al., 2024). The unchecked adoption of surveillance technology compounds these risks, creating governance vulnerabilities that could undermine the continent's sovereignty (Chakrabarty, 2024).

This chapter critically examines four key objectives to address these pressing concerns. First, it assesses FOCAC's impact on Africa's industrialisation and economic resilience, evaluating the opportunities and challenges that emerge from large-scale Chinese investments. Second, it explores the role of digital expansion in shaping Africa's innovation ecosystems, with a particular focus on data security, digital governance, and the implications of surveillance technologies. Third, the chapter analyses the economic, policy, and sovereignty challenges arising from FOCAC's involvement, with an emphasis on the implications of Chinese surveillance infrastructure. Finally, the chapter proposes policy recommendations aimed at enhancing Africa's industrial and digital resilience while safeguarding national autonomy.

To achieve these objectives, this study adopts a qualitative research approach, relying on policy analysis to critically assess the interplay between FOCAC's initiatives and the growing integration of Chinese surveillance technologies in Africa. This approach draws on secondary data sources, including government reports, bilateral agreements, and industry assessments, to examine key trends in technology transfer, infrastructure development, and digital investments. Although secondary data inherently has limitations, it provides a rich foundation for understanding the dynamics of FOCAC's role in Africa's transformation (Christodoulou et al., 2024). By synthesising insights from official documents, expert analyses, and case studies, this research seeks to offer a comprehensive understanding of Africa's strategic positioning in the evolving China-Africa partnership. Through this methodological framework, the study will provide an incisive evaluation of the opportunities and risks posed by Chinese involvement in Africa's digital and industrial evolution.

By combining policy analysis with real-world case studies and governance frameworks, this study aims to explore the dual-edged impact of FOCAC on Africa's industrial and digital future. It will also underscore the urgent need for Africa to safeguard its digital sovereignty while leveraging the opportunities presented by FOCAC. Ultimately, Africa stands at a crossroads: it can embrace FOCAC's opportunities while strengthening its governance frameworks to protect against external influence, or it risks entrenching vulnerabilities that could compromise its long-term autonomy in the global digital-industrial order.

South-South Cooperation and Development Partnerships

South-South Cooperation (SSC) has gained significant momentum in the post-colonial era as developing economies seek alternatives to traditional North-South aid dynamics (Kim, 2023). In their study, Tsikudo (2024) highlights that this shift is particularly evident in Africa, where China has emerged as a key partner, facilitating intergovernmental collaboration through mechanisms such as the Forum on China-Africa Cooperation (FOCAC). The evolution of SSC reflects both historical continuities and transformative aspirations within the Global South, offering a unique lens through which to analyse development, governance, and economic partnerships (Xu & Zhan, 2024). Muhr (2023) and Mutambik (2024) further underscore that the theoretical perspectives surrounding SSC provide critical insights into its implications for Africa's development, particularly regarding China's role in industrial and digital transformation.

Historically, SSC emerged from the collective struggle of developing nations against colonialism, imperialism, and systemic global inequalities (Haug & Kamwengo, 2023). During the 1950s and 1960s, newly independent nations sought to assert their autonomy by promoting mutual assistance, solidarity, and collective self-reliance as alternatives to Western-dominated development models (Ness, 2024). While the 1978 United Nations framework formally institutionalised SSC, emphasising non-hierarchical partnerships and equitable exchanges, Banik and Mawdsley (2023) cite that over time, SSC transitioned from its initial anti-imperialist rhetoric to a pragmatic, policy-driven model centred on economic cooperation. This evolution led to a more decentralised and flexible approach, prioritising sovereignty and context-specific development strategies. China's engagement with Africa exemplifies this transformation, as its investments in infrastructure, technology, and industrial capacity have reshaped the continent's development landscape (Mawdsley, 2024).

The dependency theory, articulated by scholars like Prebisch and Andre Frank, as cited in the study of Ahumada and Torres (2024), critiques the structural inequalities in global economic systems, arguing that underdeveloped nations remain trapped in exploitative relationships with advanced economies. SSC is often framed as a mechanism to break free from these cycles of dependency by fostering autonomous development strategies; nevertheless, China's role in Africa presents both opportunities and challenges (Apolinário, 2023).

Beyond the dependency theory, alternative development models advocate for locally tailored strategies rather than Western-centric, market-driven paradigms (Lopes, 2024). … Cheng et al. (2023) demonstrate how SSC provides African nations with a platform to prioritise industrialisation, technological advancement, and infrastructure development based on their unique socio-economic conditions, where China's engagements under FOCAC align with this perspective, allowing African states to pursue customised development paths that challenge traditional donor-driven prescriptions. However, questions persist regarding the sustainability of such partnerships and whether they genuinely empower African economies or reinforce new economic hierarchies (Juhász et al., 2023).

A more contemporary perspective on SSC draws from constructivist international relations theories (Ruffini & Krasnyak, 2023), which argue that state behaviour is shaped not only by material power but also by ideas, identities, and norms. From this viewpoint, SSC is not merely about trade and investment but about constructing new forms of solidarity, trust, and collective aspirations among developing nations. The China-Africa relationship, particularly through FOCAC, reflects this evolving dynamic, where a shared vision of South-South solidarity, mutual respect, and common prosperity is continuously articulated (Braveboy-Wagner, 2024). This constructivist lens, in accordance with the findings of Martel & Glas (2023), underscores the importance of cultural exchanges, diplomatic ties, and leadership narratives in shaping SSC. African policymakers increasingly frame their engagement with China as part of a broader effort to reposition the continent in the global order, moving beyond historical dependencies on Western powers.

The neo-Gramscian perspective offers another dimension, emphasising how power structures and global inequalities are maintained through consent rather than coercion. This theory highlights how dominant global institutions shape development norms, often reinforcing Western hegemony (Taggart & Abraham, 2024). SSC is therefore interpreted as a potential counter-hegemonic force that challenges these entrenched power dynamics. In the contention of Cai (2023), China's rise as a global economic player, particularly through initiatives like the Belt and Road Initiative (BRI), is seen as part of a broader strategy to contest Western dominance in global governance. Conversely, while China presents itself as an alternative development partner, sceptics argue that its approach does not necessarily dismantle existing hierarchies but rather reconfigures them, positioning African nations within a new framework of economic and political influence (Lim & Ikenberry, 2023; Lee et al., 2024).

Amartya Sen's theory of Development as Freedom offers a final perspective, shifting the focus from economic growth to the expansion of human capabilities and freedoms. This approach advocates for development strategies that prioritise education, healthcare, and technological empowerment (Ragkousis, 2024). Confirming from the study of Gasper (2023), within the SSC framework, China's investments in digital infrastructure, vocational training, and healthcare initiatives in Africa align with this vision. However, concerns remain about the long-term social impact of these engagements, particularly in terms of local ownership, capacity building, and equitable distribution of benefits.

Ultimately, SSC embodies a complex and evolving paradigm that blends historical struggles with contemporary aspirations. While its theoretical foundations offer diverse interpretations ranging from dependency theory to constructivism and counter-hegemonic strategies, the practical realities of SSC, particularly China's engagement in Africa, present both opportunities and challenges (Gürcan & Donduran, 2024). The success of these partnerships depends on ensuring that economic collaboration translates into sustainable development, empowering nations in the Global South to chart their own trajectories in the global order.

South-South Cooperation and Chinese Surveillance

The theoretical landscape of South-South Cooperation (SSC) offers a compelling framework for decoding the complexities of China-Africa engagements, particularly as surveillance technologies quietly reshape the continent's digital and governance architecture. In the context of the Forum on China-Africa Cooperation (FOCAC), theoretical debates move beyond abstract development paradigms to confront real and urgent issues; chief among them is the subtle consolidation of Chinese digital surveillance within Africa's industrial and digital transformation.

Dependency theory remains especially illuminating in this regard. It cautions that while SSC ostensibly promotes mutual development, it may replicate new forms of subjugation under the guise of cooperation. As China funds Africa's smart cities, builds digital ID systems, and installs surveillance-enabled infrastructure, African nations risk becoming digitally tethered to Chinese state interests (Benabdallah, 2024). This concern finds resonance in neo-Gramscian thought, which interprets FOCAC not merely as a development forum but as a site of hegemonic realignment, where China replaces Western control through technologically mediated influence (Iwata, 2025).

Nevertheless, the constructivist theory injects nuance into this narrative. By emphasising the power of discourse, identity, and normative alignment, constructivism views FOCAC's "win-win cooperation" and the language of "digital solidarity" as tools for constructing consent (Sinha, 2023). While such narratives grant Africa a seat at the digital table, they also risk concealing asymmetries, particularly when Chinese firms dominate the architecture of surveillance systems with limited transparency or accountability.

Moreover, alternative development theory offers a grounded counterweight, advocating for endogenous, community-driven growth strategies that resist externally imposed models. If African nations centre surveillance governance within locally crafted data protection laws and democratic oversight, they can reclaim agency over how digital systems serve, not surveil their citizens (Haug & Kamwengo, 2023). This aligns with Sen's *Development as Freedom*, which argues that any form of technological progress must expand, not restrict, individual liberties and human capabilities.

Taken together, these perspectives crystallise a deeper truth exhibiting that the presence of Chinese surveillance in Africa's digital transformation is not an inevitability—it is a policy choice. FOCAC's frameworks, while rich in opportunity, also embody ideological, technological, and geopolitical power plays. The task before African leaders is not to reject SSC, but to negotiate its contours, ensuring that industrial innovation and digital expansion empower rather than encroach. Only then can Africa wield SSC as a tool for sovereign transformation rather than a Trojan horse for digital dependence (Huang et al., 2023; Suleiman & Slighoua, 2024).

FOCAC's Expanding Orbit in Africa's Digital Ascent and Surveillance Alignment

FOCAC has rapidly evolved into a commanding engine of Africa's industrial and digital transformation. As Bond (2024) argues, this platform now shapes the contours of Africa's development trajectory, offering not just economic aid but a blueprint for structural advancement. Since 2000, FOCAC has transitioned from diplomatic overtures to a robust, strategic framework that enables large-scale investment in infrastructure, manufacturing, and digital economies (Li & Lu, 2024). Unlike traditional aid models that have historically entangled African nations in conditionalities, FOCAC promotes development pathways rooted in mutual interest, national sovereignty, and industrial self-strengthening (Sieren, 2023).

Indeed, industrialisation remains the fulcrum of Africa's transformation dreams. Yet, chronic deficits in infrastructure, finance, and technology continue to impede progress (Zajontz et al., 2024). To bridge these gaps, FOCAC has spearheaded targeted investments in power grids, rail networks, industrial parks, and Special Economic Zones. Under the China-Africa Industrial Capacity Cooperation framework, countries like Ethiopia, Nigeria, and Egypt have witnessed the rise of new manufacturing hubs, driving value addition, regional trade integration, and employment growth (Chakrabarty, 2024). However, these gains are not without challenges. Concerns linger around the sustainability of debt-financed infrastructure, environmental degradation, and the limited participation of local firms in value chains.

Simultaneously, FOCAC has emerged as a catalyst for Africa's digital renaissance. As the world pivots toward a knowledge-based economy, digital connectivity has become the currency of future relevance (Lendzoumbou, 2024). FOCAC has responded with vigour, propelling the continent's digital inclusion agenda through strategic partnerships in fintech, e-commerce, telecommunications, and AI (Raza & Khan, 2024a, b). Chinese tech titans like Huawei and ZTE now anchor Africa's digital infrastructure, installing data centres, undersea cables, and smart city grids across key urban corridors (Zreik, 2025). These investments have widened internet access, fuelled e-governance, and unlocked new markets for innovation.

Moreover, FOCAC's influence extends into Africa's mobile technology and financial ecosystems. Chinese-backed improvements in digital infrastructure have directly boosted mobile banking platforms like M-Pesa in Kenya and expanded Nigeria's fintech base (Arnold, 2024a, b). African e-commerce leaders, such as Jumia, now benefit from China's logistical expertise and digital trade integration. Nevertheless, this technological leap comes with new vulnerabilities. Data sovereignty, digital dependency, and the covert expansion of China's surveillance tools remain underexamined concerns (Wang et al., 2024). Through smart city installations and AI-enhanced surveillance networks, Chinese technologies blur the line between digital progress and authoritarian potential. Crucially, FOCAC's structure allows African states a degree of policy latitude rarely afforded by Western-led institutions. As Zajontz et al. (2024) observes, FOCAC's preference for non-interference and bilateral tailoring gives governments flexibility in aligning projects with national development plans. Still, this flexibility comes with asymmetry. China retains disproportionate leverage in terms of capital, technology, and strategic agenda-setting (Johnston, 2025).

As Africa stands at the crossroads of industrial rejuvenation and digital revolution, FOCAC's role is undeniably transformative. Yet, to ensure this transformation translates into long-term sovereignty and sustainability, African states must craft strategies that prioritise local innovation, regulatory transparency, and balanced partnerships. The promise of FOCAC lies not merely in infrastructure or digital hardware but in empowering Africa to shape its own future—one that is connected, industrialised, but also self-determined (Cheng et al., 2023; Roccon, 2024).

Recasting Economic Dependency and Surveillance in China-Africa Relations

The longstanding debates surrounding the economic merits and dependency risks in China-Africa relations have taken on a new and urgent dimension with the growing integration of Chinese surveillance technologies into Africa's digital and governance landscapes. While traditional critiques have centred on debt traps, extractive trade patterns, and economic sovereignty, a more contemporary threat is emerging—China's digital footprint, often disguised as development aid, is embedding surveillance capabilities that subtly extend geopolitical influence across the continent (Hönke & Yang, 2024).

Indeed, the Forum on China-Africa Cooperation (FOCAC) has catalysed large-scale infrastructure and digital connectivity projects, positioning China as Africa's dominant partner in industrialisation and technological modernisation (Obeng-Odoom, 2024). Yet, behind the allure of new highways and fibre-optic cables lies a sophisticated network of surveillance infrastructures, including facial recognition cameras, biometric ID systems, and cybersecurity architecture, which is mostly supplied by Chinese firms such as Huawei, ZTE, and Hikvision (Gilpin, 2023). These systems, while ostensibly designed to enhance state capacity and urban management, also carry the latent potential for digital authoritarianism, data harvesting, and foreign control over sovereign digital spaces.

Proponents of China-Africa economic cooperation often cite China's responsiveness to Africa's development priorities, particularly in filling investment voids left by Western actors (Lippolis & Verhoeven, 2022). However, this development model, couched in the rhetoric of "win-win partnerships," fails to critically account for the opaque terms tied to technology transfer and surveillance infrastructure deployment. Surveillance capabilities, once installed, are rarely neutral. They can entrench authoritarian governance, curtail civic freedoms, and grant external actors privileged access to sensitive data, raising alarm bells over digital sovereignty (Bagwandeen et al., 2023).

Moreover, as China bankrolls digital ecosystems through concessional loans and soft credit lines, African states risk locking themselves into a techno-economic dependency that extends beyond debt burdens. The issue is no longer just about defaulting on infrastructure loans—as seen in Kenya and Zambia—but also about forfeiting long-term control over national data infrastructures and decision-making algorithms (Hameiri & Jones, 2024). Surveillance tech, unlike roads or dams, embeds itself in the cognitive and operational layers of governance, shaping how governments manage dissent, elections, and information.

Additionally, Africa's continued reliance on China for ICT development perpetuates a skewed model of digital modernisation—one that favours rapid adoption over sustainable innovation. Instead of fostering homegrown tech ecosystems, this model risks cultivating digital dependency, wherein critical platforms and cybersecurity systems are outsourced to Chinese firms with unclear data ownership arrangements (Hairong & Sautman, 2023). This model could inhibit Africa's aspirations for digital self-determination and pose long-term barriers to industrial upgrading.

Essentially, the economic debates on dependency and benefits in China-Africa relations are inseparable from the evolving landscape of Chinese surveillance. What appears to be economic aid often doubles as strategic digital positioning. Therefore, Africa's challenge is to harness the transformative promise of FOCAC while rigorously safeguarding its digital and industrial autonomy. This requires not only debt transparency and fairer investment terms but also the development of robust digital governance frameworks that protect national data integrity, human rights, and democratic resilience (Hönke & Yang, 2024; Gilpin, 2023). The Forum on China-Africa Cooperation has become a pivotal driver of Africa's industrial and digital transformation, fostering infrastructure development, manufacturing expansion, and technological innovation (Li & Lu, 2024). While these initiatives present vast opportunities for economic resilience and strategic growth, they also raise critical questions about sustainability, governance, and technology sovereignty. Table 10.1 provides a structured analysis of key variables, highlighting positive developments, emerging opportunities, and relevant sources shaping China-Africa cooperation.

Table 10.1 Analysis of key variables under FOCAC initiatives across Africa

Key variable under FOCAC initiative	Positive developments	Opportunities	Sources
Industrial transformation Infrastructure development, manufacturing, and technology transfer	(i) Massive investment in roads, railways, and energy projects, improving regional connectivity (ii) Establishment of special economic zones fostering industrialisation (iii) Increased manufacturing capacity through joint ventures and Chinese-built factories	(i) Expansion of Africa's industrial base for global competitiveness (ii) Enhanced skills development and knowledge transfer (iii) Strengthened regional value chains for economic diversification	Mamo (2024a, b) and Bond (2024)
Digital expansion investments in ICT, digital finance, and smart cities across African economies	(i) Rapid growth of mobile banking and fintech solutions (ii) Development of smart city projects integrating AI and big data (iii) Expansion of fibre-optic networks and 5G infrastructure	(i) Strengthened digital economies driving financial inclusion (ii) AI-driven governance and smart infrastructure (iii) Creation of digital entrepreneurs,hip ecosystems	Oloyede et al. (2023) and Agaba et al. (2024)

(continued)

Table 10.1 (continued)

Key variable under FOCAC initiative	Positive developments	Opportunities	Sources
Economic and policy challenges sustainability, technology sovereignty, and governance in China-Africa cooperation	(i) Rising concerns over debt sustainability and economic dependency (ii) Limited local participation in high-tech industries (iii) Geopolitical risks related to data security and surveillance	(i) Strengthening governance frameworks for transparent partnerships (ii) Enhancing local capacity to manage infrastructure and digital investments (iii) Balancing foreign investment with domestic innovation	Nwankwo and Okoye (2023)
Opportunities for strategic growth policy recommendations for enhancing industrial and digital resilience	(i) Strengthening local manufacturing and value addition (ii) Establishing regulatory frameworks for digital sovereignty (iii) Promoting Africa-led innovations in industrial and digital transformation	(i) Expanding South-South cooperation beyond China (ii) Leveraging AI and emerging technologies for Africa's development (iii) Deepening FOCAC engagements with a focus on knowledge-based economies	Carver (2023)

Source: Author's Own Construct, 2025

FOCAC initiatives, as exhibited in Table 10.1, undoubtedly have significantly reshaped Africa's industrial and digital landscape (Cheng et al., 2023). In Ethiopia, Chinese investments in the Hawassa Industrial Park have boosted manufacturing and job creation. Kenya's Standard Gauge Railway has enhanced regional trade, while Nigeria's Lekki Free Trade Zone is attracting global investors (Lammich, 2023). In the digital sphere, Huawei's ICT expansion in South Africa and fintech advancements in Ghana showcase Africa's digital leap. However, sustainability concerns persist, requiring stronger governance and technology sovereignty. Strategic policy frameworks can maximise benefits, ensuring long-term resilience. By aligning FOCAC projects with national priorities, Africa can harness industrial transformation and digital innovation for inclusive growth.

Implications of Surveillance on Africa's Digital Sovereignty

The Forum on China-Africa Cooperation (FOCAC) has emerged as a formidable engine powering Africa's industrialisation and digital transformation. Central to this evolution is China's substantial investment in infrastructure, manufacturing zones, and digital platforms—tools heralded for enabling Africa's leap into the global industrial economy (Raza & Khan, 2024a, b). However, interwoven into this narrative of advancement is an increasingly urgent issue: the permeation of Chinese surveillance technology into Africa's critical digital systems. This phenomenon, though often underexplored, carries profound implications for the continent's industrial sovereignty and digital independence.

Through flagship initiatives such as smart city construction, e-governance frameworks, and national digital identity systems, Chinese tech giants like Huawei, ZTE, Dahua, and Hikvision have become embedded in the continent's digital DNA (Zreik, 2025). These technologies, while efficient in delivering urban safety, biometric verification, and real-time analytics, also introduce latent surveillance capabilities that can be weaponised to curtail civil liberties and influence governance patterns (Lendzoumbou, 2024). The very systems enabling African states to modernise their administrative and industrial functions are the same platforms that could potentially compromise their autonomy.

The industrial impact of this digital entanglement is multifaceted. On one hand, FOCAC's framework has spurred the creation of industrial parks, manufacturing corridors, and logistics hubs—all of which benefit from integrated ICT systems powered by Chinese technologies (Mamo, 2024a, b). On the other hand, the technological backbone of these projects often relies on proprietary Chinese infrastructure, resulting in a form of digital dependency that limits Africa's control over its industrial data flows and critical infrastructure (Wang et al., 2024). This digital reliance places African economies at a geopolitical crossroads, where industrial growth is paradoxically accompanied by the erosion of strategic autonomy.

Moreover, the data sovereignty dilemma looms large. The proliferation of Chinese surveillance technologies under FOCAC threatens to centralise data ownership in foreign hands, raising critical concerns about data harvesting, political manipulation, and algorithmic governance (Chakrabarty, 2024). In an era where data is the currency of innovation, such external control undermines Africa's potential to drive its own industrial revolution through indigenous knowledge systems, local innovation, and context-sensitive policy-making.

In response, Africa must adopt a forward-looking, self-defensive stance. Regulatory harmonisation across African Union member states, informed by comprehensive data protection laws, is vital to ensuring that digital infrastructure—no matter its origin—serves national interests first. Diversifying technological partnerships to reduce overdependence on a single actor, and enhancing the capacity of local engineers and regulators to audit foreign technologies are strategic imperatives (Johnston, 2025).

Ultimately, the intersection of surveillance and development in FOCAC presents Africa with a defining challenge: how to capitalise on industrial and digital progress without surrendering control over the tools that enable it. As Roccon (2024) cautions, technological modernity must not come at the expense of sovereign governance. Africa's industrial ascent can be sustained only if digital sovereignty is prioritised as a pillar of long-term resilience. Through a deliberate, strategic recalibration of its engagement with FOCAC, Africa can move from being a passive consumer of surveillance-laden technologies to an assertive architect of its own digital-industrial destiny.

Conclusion

FOCAC has undeniably redefined Africa's industrial and digital trajectory, ushering in a new era of accelerated infrastructure development, technological modernisation, and economic interconnectedness. Yet, interwoven with these advancements is an evolving paradox, thus the rise of Chinese surveillance technology that quietly embeds itself into Africa's digital backbone. While smart cities, AI-driven public systems, and digital financial platforms symbolise progress and modernity, they also quietly introduce layers of opacity, control, and vulnerability. The reliance on Chinese-built surveillance infrastructure, often embraced under the guise of efficiency and cost-effectiveness, risks compromising Africa's digital sovereignty, exposing national data to external scrutiny and geopolitical manipulation. As Africa stands on the cusp of the Fourth Industrial Revolution, it must not only embrace innovation but also confront the hidden intricacies of technological dependence. Therefore, the path forward demands a strategic recalibration, one where technological partnerships are pursued, not as ends in themselves, but as instruments of empowerment crafted on Africa's terms. This necessitates the development of robust regulatory frameworks that fortify cybersecurity, protect personal data, and uphold civil liberties, even as digital transformation unfolds at an unprecedented pace. Moreover, Africa must diversify its technological partnerships, invest in indigenous innovation, and enhance local capacity to govern critical digital infrastructure. The continent must reclaim agency over its digital future by building systems that reflect its values, priorities, and aspirations. The focus must shift from merely attracting foreign capital to cultivating homegrown digital ecosystems anchored in transparency, resilience, and ethical governance. In doing so, Africa can transform FOCAC from a platform of transactional dependence into a vehicle of transformative sovereignty. Ultimately, the goal is not to reject external influence but to manage it with wisdom and foresight, ensuring that every fibre of Africa's digital-industrial evolution is woven with autonomy, security, and vision. The future of the continent cannot be dictated by silent surveillance embedded within foreign frameworks; instead, it must be authored by Africa itself—boldly, securely, and uncompromisingly grounded in a future it designs, owns, and protects.

References

Agaba, H., Umeh, C. B., & Osuji, O. (2024). Assessing the gains and challenges of Nigeria's participation in the Forum On China-Africa Cooperation (FOCAC). *Global Journal of Political Science and Administration, 12*(1), 14–27.

Ahumada, J. M., & Torres, M. (2024). Dependency theory. In S. S. Jodhka & B. Rehbein (Eds.), *Global handbook of inequality* (pp. 227–247). Springer Nature. https://doi.org/10.1007/978-3-031-32152-8_80

Apolinário, L. (2023). Punctuated equilibrium in the regime complex of international development cooperation. *Contexto Internacional, 45*, e20210066. https://doi.org/10.1590/S0102-8529.20234501e20210066

Arnold, S. (2024a). African agency in ICT infrastructure provider choice: Navigating access to foreign finance and technology. *Telecommunications Policy, 48*(5), 102713. https://doi.org/10.1016/j.telpol.2024.102713

Arnold, S. (2024b). Africa's roads to digital development: Paving the way for Chinese structural power in the ICT sector? *Review of International Political Economy, 31*(4), 1148–1172. https://doi.org/10.1080/09692290.2023.2297363

Bagwandeen, M., Edyegu, C., & Otele, O. M. (2023). African agency, COVID-19 and debt renegotiations with China. *South African Journal of International Affairs, 30*(1), 1–27. https://doi.org/10.1080/10220461.2023.2180083

Banik, D., & Mawdsley, E. (2023). South–South Cooperation and global development in a multipolar world: China and India in Africa. *Journal of International Development, 35*(4), 539–548. https://doi.org/10.1002/jid.3789

Benabdallah, L. (2024). Africa–Asia: A tale of worldmaking between alterity and contestation. *African Affairs, 123*(491), 223–241. https://doi.org/10.1093/afraf/adae006

Bond, P. (2024, September 22). *Forum on China-Africa Cooperation evades contradictions at the end of the Belt and Road: Chinese investment, finance and trade controversies in Southern Africa*. CADTM. https://www.cadtm.org/Forum-on-China-Africa-Cooperation-evades-contradictions-at-the-end-of-the-Belt

Braveboy-Wagner, J. A. (2024). Incorporating global south perspectives in the study of international relations: Reflections on the field. *Polity, 56*(3), 456–471. https://doi.org/10.1086/730554

Cai, K. G. (2023). China's initiatives: A bypassing strategy for the reform of global economic governance. *Chinese Political Science Review, 8*(1), 1–17. https://doi.org/10.1007/s41111-022-00215-7

Carver, J. (2023). Developing digital "peripheries" for strategic advantage: Capacity building assistance and strategic competition in Africa. Contemporary Security Policy, 0(0), 1–42. https://doi.org/10.1080/13523260.2024.2430021.

Chakrabarty, M. (2024). China-Africa partnership: Implications for African development. In S. Damodaran & J. Ghosh (Eds.), *Development, transformations and the human condition: Essays in Honour of Jayati Ghosh*. Routledge. https://doi.org/10.4324/9781003528425

Cheng, H., Mawdsley, E., & Liu, W. (2023). Reading the Forum on China–Africa Cooperation (2000–2021): Geoeconomics, governance, and embedding 'creative involvement.' Area Development and Policy, 8(1), 60–83. https://doi.org/10.1080/23792949.2022.2092018.

Christodoulou, I., Rizomyliotis, I., Konstantoulaki, K., Nazarian, A., & Binh, D. (2024). Transforming the remittance industry: Harnessing the power of blockchain technology. *Journal of Enterprise Information Management, 37*(5), 1551–1577. https://doi.org/10.1108/JEIM-03-2023-0112

Cissé, D. (2023). Partnership for the Development of Africa's telecommunications sector under agenda 2063: African and Chinese telecommunications companies in Africa. In B. Ndzendze & D. Monyae (Eds.), *Perspectives on Africa-China infrastructural and industrial cooperation: Empirical findings and conceptual implications* (pp. 73–97). Springer. https://doi.org/10.1007/978-3-031-38395-3_5

Gasper, D. (2023). Amartya Sen as a social and political theorist—On personhood, democracy, and 'description as choice'. *Journal of Global Ethics, 19*(3), 386–409. https://doi.org/10.1080/17449626.2023.2255600

Gilpin, S. I. (2023). China, Africa and the international aid system: A challenge to (the norms underpinning) the neoliberal world order? *Journal of Asian and African Studies, 58*(3), 277–297. https://doi.org/10.1177/00219096211063804

Gürcan, E. C., & Donduran, C. (2024). *China on the rise: The transformation of structural power in the era of multipolarity*. Taylor & Francis.

Hairong, Y., & Sautman, B. (2023). China, colonialism, neocolonialism and globalised modes of accumulation. *Area Development and Policy, 8*(4), 416–449. https://doi.org/10.1080/23792949.2023.2259459

Hameiri, S., & Jones, L. (2024). China, international competition and the stalemate in sovereign debt restructuring: Beyond geopolitics. *International Affairs, 100*(2), 691–710. https://doi.org/10.1093/ia/iiae017

Haug, S., & Kamwengo, C. M. (2023). Africa beyond 'South-South cooperation': A frame with limited resonance. *Journal of International Development, 35*(4), 549–565. https://doi.org/10.1002/jid.3690

Hönke, J., & Yang, Y. (2024). Liminally positioned in/towards the South: Chinese relations with Africa. In U. Fendler & Y. Chang (Eds.), *Asia-Africa- multifaceted engagement in the contemporary world* (pp. 103–126). Springer Nature. https://doi.org/10.1007/978-981-97-0696-9_6

Huang, A., Cao, C., Xiao, A. Y., Karemere, H., Christian, M. E., Nicolas, K. K., Xue, M., & Tang, K. (2023). Opportunities and challenges of trilateral South–South cooperation for transforming development assistance for health: Evidence from a DRC–UNICEF–China maternal, newborn, and child health project. *Globalization and Health, 19*(1), 37. https://doi.org/10.1186/s12992-023-00934-9

Iwata, T. (2025). *Power and politics in Africa: A boundary generator*. Vernon Press.

Jiang, M. (2024). Models of state digital sovereignty from the global south: Diverging experiences from China, India and South Africa. *Policy & Internet, 16*(4), 727–738. https://doi.org/10.1002/poi3.427

Johnston, L. A. (2025). *The "Hunan Model": From "African Shenzhen" to China's "Africa Shenzhen"* (SSRN scholarly paper no. 5083760). Social Science Research Network. https://doi.org/10.2139/ssrn.5083760

Juhász, R., Lane, N., & Rodrik, D. (2023). *The new economics of industrial policy*.

Khan, A., Congmei, S., & Ali, F. (2024). Assessing xi Jinping's vision of modernization and its implications for global trade dynamics: A case study of the belt and road initiative. *Pakistan Journal of Humanities and Social Sciences, 12*(1), Article 1. https://doi.org/10.52131/pjhss.2024.v12i1.1962

Kim, S. (2023). Making a case for postcolonial thinking in international development studies: Towards a more critical and self-reflexive field. *国際開発研究, 31*(3), 83–103. https://doi.org/10.32204/jids.31.3_83

Lammich, G. (2023). *Development first! China's policy transfer to Africa*. https://doi.org/10.1163/1821889x-bja10089

Lee, B. T. F., Bettani, S. A., & Sims, J. P. (2024). Rise of China: Hegemony or harmony? *Chinese Political Science Review, 9*(3), 381–417. https://doi.org/10.1007/s41111-024-00253-3

Lendzoumbou, I. B. (2024). China's enduring and expanding influence: The quest for centrality in sub-Saharan Africa political economy. *The Strategic Review for Southern Africa, 46*(1 and 2), Article 1 and 2. https://doi.org/10.35293/srsa.v46i1.5314

Li, W., & Lu, S. (2024). Assessing structural transformation and the potential impacts of belt and road initiative projects in Africa. *The European Journal of Development Research, 36*(3), 548–570. https://doi.org/10.1057/s41287-024-00624-1

Lim, D. J., & Ikenberry, G. J. (2023). China and the logic of illiberal hegemony. *Security Studies, 32*(1), 1–31. https://doi.org/10.1080/09636412.2023.2178963

Lippolis, N., & Verhoeven, H. (2022). Politics by default: China and the global governance of African debt. *Survival, 64*(3), 153–178. https://doi.org/10.1080/00396338.2022.2078054

Lopes, C. (2024). *The self-deception trap: Exploring the economic dimensions of charity dependency within Africa-Europe relations*. Springer Nature. https://doi.org/10.1007/978-3-031-57591-4

Mamo, A. (2024a). A comparative perspective of the Chinese FDI in African manufacturing. In A. Mamo (Ed.), *The political economy of Chinese FDI in Africa* (pp. 239–269). Springer Nature. https://doi.org/10.1007/978-3-031-74877-6_6

Mamo, A. (2024b). Dynamics and evolution of China—Africa economic ties. In A. Mamo (Ed.), *The political economy of Chinese FDI in Africa* (pp. 87–139). Springer Nature. https://doi.org/10.1007/978-3-031-74877-6_3

Martel, S., & Glas, A. (2023). The contested meaning-making of diplomatic norms: Competence in practice in Southeast Asian multilateralism. *European Journal of International Relations, 29*(1), 227–252. https://doi.org/10.1177/13540661221133194

Mawdsley, E. (2024). South-South cooperation and decoloniality. In H. Melber, U. Kothari, L. Camfield, & K. Biekart (Eds.), *Challenging global development* (pp. 205–214). Springer Nature. https://doi.org/10.1007/978-3-031-30308-1_11

Muhr, T. (2023). Reclaiming the politics of South-South cooperation. *Globalizations, 20*(3), 347–364. https://doi.org/10.1080/14747731.2022.2082132

Mutambik, I. (2024). Unlocking the potential of sustainable smart cities: Barriers and strategies. *Sustainability, 16*(12), Article 12. https://doi.org/10.3390/su16125061

Ness, I. (2024). Western Marxism, anti-communism and imperialism. *International Critical Thought, 14*(4), 493–518. https://doi.org/10.1080/21598282.2024.2431960

Ngundu, M., Zerihun, M. F., & Nyathi, M. C. (2024). Comparing the effectiveness of the African Growth and Opportunity Act (AGOA) and Forum on China-Africa Cooperation (FOCAC) in South Africa: An application of Keynes' Macroeconomic Theory. *Asia and the Global Economy, 4*(2), 100081. https://doi.org/10.1016/j.aglobe.2024.100081

Nwankwo, O. B. C., & Okoye, U. O. (2023). Forum on China-Africa Cooperation (FOCAC) and socio-economic development of Nigeria. *Nnamdi Azikiwe Journal of Political Science, 8*(1), Article 1.

Obeng-Odoom, F. (2024). China–Africa relations in the Economist, 2019–2021. *Journal of Asian and African Studies, 59*(3), 1000–1017. https://doi.org/10.1177/00219096221125423

Oloyede, A. A., Faruk, N., Noma, N., Tebepah, E., & Nwaulune, A. K. (2023). Measuring the impact of the digital economy in developing countries: A systematic review and meta- analysis. *Heliyon, 9*(7), e17654. https://doi.org/10.1016/j.heliyon.2023.e17654

Ragkousis, A. (2024). Amartya Sen as a neoclassical economist. *Journal of Economic Issues, 58*(1), 24–58. https://doi.org/10.1080/00213624.2024.2307785

Rambe, P. (2024). Digital entrepreneurship in Africa: New frontiers, prospects, opportunities and challenges for small digital enterprises. In P. Rambe & R. E. Hinson (Eds.), *The future of entrepreneurship in southern Africa* (pp. 59–96). Springer Nature. https://doi.org/10.1007/978-3-031-55935-8_3

Raza, M. A., & Khan, A. B. (2024a). A glimpse of China-African union economic relations during 21st century. *Journal of Development and Social Sciences, 5*(3), Article 3. https://doi.org/10.47205/jdss.2024(5-III)18

Raza, M. A., & Khan, A. B. (2024b). Socio-economic development through regional organizations: A study of the implementation of agenda 2063 by the African Union (AU) in collaboration with China. *Annals of Human and Social Sciences, 5*(3), Article 3. https://doi.org/10.35484/ahss.2024(5-III)33

Roccon, M. (2024). *Foreign investment in China's cloud industry: A case study of Microsoft Azure's expansion*. https://unitesi.unive.it/handle/20.500.14247/16325

Ruffini, P.-B., & Krasnyak, O. (2023). Science diplomacy from a nation-state's perspective: A general framing and its application to Global South countries. *Science and Public Policy, 50*(4), 771–781. https://doi.org/10.1093/scipol/scad023

Sieren, A. (2023). China's role in Africa. In T. Schmidt, K. Pfaffenberger, & S. Liebing (Eds.), *Practical handbook business in Africa* (pp. 279–290). Springer Fachmedien. https://doi.org/10.1007/978-3-658-42518-0_24

Sinha, S. (2023). Addressing global challenges through South-South cooperation and science diplomacy. In *Global science's cooperation opportunities, challenges, and good practices* (pp. 1–27). IGI Global Scientific Publishing. https://doi.org/10.4018/978-1-6684-7874-5.ch001

Suleiman, M. R., & Slighoua, M. (2024). Culture as a dimension of interweaving reinvented South-South Partnership in Africa. *African Renaissance, 21*(2), 505–524. https://doi.org/10.31920/2516-5305/2024/21n2a25

Taggart, J., & Abraham, K. J. (2024). Norm dynamics in a post-hegemonic world: Multistakeholder global governance and the end of liberal international order. *Review of International Political Economy, 31*(1), 354–381. https://doi.org/10.1080/09692290.2023.2213441

Tsikudo, K. A. (2024). Different approach, same focus: How China is shaping the future of its African cooperation through education. *Human Geography, 17*(1), 88–94. https://doi.org/10.1177/19427786231173626

Wang, S., Li, Q., & Khaskheli, M. B. (2024). Management economic systems and governance to reduce potential risks in Digital Silk Road investments: Legal cooperation between Hainan Free Trade Port and Ethiopia. *Systems, 12*(8), 305. https://doi.org/10.3390/systems12080305. Retrieved April 25, 2025, from https://www.mdpi.com/2079-8954/12/8/305

Woldearegay, T. (2024). An offensive realism approach to navigate the changing dynamics of summit-level dialogue between the AU and great powers. *Cogent Social Sciences, 10*(1), 2306706. https://doi.org/10.1080/23311886.2024.2306706

Xu, L., & Zhan, G. (2024). Social self-criticism and the shaping of Chinese National Identity. *Journal of the Knowledge Economy*. https://doi.org/10.1007/s13132-024-02122-5

Zajontz, T., Carmody, P. R., Bagwandeen, M., & Leysens, A. (Eds.). (2024). *Africa's railway renaissance: The role and impact of China*. Routledge, Taylor & Francis Group.

Zreik, M. (2025). China's digital silk road and its implications for Africa's digital transformation. In *Impact of digitalization on communication dynamics* (pp. 277–298). IGI Global Scientific Publishing. https://doi.org/10.4018/979-8-3693-3579-6.ch011

Lucy Anning (PhD) is a distinguished industrial economist, SME development strategist, and researcher whose multifaceted expertise shapes China-Africa relations. With 2 years of service under Ghana's Ministry of Finance, she now serves at the Centre for Africa-China Studies, University of Johannesburg, and as Chief Economist for the Pan African Chamber of Commerce in South Africa, representing the chamber at the AfCFTA Secretariat in Ghana. Recently appointed Southern Africa Coordinator for OSAESSDA, her roles emphasise economic, social, and cultural synergies across the continent. As the current Director of DevAfrica Institute, she bridges academic and practical domains, furthering her research with the University of Electronic Science and Technology of China. Dr. Anning, an award-winning leader in research and development in Africa, holds advanced degrees in industrial economics, quantitative economics, and economics with mathematics. Her dedication to fostering academic and diplomatic exchanges underscores her pivotal role in advancing China-Africa collaboration.

Chapter 11
US-China Digital Competition in Africa: The Perspectives of IR Theories

John H. S. Åberg

Abstract This chapter shows the value of international relations (IR) theory in analysing the intensifying digital competition between the United States and China on the African continent. This chapter advocates for a pluralistic approach that draws on realism, constructivism, world-systems analysis, and postcolonialism. Each theoretical lens offers a distinct analytical perspective, revealing different dimensions of the geopolitical, economic, and normative dynamics at play. Rather than privileging a single framework, this chapter emphasizes the pedagogical and analytical utility of theoretical diversity in understanding complex global phenomena. This chapter specifically demonstrates how theoretical pluralism enhances our grasp of the digital competition between the United States and China on the African continent and invites readers to critically assess the usefulness of each perspective.

Introduction

More than a decade ago, International Relations (IR) scholars asked if IR theory is dead (Dunne et al., 2013). Some decried the increasing rejection of mainstream IR theorisation (Mearsheimer & Walt, 2013), while others asserted the "poverty of grand theory" (Brown, 2013). This was premature, and for one, a disregard of IR theories overlooks the pedagogical utility of using them as "generators of interesting insights" covering a wide range of global issues (Matthews & Callaway, 2015: 207). So, long live IR theories and let us recognise their pedagogical utility in making sense of what is unfolding in the world (see Sterling-Folker, 2013).

IR theories are grand theories that centre the analytical focus on a few core assumptions and concepts and construct an abstract arrangement of the world. Each school of thought—realism, constructivism, and so on—has several sub-schools and theoretical perspectives that contribute to the theoretical multiplicity in the

J. H. S. Åberg (✉)
Global Political Studies, Malmo University, Malmo, Sweden
e-mail: john.aberg@mau.se

G. Moyo (ed.), *An Anatomy of AI Surveillance in Africa*, Studies in Digital Politics and Governance, https://doi.org/10.1007/978-3-032-04269-9_11

discipline. The aim of the paper is to make use of different IR theories to provide different analytical "cuts" of how US-China competition plays out on the African continent in relation to digital technologies. The aim is not to arrive at a preferred theory, but to elucidate different aspects of a multifaceted reality by using various IR perspectives. As Kenneth Waltz beautifully put it: "A theory is a picture, mentally formed, of a bounded realm or domain of activity…A theory indicates that some factors are more important than others and specifies relations between them…[a theory] constructs a reality, but no one can ever say that it is the reality" (Waltz, 1979: 8–9). As our eyes, infrared lenses, X-rays, and microscopes of various kinds observe different layers of the same reality—the complex human body—IR theories are lenses that let us observe different aspects of our complex political world. We therefore need to use as many theories as possible to achieve a fuller understanding of the world (Buzan, 2024).

Yet, due to space constraints, all IR schools of thought cannot be included, instead, I have chosen to apply the perspectives I find the most useful in elucidating the issue—that is, realism, constructivism, world systems analysis, and postcolonialism. The focus is on breadth rather than depth. That is, I will not apply one theory, let's say, offensive realism, and produce an in-depth account of US-China digital competition using that analytical framework, but I will outline the central claims of each perspective and briefly show how they are analytically relevant.

Below follows a brief section on different competing digital initiatives by the United States and China. Then the four IR perspectives are applied to make sense of the US-China digital competition in Africa.

Competing Digital Initiatives

Prevailing analogies are framing US-China competition in terms of a "new cold war" (Buzan, 2024). Unlike previous eras of colonial, territorial, and ideological partition, the United States and China now compete for centrality in four interrelated networks (infrastructure, digital, production, finance) in the global capitalist system (Schindler et al., 2024). This competition threatens to turn Africa, yet again, into a geopolitical battleground. It might be an exaggeration to talk of a "new scramble for Africa" (Soulé, 2020), but top officials from the great powers are scrambling to visit the continent. In 2023, the United States sent an unprecedented number of high-level officials to the continent. The reason for this engagement lies, of course, in China. For long, China has cultivated deep political and economic ties with various African states. Frequent diplomatic visits and political forums have built consistency over the years, while economic flows have been steadily increasing. China is now definitely one of the most important political partners and the largest commercial partner of the continent—China is the largest trading partner, the primary bilateral creditor, and a top investor.

China's Digital Silk Road (DSR) aims to increase connectivity, to facilitate the global influence of China's tech giants, to support the overseas expansion of telecom infrastructure, and to disseminate Chinese digital goods and services (Shen,

2018; Greene & Triolo, 2020). China's increasing technical standardisation power is used to gain economic, legal, political, and discursive influence (Rühlig, 2023). In contrast to the domestic economic imperatives of China's "go out" policy in 1999, such as industrial overproduction, large foreign exchange surplus, and the need for natural resources to fuel China's economic growth (Dreher et al., 2022: 4), the DSR is more proactive, intentional, and externally oriented. China's Cyber Great Power strategy and China's Standards 2035 are global in scope.

Chinese technological companies are present in most of Africa's ICT infrastructure, which suggests that African states could potentially be drawn into a Chinese "technological sphere of influence" (Agbebi, 2022: 3). Motolani Agbebi (2022) shows how China's technological presence covers all levels of Africa's ICT domain, and ranges from submarine cables, data centres, and 5G, 4G, 3G, and 2G networks to internet service providers, consumer products, operating systems, apps, and media platforms. Stephanie Arnold (2024) demonstrates how China enjoys structural power in Africa's ICT space in relation to broadband networks, data centres, and research partnerships implemented through EPC + F (engineering, procurement, construction + finance) schemes. Even so, the ICT space in Africa contains multiple stakeholders, the technology stack displays heterogeneity, and digital development primarily occurs through varieties of public-private partnerships within the exploitative uniformity of US-dominated global capitalism (Åberg & Peltola, 2025).

It is clear that "digital technology is playing an increasingly crucial role in diplomacy, trade, and geopolitics" on the African continent (Eguegu, 2022: 30). The United States is responding to the large presence of Chinese companies in Africa's ICT networks through initiatives that mirror Chinese counterparts. The G7 Partnership for Global Infrastructure and Investment (PGII), which is set to mobilise US$600 billion by 2027, out of which the United States is intending to provide US$200 billion, can be viewed as an answer to China's Belt and Road Initiative (BRI). The Partnership for Global Infrastructure and Investment is labelled as "a values-driven, high-impact, and transparent infrastructure partnership" that will "meet the enormous infrastructure needs of low-and middle-income countries" (US Department of State, 2022). It is leveraging public and private financing to build "energy, physical, digital, health, and climate-resilient infrastructure" (The White House, 2023a).

The United States has so far mobilised US$30 billion, and among the initial investments, considerable attention is directed towards ICT and digital infrastructure projects in various African states. Among them a CITI bank credit facility of US$125 million to support projects by Airtel Africa in Kenya, Nigeria, Gabon, and the Democratic Republic of Congo (DRC); a loan facility from the US International Development Finance Corporation (DFC) to Africa Data Centres (ADC) to build a data center in Ghana; support from the United States Agency for International Development (USAID) and the US Trade and Development Agency (USTDA) for investments in digital infrastructure in the DRC and Angola; expansion of existing DFC financing for Africell's operations in the Gambia, Sierra Leone, and the DRC; and USAID initiatives to support Africell digital payments in Angola and fibrenetwork expansion in the DRC (The White House, 2023b).

The ICT-related initiatives of the PGII were complemented by the Digital Transformation with Africa (DTA) initiative, which can be seen as a more specific response to China's DSR. The DTA was labelled "a signature initiative of the Biden-Harris Administration," and a whole-of-government effort that included several US departments and agencies to facilitate US$450 million dollars in digital financing for Africa. It consisted of three pillars—digital economy and infrastructure, human capital development, and digital enabling institutions—that together covered nine specific objectives (The White House, 2022). Several "tech-related initiatives" were announced during the latest iteration of the US-Africa Leader's Summit to counter China's presence on the continent, and it is increasingly clear that the United States "sees technology investment and development vis-a-vis China as a zero-sum game that the U.S. cannot lose" (Howell, 2022).

With that said, let us turn to the theoretical application to make sense of US-China digital competition in Africa.

Making Sense of US-China Digital Competition in Africa

IR theories are useful to make sense of world politics. Below, I apply different IR perspectives to analyse US-China digital competition on the African continent. Let us start with realism.

Realism

The famous textbook conceptual trinity of the three S's—statism, survival, self-help—neatly covers the general analytical concern of realism, depicting an anarchic international system where states compete for power (Dunne & Schmidt, 2014). Yet realism is a mansion with many rooms. It contains different theoretical perspectives, from parsimonious frameworks to more eclectic theorising, operating at different levels of analysis. Structural realism, in both its defensive and offensive guise, is a parsimonious, great power-centric perspective that bases its theorisation of the international system on three core components—anarchy, distribution of power, and functionally undifferentiated states (Waltz, 1979; Mearsheimer, 2001). We thus get a "positional picture" that describes the system "in terms of the placement of units rather than in terms of their qualities" (Waltz, 1979: 99). In this positional picture, African states are depicted in the margins, given their lack of power. In the centre of the picture hovers the great powers, overshadowing the rest of the states struggling for survival. The realist conception of power in terms of power-as-capabilities—military strength, economic wealth, natural resources, population, and so on—connects to how both the United States and China view "AI as a powerful tool for gaining strategic advantage" (Ndzendze & Marwala, 2023: 61), while technological sovereignty is seen as key to maintain great power status (Diesen, 2021).

From a hegemonic stability perspective (Gilpin, 1981), as the distribution of power and the prestige hierarchy undergo change, while the rules of the system still reflect the declining hegemon, a disequilibrium emerges that heightens the zero-sum "positional competition" between great powers in various domains across the world (Schweller, 1999). Tech companies become subservient to the prerogatives of each great power and digital platforms are instrumentalised as geopolitical-economic agents (Rolf & Schindler, 2023). In this rendering, China is challenging US hegemony by incrementally constructing an alternative international order in Africa (Murphy, 2022), leading to the establishment of mutually exclusive "technological spheres of influence" (Agbebi, 2022). The United States could thus be seen as pursuing a wedge strategy (Izumikawa, 2013) to prevent the emergence of a China-friendly coalition among African states. Washington further advocates for the use of European original equipment manufacturers (OEMs), such as Ericsson and Nokia, and presents Open-RAN technology as an alternative to Huawei, in line with a realist geoeconomic logic.

Irrespective of their different theoretical nuances, the logical corollary of the various system-level realist accounts is that they treat African states as pawns or proxies used by great powers in their strategic games. We find little to no African agency as "the crude and derogatory neglect of differentiating small state inputs in international order is flagrant" (Chong, 2021: 180). African states are made theoretically invisible as they are conceived of having little consequential impact in the world, let alone in their own countries. Yet other realist perspectives offer theoretical space to incorporate weaker and smaller states, such as subaltern realism, classical realism, and neoclassical realism (Ayoob, 2002; Lobell et al., 2009; Williams, 2005; Marston, 2024). Given the ever-present vulnerability to the "imperialism of great powers" (Waltz, 1979: 26), militarily and economically weaker states engage in variegated self-help strategies to ensure survival in an anarchical international system. States adapt strategically to different political contexts and engage in hedging (Marston, 2024) to ensure survival, uphold autonomy, and serve national interests or more narrow regime prerogatives of the prevailing elite configuration.

A telling example is Angola. Given Angola's position as Africa's leading oil exporter to China and the continent's top recipient of Chinese loans (BU, 2024), one could reasonably expect Angola to opt for Huawei when expanding its digital networks. Yet the task was awarded to Africell, who teamed up with Nokia to deploy 2G, 3G, 4G, and 5G services in Angola alongside existing Huawei networks (Nokia, 2021). Though the reasons behind Angola's diplomatic manoeuvring are intricate, its relationship with China is evolving due to two key changes, one external and one internal—China's re-evaluation of its loan strategy, and Angolan domestic political changes (De Carvalho et al., 2022). The relationship between China and Angola is deep, but nonetheless characterized as a "marriage of convenience," which highlights a core continuity in Angola's international relations irrespective of elite configuration, namely, that "diversification of finance sources and international partners remains the bread and butter of Angola's conduct in global affairs" (De Carvalho et al., 2022: 22; see also Jura et al., 2024). It is further suggested that Angola's relations with China have increased its "bargaining power vis-à-vis the West"

(Thiombiano & Zhang, 2020). Hence, we would be wrong to assume that African engagement with great powers always comes at the expense of autonomy. In fact, "small states seek to avoid overdependence on great power protectors and diversify their security and economic relations" (Marston, 2024: 355).

This further connects to Alan Chong's study of Singapore's foreign policy, characterized by a pragmatic, flexible, and creative approach where Singapore does "not shy away from practicing an associational form of power balancing" (Chong, 2021: 199). Singapore has successfully leveraged what Chong calls "convening power"—a type of "network power"—to gather "allies, neutrals and rivals" and "converse face to face," which allows for the formation of "alliances" that one does "not always have to demonstrate tangibly" (Chong, 2021: 199).

Whatever we make of Paul Kagame's desire to develop Rwanda to become "Africa's next Singapore," it is perhaps Singaporean foreign policy that Rwanda is emulating the most. Rwanda has successfully mobilized its official genocide memory to foster good relations with Western donor countries (Munyi et al., 2020); it enjoys a good relationship with China (Lisimba & Parashar 2021); it negotiates controversial migration deals with the UK (Adamson & Greenhill, 2023); it is "one of Israel's best friends in Africa" (Bishku, 2019); it is involved in military operations and supports armed groups in its neighborhood (Cannon & Donelli, 2023); and most importantly for our purposes, Rwanda did not turn to Huawei, nor Nokia or Ericson for ICT infrastructure, but relied on Korea Telecom and Samsung to build and operate its 4G network, and is now partnering with South African MTN and Indian Airtel to expand its networks (Srikapardhi, 2023). By leveraging different relations in various issue-areas, Rwanda under Kagame arguably displays "political stability and competence"—one of Waltz vaguely defined capabilities (1979: 131)—and ensures survival through pragmatism and diplomatic diversification.

Realist perspectives that incorporate the strategic manoeuvring of smaller states grasp how African governments can influence their relationships with more powerful states and manage to make use of them to serve their own interests (Hodzi, 2018). In this way, African governments exercise agency amid great power competition as they pursue digital partnerships with both the United States and China, and a variety of other stakeholders, in line with their own national priorities (Soule, 2024).

Now, let us turn to constructivism.

Constructivism

The constructivist analytical focus is on how ideas, norms, and narratives constitute identities, interests, and institutions, and how they are crucial to understanding the actions and behaviour of states. When it comes to constructivist system theory (Wendt, 1999), it has more in common with structural realism than sometimes assumed, and differences between theories often concern explanatory emphasis rather than fundamental contradictions (Goddard & Nexon, 2005). For instance, instead of "distribution of power," constructivist hegemonic stability theory focuses on "distribution of identities" (Allan et al., 2018). This ideational dimension of hegemony effectively turns US-China competition into an international "struggle for recognition" where great powers seek to attract states who defer to their leadership (Ringmar, 2002). Rather than a "rising power" challenging the United States, China becomes a "rising identity" (Turner, 2016) seeking to enlarge its circle of recognition. In this sense, the African continent becomes an arena where the United States and China compete for "hearts and minds", for the deference of African governments.

From a relational constructivist perspective (Jackson, 2013), rhetorical commonplaces and analogies are framing US-China relations in terms of a "new cold war", part of an ongoing rhetorical "war of words" between Washington and Beijing (Winkler & Jerdén, 2023). A telling example of how this rhetorical battle plays out in relation to African states is displayed by Wendy Sherman, former US Deputy Secretary of State, when she remarked on Africell's 5G roll-out in Angola, which resulted in a diplomatic spat with China. As Wendy Sherman put it:

> We believe that when countries choose Huawei, they are potentially giving up their sovereignty. They are turning over their data to another country. They may find themselves bringing in a surveillance capability they didn't even know was there. So we've been very public about our concerns about Huawei, and so we are glad that Africell can provide to the people of Angola a safe, capable tool in their hands to reach out to the world (cited in Bartlett, 2022).

China's Foreign Ministry Spokesperson, Zhao Lijian, quickly responded by saying that China "unequivocally opposes mass surveillance of other countries by abusing information technologies", and simultaneously accused the US of failing to "respect the sovereignty of African countries and [their] right to privacy" through "long-standing cyber theft, surveillance and monitoring against foreign governments, companies, and individuals" (MFA, 2022). Examples of similar US-China whataboutism abound on social media.

In the digital media age, memes, narratives, and social constructions of threats form a master narrative of US–China rivalry associated with the meme that depicts China as "challenging the international rules-based order" (Breuer & Johnston, 2019). This filters in to strategy documents, such as the US Strategy Toward Sub-Saharan Africa, where Washington's purported "high-standards, values-driven, and transparent" approach is explicitly contrasted to China, who supposedly "sees the region as an important arena to challenge the rules-based international order, advance its own narrow commercial and geopolitical interests, [and] undermine transparency and openness" (US Strategy Toward Sub-Saharan Africa, 2022: 5).

The supposed challenge to the so-called liberal international order relates to the possibility that African states might embrace China's model of internet sovereignty and Chinese norms and technology standards. China's large financial and technological presence in Africa imbues China with the power to shape norms and spread its standards and to use the African continent as a springboard for their wider acceptance. These norms can translate into direct legislation in the form of social media or cybercrime laws modelled on Chinese practices. Exemplified by censorship on social media, digital surveillance, and the closing down of internet during times of unrest, the "Chinese model" of internet governance is seen to be spreading throughout the African continent—from Tanzania to Zimbabwe, Uganda to Sudan—so much so that the "Chinese model" might become the "African model" of digital governance (Gravett, 2020). African emulation of Chinese values and norms must thus be combated by the United States who purportedly "defend against digital authoritarianism" and offer "a digital ecosystem built on open, reliable, interoperable, and secure internet and information and communication technology across sub-Saharan Africa" (US Strategy Toward Sub-Saharan Africa, 2022: 7). Needless to say, Snowden and Assange would beg to differ.

Arguments about authoritarian norm diffusion are often supported by a power shift logic: "Counter-norms are thus grounded in changing power balances, as the post-Cold War era of US hegemony gives way to a more multipolar world" (Cooley, 2015: 50). However, the current international distribution of identity does not indicate a widespread adoption of Chinese norms (Allan et al., 2018). Moreover, China-Africa narratives often disregard the agency of African political elites, who, aside from merely emulating Chinese norms, acquire technology that can be made to function according to their own domestic norms and preferences (see Åberg, 2018; Hodzi & Åberg, 2020). Whatever we make of a so-called "China model", African perceptions of China are "not nearly as negative as Western media make out, nor as positive as official Chinese sources imply. Instead … [they] are variegated and complex … [and] eschew a binary view" (Sautman & Hairong, 2009: 730; Ishiyama, 2025).

In contrast to "digital cold war" discourses (Heeks et al., 2024: 86), narratives of "non-alignment" are common on the continent. As Chairperson of the African Union Commission Moussa Faki puts it: "Africa refuses to be seen as an arena for influence struggles…We are open to cooperation and partnerships with everyone, as long as they respect our principles, our priorities and our interests" (The North Africa Post, 2023). A normative commitment visible in the fact that not one single African government has signed on to the US Clean Network Initiative targeting Chinese technologies.

With that said, let us now continue with world systems analysis.

World Systems Analysis

World systems analysis is normally regarded as a sub-school within Marxism, focusing on the hierarchical structures of the global capitalist system. These structures are conceived in terms of core, semi-peripheral, and peripheral production processes, global value chains, and a global division of labour (Goldfrank, 2000; Babones, 2015). The state is not an autonomous actor but occupies a role defined by the global capitalist system. The world economy is characterised by four secular trends: geographic expansion of capitalist markets, commodification (primarily, commercialisation of land and proletarianisation of labour), mechanisation of production, and bureaucratisation (Goldfrank, 2000: 174–176). In line with this understanding, African governments face systemic pressures to transform social relations and institutions to facilitate capitalist accumulation (Cammack, 2015).

Yet the secular trend above all is digitalisation. The signs of the times inform us that digital connection is the new mode of dominant social relation, the new mode of being, enabled by the computer chip and the ICT revolution. The traditional economic base centred around ownership of the means of production (land, labour, capital) does not entirely capture the logic of the digital political economy, which is centred around ownership of the means of connection—the gateways to the internet (Walton & Nayak, 2021). The platform—the new mode of business organisation—has become ubiquitous in the digital age, enabling extensive spatial reach and extraterritorial governance through control over critical border-transcending infrastructure (Rolf & Schindler, 2023). In the historical context of what has been dubbed the "Fourth Industrial Revolution", digital networks, technologies, and platforms put de facto internet governance in the hands of a few external actors.

Instead of a realist "Thucydides Trap" or a liberal "Kindleberger Trap", a world systems perspective puts the analytical focus on the emergence of new core economic processes in the digital age and how the United States and China politically try to "capture" those very processes (Flint & Zhang, 2021). Scholars who analyse US corporate power claim that US structural power has increased (Starrs, 2013), and especially so in the digital-intensive "new economy" sectors (Schwartz, 2019). Other scholars have shown that China is making great strides in increasing its power in the production structure (Malkin, 2022), while China's power in the credit structure is particularly pronounced on the African continent, where it is the largest bilateral creditor. Although US tech firms—Alphabet, Amazon, Apple, Meta, Microsoft, and Nvidia—remain dominant, "there is also no question that Chinese capacities are developing rapidly and, in some areas, displacing US platform power" (Rolf & Schindler, 2023: 18).

For one, Chinese digital infrastructure enables the dissemination of China's digital yuan, the first central bank digital currency (CBDC) of a major economy, which exemplifies China's influence over the technological–financial–business infrastructures of digitalised economies (Slawotsky, 2022). In Africa, we see how Huawei's Mobile Money Platform provides the technology behind the African mobile money giant M-Pesa, as well as for Telebirr and smaller mobile money players in 19 African countries (Adeyemi, 2021). Yet this arose as a cooperative project between Afro-Anglo-American (Safaricom and Vodafone) and Chinese (Huawei) firms, highlighting their at times common interests in exploiting opportunities in African markets.

China's presence in Africa is part of an ongoing restructuring of core–periphery relations, and US-China intra-core competition (Xing & Bernal-Meza, 2021) occurs in a specific historical context defined by the emergence of state platform capitalism (Rolf & Schindler, 2023). The United States and China compete to gain access to African resources, data, and markets. African countries are financially and technologically dependent on external powers for their digital infrastructure, and Chinese firms have been indispensable to the ICT development in several African countries (Arnold, 2024). Even so, the ICT space in Africa contains multiple stakeholders, the technology stack displays heterogeneity, and digital development occurs through varieties of public–private partnerships within the exploitative uniformity of US-dominated global capitalism (Åberg & Peltola, 2025).

We observe Africa's uneven insertion into the global economy through value chain analysis, showing the peripheral and low-value-added productive roles that African states occupy. First of all, the digital revolution is powered by critical minerals—cobalt, coltan, copper, lithium, and so on—excavated in several African countries under harsh social conditions and with severe environmental consequences, making it abundantly clear how "the new extractivism of data mining also encompasses and propels the old extractivism of traditional mining" (Crawford, 2021: 31). The DRC has long been the tragic example of this exploitation given reoccurring hostilities and wars to control its mineral abundance (Mantz, 2008). Africa's position in the global division of digital labour is further illustrated by how African microworkers are used to train AI systems. Microworkers carry out various repetitive and dreary tasks such as labelling, tagging, sorting, moderating—crucial for the performance of AI systems. Microworkers suffer from poor working conditions, including long hours, meagre compensation, and the psychologically damaging effects of cleaning up the "dark side" of the internet. In Kenya, dubbed the "Silicon Savannah" of Africa, American tech firms have made extensive use of this kind of work (Stahl et al., 2024). We also see how the externalities of the digital age, in the form of e-waste, end up in African cities, creating toxic wastelands of used products that many Africans never got the chance to use themselves. For several years, the Ghanaian capital Accra was home to the largest e-waste site in Africa, receiving around 15,000 tons of used electronics, phones, and computers annually (Lambert, 2024). The unequal structures of global capitalism are further evident in the digital divide on the African continent, where internet usage (40 %) and 4G coverage (50 %) are low and unevenly distributed (ITU2022).

With that said, much of what is described above is compatible with postcolonial perspectives, highlighting the colonial continuities in the world economy.

Postcolonialism

Postcolonialism is a rich school of thought with a wide range of scholars putting the analytical focus on various colonial legacies and their enduring effects in a formally decolonized world—from a focus on how former colonial powers continue to control African economies through various neo-colonial schemes (Nkrumah, 1966) to how Western knowledge production, narratives, and representations of the "Other" are distorted, stereotypical, and used to justify imperial dominance (Said, 1978). Colonial patterns remain, and former colonial powers maintain monopolies over military technology, financial assets, natural resources, weapons of mass destruction, and communication and media channels that reproduce capitalism and inequality (Ghosh, 2021). Other core postcolonial concepts include subalternity—focusing on the capacity of groups to have voice and representation (Spivak, 1988)—and hybridity—describing the creation of new cultural practices through the blending of colonial and indigenous traditions (Bhabha, 2012). Postcolonial perspectives for the study of the digital age emphasise cyberspace as a new frontier, neocolonialism in the digital space, digital diasporas, and digital hybridity (Enein, 2023).

The colonial legacies are apparent in Africa's value-extractive position in the global economy (Amir Anwar & Graham, 2022). As was highlighted in the world systems analysis above: "African minerals are still extracted to serve and profit consumers and corporations of the global North as was done under colonialism" (Bernal, 2021: 54). On top of this, a new form of colonialism—"data colonialism"—transforms human life into data that is extracted and commodified (Couldry & Mejias, 2019: 343). The concept of digital coloniality captures the continuous process of economic and cultural control and highlights new patterns of exploitation, the takeover of communication spaces, and the geographical spread of technology companies throughout Africa (Oyedemi, 2024). These patterns are well exemplified by the Equiano and 2Africa subsea cable projects, controlled by Google and led by Meta, respectively. These projects allow American tech giants to own and control infrastructure for mass data harvesting. The implementation of these projects is opaque and was developed without involving local communities. The projects monopolise vital digital infrastructure and maintain historical patterns of exploitative practices, exemplifying the central position of US tech firms and the extractive logic of global capitalism. On top of that, the Equiano cable is named after the African abolitionist Olaudah Equiano, representing a blatant example of settler appropriation, while the corporations adopt the language of white saviourism (Mwema & Birhane, 2024). Digital infrastructures are aimed at securing long-term market dominance, a strategy referred to as "infrastructure-as-debt," and technological supremacy is reinforced by a neocolonial missionary-like ideology promoted by tech evangelists (Kwet, 2022). When large foreign firms enter African markets through acquisitions, as when American data centre firms Digital Realty and Equinix acquired South African firm Teraco and Nigerian firm MainOne, respectively, they do so to incorporate "local operators [into] their empire".

China is not a former colonial power, but it can be conceived as a sub-imperial power performing a crucial role in the exploitation of the global south (Bond, 2017). Adem and Babagana (2023: 1375) further caution against the potential that "Africa could become China's neo-dependency in which feudo-imperial interdependence is reproduced, consolidated and perpetuated." The paradigm of "surveillance capitalism"(Zuboff, 2019)—the monetisation of data through tracking and analysis of online behaviour and interactions – initially pioneered by American technology corporations, is now being adopted by Chinese enterprises. While Western companies have utilised Africa as a "testing ground for surveillance technologies"; however, there is a burgeoning presence of Chinese firms in this domain (Roberts & Mare, 2025, 6). The agreement between Chinese firm, Cloud Walk Technology, and the Zimbabwean government is instructive. It stipulates that Zimbabwe will send biometric data on its citizens to Cloud Walk for the development of facial recognition algorithms that can recognise different ethnicities. It enables the dissemination of Cloud Walk's technology and exemplifies how raw information is "harvested from developing countries for the commercial and strategic benefit of richer, more powerful nations that hold AI supremacy" (Cave et al., 2019). With Chinese tech giants—Huawei, ZTE, Tencent, Alibaba, Baidu, China Telecom, China Mobile, Transsion, etc.—increasingly providing tech solutions in African countries, it sets the stage for dependence on Chinese technology systems, enabling data harvesting.

The use of AI to monitor traffic in various ways is further embedded into the Chinese concept and practice of "smart cities" spread across the continent.

Overall, Gravett (2020: 127–128) argues that Chinese digital neo-colonialism in Africa takes three particular forms: "(i) advocating the Chinese model of 'internet sovereignty' in African nations; (ii) exporting authoritarian surveillance technology to African states, and (iii) deploying artificial intelligence technology and data-mining techniques across Africa." However, Western and Chinese firms alike engage in digital surveillance in five different ways: "(1) internet interception, (2) mobile interception, (3) social media monitoring, (4) public space surveillance, and (5) biometric digital-ID systems" (Roberts & Mare, 2025, 8). As they compete for influence and profit, the United States and China incorporate African states into different extraterritorial border-transcending schemes that monitor populations, extract data, and colonise the continent digitally.

Furthermore, knowledge production is intertwined with power, maintaining Western hegemony over formerly colonised peoples while silencing other ways of knowing and being (Mantz, 2019). The internet in particular, is a US-dominated English-language domain (Babones & Åberg, 2019: 308–309) that "superimposes American lifestyles" while commodifying and stereotyping African men and women (Fonyuy, 2024: 80). The dominant "artificial intelligentsia" that operates within the distant realm of computing generates information that appears neutral but is inherently biased (Tuzcu, 2021). Studies show how American large language models continue to reinforce a wide range of explicit and covert racial biases and stereotypes, from images to dialects (Hofmann et al., 2024). At the same time, anti-black sentiments are disseminated on Chinese social media platforms, with discourses justifying exclusionary practices alongside negative racial stereotypes (Gu & Ho, 2024). Biases, whether Western or Chinese, are not innocent misrepresentations or coding errors, but are deeply embedded in global power dynamics where African countries become subject to "algorithmic colonialism driven by corporate agendas" that preclude ownership, control, and sensitivity to local contexts (Birhane, 2020). Digital technologies thus "facilitate the coloniality of knowledge in the global South in general and Africa in particular" (Ndayisenga, 2024: 4) by introducing new mechanisms that silence the "cybaltern" in cyberspace (Tuzcu, 2021). Yet colonial remnants are also deeply ingrained in many African legal systems that criminalise false information, sedition, and insults, as well as in newer "cybercrime and electronic communication laws", which result in online expression being "continuously violated by colonial laws" (Ilori, 2024: 300).

Ultimately, there is an emancipatory element in postcolonial scholarship that urges us to challenge unjust power structures and the universalisation of Western experiences and knowledge as the standard for all societies (Mantz, 2008). In relation to digital technologies, Enein (2023) emphasises four emancipatory perspectives: digital empowerment and agency, counter narratives in digital storytelling, digital transnationalism, and digital archiving and cultural preservation. A number of responses have also developed in relation to the biases in artificial intelligence, such as the development of decolonial AI frameworks and the promotion of diverse datasets (Mohamed et al., 2020; Kam et al., 2024). These initiatives challenge the colonial and racial biases that historically have shaped technology, its applications, and its use in maintaining dominance.

Conclusion

IR theory provides invaluable perspectives for understanding the complex dynamics of global politics. The multifaceted nature of IR theory helps us to make sense of the world by organising knowledge, by predicting and interpreting the behaviour of a range of different actors, and by facilitating critical examination and reflection. The sections above offer four different analytical cuts provided by realism, constructivism, world systems analysis, and postcolonialism, providing various insights into the issue of US-China digital competition on the African continent. Viewing issues from different theoretical perspectives enhances our understanding of the problems at stake, and I hope the theoretical applications have contributed to that aim. Ultimately, it is up to informed readers and observers to cast value judgements of where theoretical usefulness lies, according to the questions and purposes that animate their interests.

References

Aberg, J. H. S., & Peltola, M. (2025). A digital cold war in Africa? Capitalist multiplicity, digital transformation, and shifting dependencies amid US–China tech rivalry. *Third World Quarterly*, 1–26. https://doi.org/10.1080/01436597.2025.2546668

Adamson, F. B., & Greenhill, K. M. (2023). Deal-making, diplomacy and transactional forced migration. *International Affairs, 99*(2), 707–725. https://doi.org/10.1093/ia/iiad017

Adem, S., & Babagana, A. W. (2023). Is Africa China's neo-dependency in the making? *Third World Quarterly, 44*(7), 1363–1379. https://doi.org/10.1080/01436597.2023.2189579

Adeyemi, D. (2021). *M-Pesa. Opay, Telebirr, Palmpay: How Chinese tech is powering African Fintech*. Techcabal.

Agbebi, M. (2022). China's Digital Silk Road and Africa's Technological Future. Council on Foreign Relations. Accessed 01 February 2022. https://www.cfr.org/blog/chinas-digital-silk-road-and-africas-technological-future

Allan, B. B., Vucetic, S., & Hopf, T. (2018). The distribution of identity and the future of international order: China's hegemonic prospects. *International Organization, 72*(4), 839–869. https://doi.org/10.1017/S0020818318000267

Amir Anwar, M., & Graham, M. (2022). *The digital continent: Placing Africa in planetary networks of work* (1st ed.). Oxford University Press. https://doi.org/10.1093/oso/9780198840800.001.0001

Arnold, S. (2024). Africa's roads to digital development: Paving the way for Chinese structural power in the ICT sector? *Review of International Political Economy, 31*(4), 1148–1172. https://doi.org/10.1080/09692290.2023.2297363

Ayoob, M. (2002). Inequality and theorizing in international relations: The case for subaltern realism. *International Studies Review, 4*(3), 27–48. https://doi.org/10.1111/1521-9488.00263

Babones, S. (2015). What is world-systems analysis? Distinguishing theory from perspective. *Thesis Eleven, 127*(1), 3–20. https://doi.org/10.1177/0725513615575324

Babones, S., & Åberg, J. H. S. (2019). Globalization and the rise of integrated world society: Deterritorialization, structural power, and the endogenization of international society. *International Theory, 11*(3), 293–317. https://doi.org/10.1017/S1752971919000125

Bartlett, K. (2022, May 13). *US, China vie for Africa mobile phone sector*. Voice of America. https://www.voanews.com/a/us-china-vie-for-africa-mobile-phone-sector/6569971.html

Bernal, V. (2021). Digitality and decolonization: A response to Achille Mbembe. *African Studies Review, 64*(1), 41–56. https://doi.org/10.1017/asr.2020.90

Bhabha, H. K. (2012). *The location of culture* (2nd ed.). https://doi.org/10.4324/9780203820551

Birhane, A. (2020). Algorithmic colonization of Africa. *SCRIPTed: A Journal of Law, Technology and Society, 17*, 389.

Bishku, M. B. Israel & Rwanda (2019). The Development of a Special Relationship. *The Maghreb Review, 44*(3), 335–356.

Bond, P. (2017). BRICS banking and the debate over sub-imperialism. In *Rising powers and South-South cooperation*. Routledge.

Breuer, A., & Johnston, A. I. (2019). Memes, narratives and the emergent US–China security dilemma. *Cambridge Review of International Affairs, 32*(4), 429–455. https://doi.org/10.1080/09557571.2019.1622083. Retrieved April 21, 2025, from https://www.tandfonline.com/doi/epdf/10.1080/09557571.2019.1622083?needAccess=true

Brown, C. (2013). The poverty of grand theory. *European Journal of International Relations, 19*(3), 483–497. https://doi.org/10.1177/1354066113494321

BU. (2024). *Policy research for a better world*. Global Development Policy Center. Retrieved April 21, 2025, from https://www.bu.edu/gdp/

Buzan, B. (2024). A new cold war? The case for a general concept. *International Politics, 61*(2), Article 2.

Cammack, P. (2015). What international organizations do, and why they do it. *Spectrum: Journal of Global Studies, 7*(1), Article 1.

Cannon, B. J., & Donelli, F. (2023). Rwanda's military deployments in Sub-Saharan Africa: A neoclassical realist account. *The International Spectator, 58*(1), 109–127. https://doi.org/10.1080/03932729.2022.2132046

Cave, D., Hoffman, S., Joske, A., Ryan, F., & Thomas, E. (2019). *Mapping China's technology giants*. Mapping China. Retrieved April 21, 2025, from http://www.aspi.org.au/report/mapping-chinas-tech-giants

Chong, A. (2021). 'Small sees big': International order through small state leaders' insights via the intellectual propaganda of Czechoslovak, Ghanaian and Singaporean leaders. *Global Change, Peace & Security, 33*(2), 177–199. https://doi.org/10.1080/14781158.2021.1934430

Cooley, A. (2015). Authoritarianism goes global: Countering democratic norms. *Journal of Democracy, 26*(3), 49–63.

Couldry, N., & Mejias, U. A. (2019). Data colonialism: Rethinking Big Data's relation to the contemporary subject. *Television & New Media, 20*(4), 336–349. https://doi.org/10.1177/1527476418796632

Crawford, K. (2021). *The atlas of AI: Power, politics, and the planetary costs of artificial intelligence*. Yale University Press.

De Carvalho, P., Kopiński, D., & Taylor, I. (2022). A marriage of convenience on the rocks? Revisiting the Sino–Angolan relationship. *Africa Spectrum, 57*(1), 5–29. https://doi.org/10.1177/00020397211042384

Diesen, G. (2021). *Great power politics in the fourth industrial revolution* (pp. 1–272). Bloomsbury Publishing Plc.

Dreher, A., Fuchs, A., Parks, B., Strange, A., & Tierney, M. J. (2022). *Banking on Beijing: The aims and impacts of China's overseas development program* (1st ed.). Cambridge University Press. https://doi.org/10.1017/9781108564496

Dunne, T., Schmidt, B. C. Realism. (2014). In The Globalization of World Politics: An Introduction to International Relations; Baylis, J., Smith, S., Owens, P., Eds., Oxford University Press: Oxford, pp 99–112

Dunne, T., Hansen, L., & Wight, C. (2013). The end of international relations theory? *European Journal of International Relations, 19*(3), 405–425. https://doi.org/10.1177/1354066113495485

Eguegu, O. (2022). The Digital Silk Road: Connecting Africa with new norms of digital development. *Asia Policy, 17*(3), 30–39. https://doi.org/10.1353/asp.2022.0049

Enein, D. G. F. R. A. (2023). Post-colonialism and the digital age. *Journal of Namibian Studies: History Politics Culture, 38*, 262–277. https://doi.org/10.59670/jns.v38i.5370

Flint, C., & Zhang, X. (2021). Why and whither the US-China trade war?: Not realist 'traps' but political geography 'capture' as explanation. *Journal of World Trade, 55*(2) https://kluwerlawonline.com/api/Product/CitationPDFURL?file=Journals\TRAD\TRAD2021013.pdf

Fonyuy, B. S. (2024). Oscillating between racism, colonialism, and digital colonialism: Towards theorizing Digi-Africanism. *International Journal of Humanities, Social Sciences and Education, 11*(5), 74–83. https://doi.org/10.20431/2349-0381.1105008

Ministry of Foreign Affairs of the People's Republic of China. (2022). *Foreign Ministry spokesperson Zhao Lijian's regular press conference on May 9, 2022* [Ministry of Foreign Affairs of the People's Republic of China]. Retrieved April 21, 2025, from https://www.mfa.gov.cn/eng/xw/fyrbt/lxjzh/202405/t20240530_11347277.html

Gardner, T. (2024). *The Abiy project: God, power and war in the new Ethiopia*. Oxford University Press.

Ghosh, J. (2021). Interpreting contemporary imperialism: Lessons from Samir Amin. *Review of African Political Economy, 48*(167), 8–14. https://doi.org/10.1080/03056244.2021.1895535

Gilpin, R. (1981). War and change in world politics. *Cambridge University Press*. https://doi.org/10.1017/CBO9780511664267

Goddard, S. E., & Nexon, D. H. (2005). Paradigm lost? Reassessing theory of international politics. *European Journal of International Relations, 11*(1), 9–61. https://doi.org/10.1177/1354066105050136

Goldfrank, W. L. (2000). Paradigm regained? The rules of Wallerstein's world-system method. *Journal of World-Systems Research, 1/2*(2), 150–195. https://doi.org/10.5195/jwsr.2000.223

Gravett, W. (2020). Digital neo-colonialism: The Chinese model of internet sovereignty in Africa. *African Human Rights Law Journal, 20*(1), 125–146. https://doi.org/10.17159/1996-2096/2020/v20n1a5

Greene, R., & Triolo, P. (2020). *Will China control the global internet via its Digital Silk Road?* https://policycommons.net/artifacts/434249/will-china-control-the-global-internet-via-its-digital-silk-road/1405307/

Gu, J., Ho, J. (2024). Anti-Black Sentiments in Chinese Weibo Discourse: A Critical Discourse Historical Analysis. *Social Semiotics 2024, 34*(5), 846–869. https://doi.org/10.1080/10350330.2023.2210506

Heeks, R., Ospina, A. V., Foster, C., Gao, P., Han, X., Jepson, N., Schindler, S., Zhou, Q. (2024). China's Digital Expansion in the Global South: Systematic Literature Review and Future Research Agenda. *The Information Society, 40*(2), 69–95. https://doi.org/10.1080/01972243.2024.2315875

Hodzi, O. (2018). China and Africa: Economic growth and a non-transformative political elite. *Journal of Contemporary African Studies, 36*(2), 191–206. https://doi.org/10.1080/02589001.2017.1406191

Hodzi, O., & Åberg, J. H. S. (2020). Introduction to the special issue: Strategic deployment of the China model in Africa. *Politics & Policy, 48*(5), 804–814. https://doi.org/10.1111/polp.12378

Hofmann, V., Kalluri, P. R., Jurafsky, D., & King, S. (2024). AI generates covertly racist decisions about people based on their dialect. *Nature, 633*(8028), 147–154. https://doi.org/10.1038/s41586-024-07856-5

Howell, S. (2022). *Countering China in Africa by reaffirming US tech leadership*. The Diplomat. https://thediplomat.com/2022/12/countering-china-in-africa-by-reaffirming-us-tech-leadership/

Ilori, T. (2024). A postcolonial legal critique of online expression in Africa. *Journal of African Law, 68*(3), 283–300. https://doi.org/10.1017/S0021855324000111

Ishiyama, J. (2025). Who is attracted to the Chinese model in Africa? *Journal of Asian and African Studies, 60*(1), 310–323. https://doi.org/10.1177/00219096231171544

ITU. (2022). *Facts and digures 2022*. https://www.itu.int/itu-d/reports/statistics/facts-figures-2022

Izumikawa, Y. (2013). To coerce or reward? Theorizing wedge strategies in Alliance politics. *Security Studies, 22*(3), 498–531. https://doi.org/10.1080/09636412.2013.816121

Jackson, P. T. (2013). Relational Constructivism: A War of Words. In Making Sense of International Relations Theory; Sterling-Folker, J., Ed., Lynne Rienner Publishers: Boulder, pp 152–168

Jura, J., D. Kopiński, A. Polus, & W. Tycholiz. (2024). Examining Shifts in the Angola–China Relations in the Post-Dos Santos Era. *African Affairs, 123*(491), 193–221.

Kam, J. W. Y., Badhwar, A., Borghesani, V., Lee, K., Noble, S., Raamana, P. R., Ratnanather, J. T., Tan, D. G. H., Oestreich, L. K. L., Lee, H. W., Marzetti, L., Nakua, H., Rippon, G., Olsen, R., Pozzobon, A., Uddin, L. Q., Yanes, J. A., Tzovara, A. (2024). Creating Diverse and Inclusive Scientific Practices for Research Datasets and Dissemination. *Imaging Neuroscience, 2*, 1–14. https://doi.org/10.1162/imag_a_00216

Kwet, M. (2022). *Digital colonialism and infrastructure-as-debt* (SSRN scholarly paper no. 4004594). Social Science Research Network. https://papers.ssrn.com/abstract=4004594

Lambert, J. (2024). Stunning Photos of a Vast E-Waste Dumping Ground — and Those Who Make a Living off It. NPR. October 5, 2024. https://www.npr.org/sections/goats-and-soda/2024/10/05/g-s1-6411/electronics-public-health-wasteghana-phones-computers (accessed 2024-12-05).

Lisimba, A. F., & Parashar, S. (2021). The 'state' of postcolonial development: China–Rwanda 'dependency' in perspective. *Third World Quarterly, 42*(5), 1105–1123. https://doi.org/10.1080/01436597.2020.1815527

Lobell, S. E., Ripsman, N. M., & Taliaferro, J. W. (2009). *Neoclassical realism, the state, and foreign policy*. Cambridge University Press.

Malkin, A. (2022). The made in China challenge to US structural power: Industrial policy, intellectual property and multinational corporations. *Review of International Political Economy, 29*(2), 538–570. https://doi.org/10.1080/09692290.2020.1824930

Mantz, J. W. (2008). *Improvisational economies*. https://www.berghahnjournals.com/view/journals/saas/16/1/j.1469-8676.2008.00035.x.xml

Mantz, F. (2019). Decolonizing the IPE syllabus: Eurocentrism and the coloniality of knowledge in International Political Economy. *Review of International Political Economy, 26*(6), 1361–1378. https://doi.org/10.1080/09692290.2019.1647870

Marston, H. S. (2024). Navigating great power competition: A neoclassical realist view of hedging. *International Relations of the Asia-Pacific, 24*(1), 29–63. https://doi.org/10.1093/irap/lcad001

Matthews, E. G., & Callaway, R. L. (2015). Where have all the theories gone? Teaching theory in introductory courses in international relations. *International Studies Perspectives, 16*(2), 190–209. https://doi.org/10.1111/insp.12086

Mearsheimer, J. J. (2001). *S2-mearsheimer-2001*. Norton & Company. https://samuelbhfaure.com/wp-content/uploads/2015/10/s2-mearsheimer-2001.pdf

Mearsheimer, J. J., & Walt, S. M. (2013). Leaving theory behind: Why simplistic hypothesis testing is bad for international relations. *European Journal of International Relations, 19*(3), 427–457. https://doi.org/10.1177/1354066113494320

Mohamed, S., Png, M.-T., & Isaac, W. (2020). Decolonial AI: Decolonial theory as sociotechnical foresight in artificial intelligence. *Philosophy & Technology, 33*(4), 659–684. https://doi.org/10.1007/s13347-020-00405-8

Munyi, E. N., Mwambari, D., & Ylönen, A. (2020). *Beyond history: African Agency in development, diplomacy, and conflict resolution*. Rowman & Littlefield.

Murphy, D. C. (2022). China's Rise in the Global South: The Middle East, Africa, and Beijing's Alternative World Order. In China's Rise in the Global South; Stanford University Press. https://doi.org/10.1515/9781503630604

Mwema, E., & Birhane, A. (2024). Undersea cables in Africa: The new frontiers of digital colonialism. *First Monday*. https://doi.org/10.5210/fm.v29i4.13637

Ndayisenga, Z. (2024). Decolonizing digital Technology in Africa: A political thought. *Journal of Humanities & Social Sciences, 7*, 2024.

Ndzendze, B., & Marwala, T. (Eds.). (2023). *Artificial intelligence and international relations theories* (pp. 33–54). Springer Nature. https://doi.org/10.1007/978-981-19-4877-0_3

Nkrumah, K. (1966). *Neocolonialism, the last stage of imperialism*. International Publishers Co. Inc, https://www.scholar.google.com.

Nokia. (2021). *Nokia and Africell to deploy a brand-new 5G-ready network in Angola*. Nokia.com. https://www.nokia.com/

Oyedemi, T. D. (2024). Africa and Digital Coloniality. In Media in Africa: Issues and Critique; Oyedemi, T. D., Smith, R. A., Eds., Routledge.

Ringmar, E. (2002). The recognition game: Soviet Russia against the west. *Cooperation and Conflict, 37*(2), 115–136. https://doi.org/10.1177/0010836702037002973

Roberts, T., & Mare, A. (2025). *Digital surveillance in Africa: Power, agency, and rights*. Zed Books.

Rolf, S., & Schindler, S. (2023). The US–China rivalry and the emergence of state platform capitalism. *Environment and Planning A, 55*(5), 1255–1280. https://doi.org/10.1177/0308518X221146545

Rühlig, T. (2023). Chinese Influence through Technical Standardization Power. *Journal of Contemporary China 2023, 32*(139), 54–72. https://doi.org/10.1080/10670564.2022.2052439

Said, E. W. (1978). Orientalism. New York: Pantheon Books.

Sautman, B., Hairong, Y. (2009). African Perspectives on China–Africa Links. *The China Quarterly, 199*, 728–759. https://doi.org/10.1017/S030574100999018X

Schindler, S., Alami, I., DiCarlo, J., Jepson, N., Rolf, S., Bayırbağ, M. K., Cyuzuzo, L., DeBoom, M., Farahani, A. F., Liu, I. T., McNicol, H., Miao, J. T., Nock, P., Teri, G., Vila Seoane, M. F., Ward, K., Zajontz, T., & Zhao, Y. (2024). The second cold war: US-China competition for centrality in infrastructure, digital, production, and finance networks. *Geopolitics, 29*(4), 1083–1120. https://doi.org/10.1080/14650045.2023.2253432

Schwartz, H. M. (2019). American hegemony: Intellectual property rights, dollar centrality, and infrastructural power. *Review of International Political Economy, 26*(3), 490–519. https://doi.org/10.1080/09692290.2019.1597754

Schweller, R. L. (1999). Realism and the present great power system: Growth and positional conflict over scarce resources. In *Unipolar politics: Realism and state strategies after the cold war* (pp. 28–68). Columbia University Press.

Shen, H. (2018). Building a Digital Silk Road? Situating the Internet in China's Belt and Road Initiative. *International Journal of Communication, 12*(19), 2683–2710.

Slawotsky, J. (2022). Digital currencies and great power rivalry: China as a disseminator in the digital age. *Asia Pacific Law Review, 30*(2), 242–264. https://doi.org/10.1080/10192557.2022.2085412

Soulé, F. (2020). 'Africa+1' summit diplomacy and the 'new scramble' narrative: Recentering African agency. *African Affairs, 119*(477), 633–646. https://doi.org/10.1093/afraf/adaa015

Soulé, F. (2024). Negotiating Africa's Digital Partnerships amid Geopolitical Competition. Centre for International Governance Innovation. Special Report.

Spivak, G. C. (1988). Can the subaltern speak? In C. Nelson & L. Grossberg (Eds.), *Marxism and the interpretation of culture* (Vol. 1). University of Illinois Press.

Srikapardhi. (2023). *Airtel Rwanda Launches Affordable 4G Smartphone Under ConnectRwanda2.0 Initiative*. TelecomTalk. Retrieved April 21, 2025, from https://telecomtalk.info/airtel-rwanda-launches-affordable-4g-smartphone-connectrwanda/886551/

Stahl, L., Chasan, A., Bar-On, S., & Jung, J. (2024, November 24). *Kenyan workers with AI jobs thought they had tickets to the future until the grim reality set in*. CBS News. https://www.cbsnews.com/news/ai-work-kenya-exploitation-60-minutes/

Starrs, S. (2013). American economic power hasn't declined—It globalized! Summoning the data and taking globalization seriously. *International Studies Quarterly, 57*(4), 817–830. https://doi.org/10.1111/isqu.12053

Sterling-Folker, J. A. (Ed.). (2013). *Making sense of international relations theory* (2nd ed.). Lynne Rienner Publishers, Inc..

The North Africa Post. (2023, January 26). *'Africa is no one's pawn', says AU chief, as top US, Chinese, Russian officials tour continent*. https://northafricapost.com/64737-africa-is-no-ones-pawn-says-au-chief-as-top-us-chinese-russian-officials-tour-continent.html

The White House. (2022, December 14). *New initiative on Digital Transformation with Africa (DTA)*. The White House. https://bidenwhitehouse.archives.gov/briefing-room/statements-releases/2022/12/14/fact-sheet-new-initiative-on-digital-transformation-with-africa-dta/

The White House. (2023a, June 8). *Vice President Harris announces new initiatives to strengthen U.S-Caribbean partnership*. The White House. https://bidenwhitehouse.archives.gov/briefing-room/statements-releases/2023/06/08/fact-sheet-vice-president-harris-announces-new-initiatives-to-strengthen-u-s-caribbean-partnership/

The White House. (2023b, May 20). *Partnership for global infrastructure and investment at the G7 Summit*. The White House. https://bidenwhitehouse.archives.gov/briefing-room/statements-releases/2023/05/20/fact-sheet-partnership-for-global-infrastructure-and-investment-at-the-g7-summit/

Thiombiano, D., & Zhang, Z. (2020). The impact of China on the agency and negotiating power of African countries: Cases of Angola and Niger. *African Journal of Political Science and International Relations, 14*(1), 1–12. https://doi.org/10.5897/AJPSIR2018.1130

Turner, O. (2016). China, India and the US rebalance to the Asia Pacific: The geopolitics of rising identities. *Geopolitics, 21*(4), 922–944. https://doi.org/10.1080/14650045.2016.1190708

Tuzcu, P. (2021). Decoding the cybaltern: Cybercolonialism and postcolonial intellectuals in the digital age. *Postcolonial Studies, 24*(4), 514–527. https://doi.org/10.1080/13688790.2021.1985264

US Department of State (2022). https://www.state.gov/about-us-office-of-the-u-s-special-coordinator-for-the-partnershipfor-global-infrastructure-andinvestment/#:~:text=Investing%20in%20the%20World:%20A,and%20leveraging%20private%20sector%20investments

US Strategy Toward Sub-Saharan Africa. (2022). *U.S.-Strategy-Toward-Sub-Saharan-Africa-FINAL*. The White House. https://bidenwhitehouse.archives.gov/wp-content/uploads/2022/08/U.S.-Strategy-Toward-Sub-Saharan-Africa-FINAL.pdf

Walton, N., & Nayak, B. S. (2021). Rethinking of Marxist perspectives on big data, artificial intelligence (AI) and capitalist economic development. *Technological Forecasting and Social Change, 166*, 120576. https://doi.org/10.1016/j.techfore.2021.120576

Waltz, K. (1979). *Theory of international politics Reading*. Addison-Wesley.

Wendt, A. (1999). *Social theory of international politics*. Cambridge University Press.

Williams, M. C. (2005). *The realist tradition and the limits of international relations*. Cambridge University Press.

Winkler, S. C., & Jerdén, B. (2023). US foreign policy elites and the great rejuvenation of the ideological China threat: The role of rhetoric and the ideologization of geopolitical threats. *Journal of International Relations and Development, 26*(1), 159–184. https://doi.org/10.1057/s41268-022-00288-6

Xing, L., & Bernal-Meza, R. (2021). China-US rivalry: A new Cold War or capitalism's intra-core competition? *Revista Brasileira de Política Internacional, 64*(1), e010. https://doi.org/10.1590/0034-7329202100110

Zhang, B. (2024). Polarity and strategic competition: A structural explanation of renewed great power rivalry. *The Chinese Journal of International Politics, 16*(4), 383–405. https://doi.org/10.1093/cjip/poad012

Zuboff, S. (2019). Surveillance capitalism and the challenge of collective action. *New Labor Forum, 28*(1), 10–29. https://doi.org/10.1177/1095796018819461

John H. S. Åberg is a senior lecturer in the Department of Global Political Studies (GPS) at Malmö University, Sweden. His research interests include global political economy, Africa-China relations, and US-China relations. John is a founding member of the Africa-China Research Network (ACRN).

Chapter 12
Towards the Decolonisation of Surveillance Technologies in Africa: A Postscript

Philani Moyo and Gorden Moyo

Abstract This concluding chapter is highly schematic. It poses more questions than it attempts to answer. It provides an overview of both the demand and supply factors that have contributed to the rapid proliferation of Artificial Intelligence (AI) surveillance technologies in Africa. It also offers a synthesis of the implications of AI surveillance technologies on human rights, civil liberties, and political freedoms of the affected African populations. At the same time it reinforces the argument made throughout the book that AI surveillance technologies in Africa have been deployed in ways that violate the fundamental rights of the citizens despite the fact that these rights are guaranteed in national constitutions, regional and international conventions as well as in domestic laws (Munoriyarwa and Mare, Digital surveillance in Southern Africa: policies, politics and practices, Palgrave Macmillan, https://link.springer.com/book/10.1007/978-3-031-16636-5, 2022; Roberts and Mare, Digital surveillance in Africa: power, agency, and rights (1st edn), Bloomsbury Publishing Plc. https://doi.org/10.5040/9781350422117, 2025). The major concern raised in this chapter is that surveillance technologies have added to a long history of human rights abuse, impunity, and the criminalization of groups that are opposed to power structures in their respective African countries. In net, the issues covered in this chapter include summaries of actors, motives, and contradictions of AI surveillance practices in Africa.

Introduction

This concluding chapter is highly schematic. It poses more questions than it attempts to answer. It provides an overview of both the demand and supply factors that have contributed to the rapid proliferation of Artificial Intelligence (AI) surveillance

---

P. Moyo · G. Moyo (✉)
Fort Hare Institute for Social and Economic Research, University of Fort Hare, East London, South Africa
e-mail: pmoyo@ufh.ac.za

G. Moyo (ed.), *An Anatomy of AI Surveillance in Africa*, Studies in Digital Politics and Governance, https://doi.org/10.1007/978-3-032-04269-9_12

technologies in Africa. It also offers a synthesis of the implications of AI surveillance technologies on human rights, civil liberties, and political freedoms of the affected African populations. At the same time, it reinforces the argument made throughout the book that AI surveillance technologies in Africa have been deployed in ways that violate the fundamental rights of the citizens despite the fact that these rights are guaranteed in national constitutions, regional and international conventions as well as in domestic laws (Munoriyarwa & Mare, 2022; Roberts & Mare, 2025). The major concern raised in this chapter is that surveillance technologies have added to a long history of human rights abuse, impunity, and the criminalization of groups that are opposed to power structures in their respective African countries. In net, the issues covered in this chapter include summaries of actors, motives, and contradictions of AI surveillance practices in Africa.

The perspectives and themes of this book have been analysed through the lens of heterodox theoretical traditions, including dependency, core-periphery, world systems, and neo-Marxian theories, as well as Afro-decolonial thought. Arguing from heterodox approaches, especially Afro-decolonial perspectives, the authors in this volume contend that the biographies, histories, and lineages of surveillance practices in Africa are traceable back to the time of slavery, colonialism, apartheidism, and imperialism. In other words, the proliferation of AI surveillance tools that are deployed to telemonitor and control populations is anchored on colonial practices, approaches, systems, institutions, laws, and legacies (Bertoni & Kurre, 2017). For the avoidance of doubt, it would be recalled that colonial and apartheid surveillance mechanisms consisted of eavesdropping, opening of private correspondences, monitoring of movements of activists, passbooks, national identification cards, spatial containment, profiling of suspected enemies of the state, conducting stop and search, spying on and infiltration of activist groups by law enforcement agents. The whole purpose was to control, dominate, subjugate, oppress, and repress the colonised populations. The authors in this book have identified seamless parallels between the colonial and the post-colonial mechanics, objectives, and veracity of surveillance practices in Africa.

There is no doubt that surveillance practices and techniques have evolved with changing digital technology, data environments, and AI. Today, state surveillance has been digitised and automated compared to the analogue surveillance of the colonial and apartheid era. Examples of contemporary surveillance tools include closed-circuit television (CCTV) cameras, drones, biometric identification systems, border management technology, automated vehicle plate readers, facial recognition technologies, and video analytics. These tools provide African governments, militaries, security agencies, and tech companies with unprecedented capacity for panoptic real-time surveillance of offline and online citizens' lives. AI surveillance technologies have been presented as positive tools that can promote and enhance national security, digital development, cybersecurity, and public order. However, the discussions contained in this volume tell a different story. They show that some African governments have repurposed, weaponised, and instrumentalised the AI surveillance tools and deployed them for controlling, dominating, subjugating and repressing legitimate political opposition, judges, government critics, academics, journalists and civic society activists among others (see Gravett, 2020; Munoriyarwa & Mare, 2022; Sheombar & Skelton, 2023; 2025; Sakarombe et al., 2025). This use of AI surveillance disproportionately affects marginalised communities and peoples (Gürses et al., 2016), contributing towards democratic regression, shrinking of the civic space, and rise of authoritarian regimes on the continent.

It was reified throughout this volume that Africa is a consumer of foreign technologies, and it is not known for its local production and copyrights. This is in line with the international division of labour, where Africa remains at the lower rungs of global governance as an exporter of commodities and importer of finished goods (Moyo, 2021, 2024). Viewed from this perspective, it is not surprising that today's AI surveillance tools are owned and controlled by foreign governments and foreign companies. In particular, the three core pillars of the digital ecosystem, namely, software, hardware and network connectivity, are foreign-produced, foreign-owned, and foreign-controlled. In this context, there is considerable concern that African countries have become a privileged market for foreign manufacturers, exporters, promoters, distributors, and installers of surveillance technologies. In this context, foreign tech companies and governments have more detailed information on African populations than national governments have on their own citizens (Roberts & Mare, 2025). This simply means that the ongoing telemonitoring of citizens represents the continuities of the colonial era practices, systems, laws, and institutions. Decolonial thinkers, such as Anibal Quijano, Arturo Escobar, Enrique Dussel, Nelson Maldonado-Torres, Ramon Grosfoguel, Sabelo Ndlovu-Gatsheni, Steve Martinot, Madina Tlostanova, and Walter Mignolo, have long argued that colonialism did not reach its expiry date when African countries got their independence in the 1960s, 1970s, 1980s, and 1990s. Instead, colonialism has outlived administrative colonialism. Today, it exists in the form of foreign control of Africa's economy, finance, trade, investments, and technology, among others. Thus, viewing AI surveillance technologies from heterodox theoretical perspectives has enabled the authors in this volume to invisibilise the hidden colonialities of surveillance technologies in Africa and the rest of the Global South.

Expanding Footprint of AI Surveillance Technologies

AI surveillance was used in this volume to mean the deployment of digital technology to monitor, intercept, or exploit sensitive data, information or communication, movements, activities, conversations, correspondences, and recording of metadata by state agents using digital devices (Gravett, 2020; Königs, 2022; Munoriyarwa & Mare, 2022; Jimoh, 2023; Sheombar & Skelton, 2023). Chapter 1 of this book traces the biography of surveillance systems to the colonial and apartheid eras. As explained, colonial and apartheid surveillance practices took the form of eavesdropping, monitoring of movements, passbooks, national identification cards, spatial containment, profiling of suspected enemies of the state, conducting stop and search, and spying on activist groups by law enforcement agents. Like their colonial predecessors, today African governments are increasingly engaged in processes of surveilling, profiling, and targeting ordinary citizens as well as political opposition, government critics, judges, journalists, and civic society activists. Generally speaking, the digital surveillance usually takes the form of the malicious use of audios, cameras, videos, GPS, and hacking, among others. Again, it was noted throughout this book that whilst many Euro-Western countries, including Germany, France, Israel, Italy, Japan, the United Kingdom, and the United States are big players in the AI surveillance world, the major manufacturer, promoter, supplier, and installer of AI surveillance technologies in Africa is China. African governments are heavily reliant on Chinese surveillance technologies. This is adding to already emerging signs of a neo-colonial relationship between China and Africa. It is not unreasonable to argue that Africa's dependence on Chinese technology is likely to compromise its digital sovereignty, economic and political agency (see Sakarombe et al., 2025).

Apparently, many African governments prefer Chinese surveillance technologies largely because they are more affordable. China offers attractive loan facilities for African governments to purchase these technologies. In addition, China enjoys strong historical ties with some African countries dating back to the time of the liberation struggle. To put it into perspective, China-Africa geoeconomic relations are negotiated within the Forum for China-Africa Cooperation (FOCAC). This Forum is guided by principles such as win-win, mutual respect, and the doctrine of non-interference in each other's internal affairs (Moyo et al., 2020; Moyo, 2022).In this context, Beijing has framed its geoeconomic relations with Africa as a practical partnership aimed at enabling African countries to achieve their development goals and aspirations. However, with China's growing presence in Africa's digital surveillance sector, there are concerns that Beijing could be reshaping the older patterns of colonialism through its AI surveillance tools in Africa. Again, it was argued throughout this book that African governments have turned a blind eye to the malign activities of China in Africa. This is because the ruling elites are benefiting from the AI surveillance technologies from China, including closed-circuit television (CCTV) cameras, drones, biometric identification systems, border management technology, automated vehicle plate readers, facial recognition technologies, and video analytics. As explained, these tools are used to track and monitor, scan, capture, and transmit fragments of information and remote images of citizens, government critics, opposition leaders, independent journalists and civil society who are perceived as the enemies of the state.

Although most of the authors in this volume tend to apportion blame on China for exporting its model of surveillance to Africa, a few chapters, including Chaps. 7 and 9, contend that African governments are not coerced into purchasing the intrusive technologies. Instead, it is out of their volition, choice, and invested interest that they have imported, installed, and repurposed surveillance technologies in their countries. It was also argued that the construction of the "surveillance states," also known by the moniker "panoptic state," in countries such as Cameroon, Uganda, and Zimbabwe, was a deliberate policy option by the ruling elite to sustain themselves in power in perpetuity by tightly monitoring the opposition leaders. It is worth reiterating that while surveillance can be used for legitimate purposes such as crime prevention, traffic management, emergency response, counter-terrorism, counter-intelligence, border control, cybersecurity, business security, and infrastructure protection, this volume has raised concerns that AI surveillance systems are, instead, used as tools for repression, suppression, subjugation and the victimisation of government critics as well as the general members of the public in Africa. The rhetoric about the brighter side of surveillance technologies is often deployed to defend both the purchase of a wide variety of surveillance technologies and reforms to norms that allow its use.

Financing of Surveillance Technologies

What is evident throughout this book is that the construction of the surveillance state in Africa is largely financed by Chinese policy banks. These include the National Aero-Technology Import and Export Corporation, China Exim Bank, and China Development Bank, as well as the China Export and Credit Insurance Corporation, which offer loans to African governments. It was noted that on average, China supplies approximately US$1 billion worth of digital surveillance tools annually in the form of loans and the major recipient countries include Cameroon, Chad, Cote d'Ivoire, Egypt, Ethiopia, Kenya, Malawi, Morocco, Nigeria, Rwanda, South Africa, Zambia, and Zimbabwe (Matsengarwodzi, 2023). The surveillance tools are typically purchased as part of a package of ICT systems, which include CCTV systems and high-tech biometrics that are integrated and used in tandem with AI products touted as supportive of public security and development ambitions of African countries (Jili, 2023). In most cases, AI surveillance technologies are imported under the banner of smart city initiatives. Needless to say, by bundling AI surveillance technologies with the other ICT solutions, African governments can hide the surveillance tools and their real motives from the public.

On the other side of the ledger, China's surveillance technologies offer opportunities for an emerging class of 'middlemen' involved in the digital technologies trade in Africa. These middlemen encourage this trade and spur it on, as it offers huge financial rewards. The middlemen are generally linked to some corrupt political leaders and politically exposed persons. These middlemen have identified some opportunities for huge financial rewards and have been at the centre of sustaining trade in AI surveillance technologies in Africa and the rest of the Global South (Munoriyarwa & Mare, 2022).

Worryingly, the Chinese loans offered to African countries have added to the problem of debt distress on the continent. For example, Egypt, Ethiopia, Kenya, Nigeria, and Zimbabwe are among the countries that have serious debt sustainability problems. These countries have embraced the Safe Cities initiative, and they have been offered some loans to construct their safe cities. Unfortunately, the chapters in the volume did not explore in detail the extent to which these loans have exacerbated the debt problems in quantitative terms. However, given the extent to which some African countries have installed surveillance technologies, there is little doubt that their total debt stock will continue to balloon as a result of Chinese loans for surveillance apparatuses.

Regulating Surveillance Practices

There is a general agreement in literature (see Gravett, 2020; Munoriyarwa & Mare, 2022; Sheombar & Skelton, 2023, 2025; Sakarombe et al., 2025) that the adoption of surveillance technologies in Africa have not been accompanied by the corresponding data protection measures. Plainly put, the existing legislation and norms do not necessarily provide the guarantees needed for AI surveillance technologies. The current laws are not aligned with the adherence to human rights as enshrined in the national constitutions, regional and international conventions and domestic laws.

It is, however, instructive to note that in countries like the United Kingdom, the United States, and the European Union, digital technologies are governed by laws that promote privacy rights and protect human rights, including civil liberties and political freedoms. As Jimoh (2023) rightly observed, surveillance laws should be enacted to protect public interest, including national security, public health data protection, electronic transactions, and cybersecurity. Paradoxically, most of the laws intended to govern the digital lives of the people in Africa suffer from colonial and apartheid hangover. Some of these laws do not only allow surveillance to be brazenly implemented but also make it mandatory for mobile phone companies to collect personal identification details from anyone using a mobile phone SIM card; compel providers of telecommunication services to facilitate communication interception; restrict encryption usage; stipulate the mandatory collection of biometric data; and bestow law enforcement agents broad search and seizure powers (Roberts & Mare, 2025). This is reminiscent of the apartheid era where blacks were subjected to inhumane treatment by state agencies. Without digital technology protection laws, African peoples are "stripped naked". They have no privacy, and their rights only exist on paper. Worse still, even in countries that have laws protecting the rights of citizens, those laws are violated with impunity.

While noting the challenge of impunity, the authors in this volume have called for the enactment of comprehensive surveillance legislation in Africa. Some observers posit that implementing effective surveillance legislation in Africa requires careful consideration of the balance between national security, public safety, and human rights. Given the advances of AI surveillance technologies in Africa, there is a need to rethink the rules that are required to mitigate risks to human rights, privacy, and civil liberties. In addition, the law must pass the test of accountability and transparency, oversight, and legal punishments for illegitimate surveillance. At the same time, Africa needs more debate about the use of surveillance technology, given the huge negative ramifications on people's offline and online lives.

Revisiting the Actors, Drivers, and Motivations

As explained, this book privileged the key actors, motives, contradictions, and implications behind the adoption, deployment, and expansion of AI surveillance tools in Africa. One of the actors that were reified in the book is China. This country uses the exportation of electronic surveillance tools as part of its diplomatic strategy, technological ambitions, and growing corporate expansion in Africa (Jili, 2023). The authors in this book question the degree to which the Chinese Communist Party (CCP), in partnership with tech corporations such as Dahua Technology, CloudWalk, Hikvision, Huawei, and ZTE, enables autocratic digital practices to take root in Africa. The Chinese tech companies sit at the centre of many state surveillance technologies, systems, and practices in Africa. They are the major suppliers of surveillance technologies to African governments. It is also instructive to note that these tech companies are inherently part of the CCP's foreign policy because they help the party realise its ideals (Lumumba-Kasongo, 2011), especially the imperative to strangle any forms of democracy like privacy, free speech, freedom of movement, and thought. These "Red Techs" have been implicated in the rise of malign surveillance practices in Africa.

While the degree of coordination between Beijing and tech corporations cannot be fixed, financial incentives in the form of loans and aid provided by policy banks are used to incentivise African state procurement and proliferation of surveillance technologies on the continent. The Chinese tech corporations, such as Cloud Walk and Huawei, expanded into African ICT markets in the 2000s ostensibly to expand internet connectivity in countries like Ethiopia, Ghana, and Kenya. Today, they have expanded their portfolios into promoting smart cities that use AI surveillance technologies. China's motive in exporting its surveillance technologies to Africa includes a combination of geostrategic goals of expanding its global influence, the need to strengthen its position as a global leader in the digital sector, and enhancing its diplomatic strength to access Africa's natural resources and minerals ahead of the Euro-Western powers. Moreover, China aims to advance its diplomatic ambitions, corporate interests and technological prowess in its direct geopolitical and geoeconomic competition with the Euro-Western countries.

However, contrary to the conventional wisdom that China is the culprit when it comes to the expansion of AI surveillance technologies in Africa, the authors in this book have identified African governments, militaries, and local governments as the primary actors behind the explosion of malign surveillance practices on the continent. A combination of global polycrisis, such as international terrorism, COVID-19, and climate change, provided an excuse for African governments to grant themselves additional surveillance rights and significantly increase their collection of monitoring apparatus and technologies (Roberts et al., 2021; Sheombar & Skelton, 2025). It should also be noted that African governments use AI surveillance tools as a strategy to shrink the civic space and lobotomise the opposition political parties so as to extend their rule beyond the constitutional limits. This explains why African governments adopt and help drive the proliferation and use of Chinese digital surveillance technology on the continent.

This volume also examined the motivations for the procurement, installation and use of digital surveillance apparatuses in Africa. As previously mentioned, the official rhetoric is that African governments need surveillance technologies in order to combat crime and terrorism, scale public security capabilities, and national security. Whilst all these things are legitimate, the evidence presented by various authors in this volume tells a different story. The real motive for the rapid expansion of AI surveillance technologies has been to control and dominate the population. To this extent, the decolonial researchers were right in arguing that surveillance in Africa represents the continuities of the colonial and apartheid governments that sought to control, repress, and exploit Africans. As such, the Chinese surveillance tools have dramatically empowered governments, especially the authoritarian ones such as Cameroon, Egypt, Uganda, and Zimbabwe, to telemonitor government critics, opposition leaders and civil society activists, among others.

Tackling the Implications of Digital Surveillance

Today, many kinds of data are generated, captured, and used without consent and sometimes without the knowledge of those from whom the data originated. This has had adverse implications on privacy, human rights, civil liberties, and political freedoms in Africa. It is clear that the violation of human rights starts in the digital environment then moves to the physical world. With a population of approximately 1.5 billion people, Africa is a continent where many citizens face surveillance with malicious intent (Sheombar & Skelton, 2025). As explained, countries such as Cameroon, Chad, Cote d'Ivoire, Egypt, Ethiopia, Kenya, Malawi, Morocco, Nigeria, Rwanda, South Africa, Zambia, and Zimbabwe have invested a lot in AI surveillance technologies. The authors in this volume have argued that there is a power imbalance between African governments and their citizens. These power dynamics have increased the potential for persecution, repression, and subjugation of ordinary citizens. Notably, surveillance technologies have been procured and installed without the knowledge of the legislative arm of government and ordinary citizens. Such secretive and opaque installations create the risk of abuse by the ruling elite.

Throughout this book, a case has been made to the fact that the ubiquitous and underregulated use of digital surveillance apparatuses threatens privacy rights. What began as a promise of security and modernisation through China's Smart City and Safe City projects has morphed into an omnipresent watchtower, altering the very fabric of privacy and civil liberties in many African countries.

It was also noted in this volume that permitting African governments some unfettered access to citizens' private communication, tracking their movements, activities, conversations, correspondences, and communications, including recording of metadata, violates fundamental human rights, jeopardises democratic institutions, and creates a culture of fear and self-censorship (Bertoni & Kurre, 2017). It should be recalled that the most egregious violations of human rights under colonialism and apartheid were fundamentally linked to surveillance operations conducted by intelligence agents and secret police (Bertoni & Kurre, 2017). Sadly, this is still the case today, many years after Africa's juridical independence.

At the same time, it was also discussed that the oversized role of China in Africa is steadily engendering a dependence on their products and expertise. Some observers have raised a concern "that Africa runs a risk of becoming China's neo-colony". It is not unreasonable to suggest that AI surveillance systems have been repurposed by African governments with the aid of China as a neo-colonial power. To this extent, African governments run a risk of unwittingly reproducing and maintaining imbalanced power relations with China, where Africa is juniorised and inferiorised. However, it should be clearly stated that this book does not seek to perpetuate Coupland's myth of Africans as agency-less bystanders and hapless objects in their own history, present, and future. On the contrary, the book acknowledges the agency of Africa and Africans in pursuit of their economic, cultural, political, and technological destinies. This is important because it gives room for Africa to rethink its digital governance.

Overall, the authors in this volume contend that the consequences of increased AI surveillance practices tend to deepen socioeconomic inequalities and asymmetries in Africa, thereby hindering debates for social justice, human rights, and democracy, among others. State surveillance systems create grave risks to freedom and censorship, with a tangible reticence to debate publicly, and people censoring themselves because they know they are being surveilled. This is evident among academics, civil society activists, and journalists as well as human rights defenders in countries such as Egypt, Uganda, and Zimbabwe. Moreover, surveillance technologies perpetuate conditions whereby the citizens are always known, never able to be unknown, and never be knowers. In this regard, surveillance reinforces colonial hierarchies of power and reinscribes subjectivity and subalternity in the general population.

Decolonising Surveillance Technologies

The book unfolded as a major critique of African governments, along with Beijing, as key actors and drivers of controversial AI surveillance technologies in Africa. The book may not have answered all the questions pertaining to the actors, drivers, motives, contradictions, and implications of the rapid rise of AI surveillance in Africa, but it has initiated some critical thinking about the intrusive AI surveillance practices and surveillance colonialism in Africa. To this extent, the book is relevant to scholars, researchers, diplomats, and anybody interested in the geoeconomics of technology in this Era of Global Surveillance.

It was noted that in Africa, surveillance is an enduring characteristic of colonialism and apartheid. The reproduction of colonial and apartheid systems is undesirable in Africa. The discussions in this book argue against the abuse of technology for the nefarious ends of the ruling elite. This stance is based on the observed reality in Africa, where digital surveillance tools have been deployed to sustain what Spivak (1990: 166) termed “post-colonial neo-colonial world”. In this context, there is a need for a new breed of African leaders—decolonial agency. In line with the work of decolonial scholars (Grosfoguel, 2004; Mignolo, 2007; Quijano, 2007), the current practice of surveillance is part of coloniality that needs to be flushed out of the body politic of Africa and the rest of the Global South. Accordingly, African governments must use their agency to ensure that surveillance technologies are used for the good of society and not for the ruling elite.

Pursuant to this objective, African legislators and digital rights advocacy groups should work towards strengthening the norms and practices of surveillance technology on the continent (Jili, 2020). Regrettably, the African Union Convention on Cyber Security and Personal Data Protection, which was established over a decade ago, is yet to be fully operationalised in many African countries. Only Namibia, Senegal, Ghana, Guinea, and Mauritius have ratified this Convention. To be clear, the Convention requires the member states to establish national security policies as well as regulatory and institutional frameworks for democratic cybersecurity governance. What is even more worrying is that some African governments, such as Mozambique and Zimbabwe, have come up with their cyber laws that allow them to conduct unethical surveillance on their citizens. In this context, Africa needs agency-African agency that is driven by democratic and ethical values to use digital surveillance tools in pursuit of the public goods rather than the narrow and parochial interests of the ruling elite. Specifically, the policy makers should draft policies and laws that will promote the use of AI surveillance technologies in ways that protect the interests of the state and its citizens against cyber-criminals, cyber-terrorists, and cyber-espionage. To achieve this, there is a need for concerted effort by policy makers, digital rights groups, civil society, academics, and security professionals to work together in transforming, redirecting, and repurposing the AI surveillance apparatuses towards public interest.

In fact, surveillance governance should be decolonised. A decolonised surveillance law will ensure that surveillance tools are used to uplift the lives of the people rather than turning a country into a panopticon state where everyone is under the “all seeing eye of the Osiris”. In the past, Africans exercised their agency to get rid of administrative colonialism and apartheid (Moyo, 2024). Today they need the same kind of energy, attitude, perspectives, and commitment to liberate themselves from surveillance colonialism and digital repression, among other malign uses of AI surveillance practices. It is reasoned in this volume that AI surveillance systems and practices are part of the neo-colonial revolution or revolution of coloniality, and internal colonialism that can only be diminished by decolonial agency armed with decolonial consciousness. In this regard, checks, balances, and safeguards against intrusive surveillance must be established, legally and systematically, to ensure the dignity of Africa and Africans.

It is encouraging that some countries are already making considerable progress in adopting citizen-centric cybersecurity policies. For example, South Africa’s cybercrimes and personal data protection legislation makes purposeful attempts to establish rights-respecting standards for combating cybercrime. Similarly, civil society organisations in countries like Senegal and Kenya are also putting pressure on their respective governments to have digital governance that is respectful of the citizens' rights. This should be augmented by the enactment of transparency laws that will provide for clear disclosures and better transparency from tech companies. By adopting citizen-centric digital policies, African governments will safeguard democracy, further peace, and rebuild public trust.

Final Reflection

In sum, surveillance has taken a dramatic turn in the digitally enhanced era of AI, Internet of Things, Robotics, and big data, with myriad possibilities for monitoring individuals and groups. It was demonstrated in this book that African governments are currently making large investments in AI surveillance technologies, passing laws that expand their legal powers, and conducting illegal algorithmic surveillance of their citizens. It was also revealed that China is the largest manufacturer, exporter, promoter, financier, supplier, distributor, and installer of mass electronic surveillance equipment across the African continent. These tools have been weaponised against opinion makers, government critics, public intellectuals, civil society activists, journalists, human rights defenders, and opposition leaders, as well as ordinary people in general. To address these challenges, the authors in this book have recommended the establishment of clear surveillance regulations, robust national data protection laws, and independent oversight and transparency in the procurement of AI surveillance technologies. In other words, there is a need for the decolonisation of surveillance technologies by regulating the procurement of these tools to ensure the protection of fundamental human rights, privacy, civil liberties, and democratic principles. This will ensure that technology serves the interests of Africa and Africans. Without such safeguards, the digital landscape in Africa will remain a terrain of suppression, oppression, and subjugation of the people under the guise of public safety, public order, and public security, among other public goods that are said to be secured by AI surveillance technology.

References

Bertoni, E., & Kurre, C. (2017). Surveillance and privacy protection in Latin America: Examples, principles, and suggestions. In F. H. Cate & J. X. Dempsey (Eds.), *Bulk collection* (1st ed., pp. 325–342). Oxford University Press. https://doi.org/10.1093/oso/9780190685515.003.0016

Gravett, W. H. (2020). Digital neocolonialism: The Chinese surveillance state in Africa. *African Journal of International and Comparative Law, 30*(1), 39–58. https://doi.org/10.3366/ajicl.2022.0393

Grosfoguel, R. (2004). Race and ethnicity or racialized ethnicities?: Identities within global coloniality. *Ethnicities, 4*(3), 315–336. https://doi.org/10.1177/1468796804045237

Gürses, S., Kundnani, A., & Van Hoboken, J. (2016). Crypto and empire: The contradictions of counter-surveillance advocacy. *Media, Culture & Society, 38*(4), 576–590. https://doi.org/10.1177/0163443716643006

Jili, B. (2020). *The spread of surveillance technology in Africa stirs security concerns*. https://africacenter.org/spotlight/surveillance-technology-in-africa-security-concerns/

Jili, B. (2023). *Africas demand for an adoption of Chinese surveillance technology*. Digital Forensic Research Lab (DFRLab), Issue Brief. https://dfrlab.org/wp-content/uploads/sites/3/2023/05/Africas-Demand-for-an-Adoption-of-Chinese-Surveillance-Technology.pdf

Jimoh, M. (2023). The place of digital surveillance under the African charter on human and peoples' rights and the African human rights system in the era of technology. *SSRN Electronic Journal*. https://doi.org/10.2139/ssrn.4458550

Königs, P. (2022). Government surveillance, privacy, and legitimacy. *Philosophy & Technology, 35*(1), 8. https://doi.org/10.1007/s13347-022-00503-9

Lumumba-Kasongo, T. (2011). China-Africa relations: A neo-imperialism or a neo-colonialism? A reflection*. *African and Asian Studies, 10*(2), 234–266. https://doi.org/10.1163/156921011X587040

Matsengarwodzi, D. (2023). *Colonial legacy of surveillance: Hidden world of surveillance technology in the African continent*. Al Jazeera Media Institute. https://institute.aljazeera.net/en/ajr/article/2423

Mignolo, W. D. (2007). Introduction: Coloniality of power and de-colonial thinking. *Cultural Studies, 21*(2–3), 155–167. https://doi.org/10.1080/09502380601162498

Moyo, G. (2021). *African agency, finance and developmental states*. Palgrave Macmillan. https://doi.org/10.1007/978-3-030-72412-2

Moyo, G. (2022). China-Taiwan geoeconomic competition for diplomatic recognition: Battling for the soul of Africa. In *Taiwan in Africa: Seven decades of certainty and uncertainties* (pp. 119–142). https://doi.org/10.5040/9781978726703.ch-7

Moyo, G. (2024). *Africa in the global economy: Capital flight, enablers, and decolonial responses*. Springer. https://doi.org/10.1007/978-3-031-51000-7

Moyo, G., Nhliziyo, M., & Fayayo, R. (2020). The entanglement of Zimbabwe in the US-China Geoeconomic frictions: Defining winners and losers. *iBusiness, 12*(03), 81–102. https://doi.org/10.4236/ib.2020.123006

Munoriyarwa, A., & Mare, A. (2022). *Digital surveillance in Southern Africa: Policies, politics and practices*. Palgrave Macmillan. https://doi.org/10.1007/978-3-031-16636-5

Quijano, A. (2007). Coloniality and modernity/rationality. *Cultural Studies, 21*(2–3), 168–178. https://doi.org/10.1080/09502380601164353

Roberts, T., & Mare, A. (Eds.). (2025). *Digital surveillance in Africa: Power, agency, and rights* (1st ed.). Bloomsbury Publishing Plc. https://doi.org/10.5040/9781350422117

Roberts, T., Mohamed Ali, A., Farahat, M., Oloyede, R., & Mutung'u, G. (2021). *Surveillance law in Africa: A review of six countries*. Institute of Development Studies. https://doi.org/10.19088/IDS.2021.059

Sakarombe, E., Chimwamurombe, F., Masuku, S., Mupanga, J., & Mutume, T. E. (2025). The coloniality of Chinese surveillance technologies in Africa. *International Journal of Research and Innovation in Social Science, IX*(II), 1325–1336. https://doi.org/10.47772/IJRISS.2025.9020107

Sheombar, A., & Skelton, S. K. (2023). Follow the surveillance: A breadcrumb trail of surveillance technology exports to Africa. In *IFIP Advances in Information and Communication Technology, 696 AICT* (pp. 241–261). https://doi.org/10.1007/978-3-031-50154-8_19

Sheombar, A., & Skelton, S. (2025). Who supplies digital surveillance technologies to African governments?: Pathways for resistance. In *Digital surveillance in Africa: Power, agency, and rights* (pp. 183–210). Bloomsbury Publishing Plc. https://doi.org/10.5040/9781350422117.ch-8

Spivak, G. C. (1990). *The postcolonial critic: Interviews, strategies, dialogue*. Routledge.

Philani Moyo is a Professor of Sociology and Director of the Fort Hare Institute for Social and Economic Research at the University of Fort Hare in South Africa. He holds a DPhil and MA from the University of Leeds (UK), a Master of Social Sciences from the University of Fort Hare, and a BA Honours from the University of Zimbabwe. He has published extensively on climate change adaptation and resilience, climate justice, and food systems. His three most recent books are Socio-Ecological-Economic Reflections on the Impacts of COVID-19 in Africa (2025), co-edited with W. Chinyamurindi, https://doi.org/10.4102/aosis.2025.BK488; *Climate Action in Southern Africa: Implications for Climate Justice and Just Transition* (Routledge, 2024); and *Revisiting Environmental and Natural Resource Questions in Sub-Saharan Africa* (2017), co-edited with W. Akpan. An exhaustive list of his publications can be found here: https://orcid.org/0000-0002-9089-7565 and https://scholar.google.com/citations?User=BUVAJKkAAAAJ&hl=en. His research has been funded by the Social Science Research Council (USA), National Research Foundation (South Africa), National Institute for the Humanities and Social Sciences (South Africa), Government of South Africa, and Oxfam, among others. Prof. Moyo sits on the Board of Directors for the Association for Applied and Clinical Sociology (USA) and is a Member of the Standing Committee on Science for the Reduction of Poverty and Inequality of the Academy of Science of South Africa, Member of the Development Studies Association of the UK, Member of the South African Sociological Association, former Co-Chair of the South African Young Academy of Science, and former Secretary of the South African Sociological Association.

Gorden Moyo (PhD) is currently a Research Fellow at the Fort Hare Institute for Social and Economic Research at the University of Fort Hare in South Africa; Fellow at the University of the Free State in South Africa; Senior Lecturer in the Faculty of Humanities and Social Sciences at Lupane State University in Zimbabwe; Director of the Public Policy and Research Institute of Zimbabwe (PPRIZ); Member of the Editorial Board of the Sabella Abidde Publishing House, University of Alabama (USA); Member of the Board of Trustees of the Mass Public Opinion Institute (MPOI); Associate Member of the International Society for Development and Sustainability (ISDS), Japan; President of the Development Studies Association of Zimbabwe (DeSAZ); Member of the Southern African Development Parliamentary Forum Technical Group on Public Financial Management; ex-Minister of State in the Prime Minister's Office, ex-Minister of State Enterprises and Parastatals, and former Member of Parliament of the Republic of Zimbabwe (2009–2013); and former British Council Facilitator of the Pan-African Leadership Programme in 19 countries across Africa, including Botswana, Cameroon, Eritrea, Ethiopia, eSwatini, Ghana, Kenya, Lesotho, Liberia, Malawi, Mauritius, Namibia, Nigeria, South Africa, Tanzania, Uganda, Zambia, and Zimbabwe. He is a Chevening Scholar whose primary research interests are in global finance, international economic relations, developmental states, public leadership, military commercialism, Africa-China relations, and African agency, among others. He has published several articles in peer-reviewed journals and several book chapters. His most recent books include African Agency, Finance, and Developmental States (Palgrave Macmillan, 2021); Making Politics in Zimbabwe's Second Republic: The Formative Project by Emmerson Mnangagwa (Springer, 2023), co-edited with Prof. Kirk Helliker; Africa in the Global Economy: Capital Outflows, Enablers and Decolonial Responses (Springer, 2024); and Global Storms and Africa in Global Politics: Contemporary Challenges and Decolonial Responses, co-edited with Sabelo J. Ndlovu-Gatsheni (Springer, 2025).

GPSR Compliance
The European Union's (EU) General Product Safety Regulation (GPSR) is a set of rules that requires consumer products to be safe and our obligations to ensure this.

If you have any concerns about our products, you can contact us on

ProductSafety@springernature.com

In case Publisher is established outside the EU, the EU authorized representative is:

Springer Nature Customer Service Center GmbH
Europaplatz 3
69115 Heidelberg, Germany

www.ingramcontent.com/pod-product-compliance
Lightning Source LLC
Chambersburg PA
CBHW071605011225
36161CB00002B/39
* 9 7 8 3 0 3 2 0 4 2 6 8 2 *